MANCHESTER UNITED OFFICIAL YEARBOOK 2001

Compiled and Edited by Cliff Butler
Assisted by Ivan Ponting

Contributors
MARTIN EDWARDS
SIR ALEX FERGUSON
BARRY MOORHOUSE
CLIFF BUTLER
IVAN PONTING

Thanks to
ARTHUR ALBISTON, NEIL BAILEY, RUTH BAYLEY, ADAM BOSTOCK, PHIL BROGAN, DAVE BUSHELL, DIANE
CLIFFORD, JOHN COOKE, MARTIN CORTEEL, SARAH CORTEEL, TONY COTON, MIKE COX, RACHEL CROSS, JIMMY
CURRAN, PAUL DAVIES, SIMON DAVIES, MARK DEMPSEY, KERRIN EDWARDS, MARK EDWARDS, SHARON
FAULKNER, JULIAN FLANDERS, LES KERSHAW, TREVOR LEA, EDDIE LEACH, MARK LLOYD, STEPHANIE McCAIG,
PAUL MCGUINNESS, TOMMY MARTIN, STUART MATHIESON, DAVID MEEK, ROSS MILLARD, ALBERT MORGAN,
DEREK NASSARI, CLARE NICHOLAS, TOMMY O'NEIL, MIKE PHELAN, MICK PRIEST, MATT PROCTOR, DAVID PUGH,
KEN RAMSDEN, MARIE RILEY, ARTHUR ROBERTS, CARLY ROGERS, DAVE ROUSE, DAVID RYAN, JIMMY RYAN, JIM
SANDFORD, ANDY SMITH, TOM STATHAM, CRAIG STEVENS, REBECCA TOW, TONY WHELAN, DAVID WILLIAMS,
KATHIE WILSON, NEIL WITHERS, STUART WORTHINGTON, ALEC WYLIE, ANNE WYLIE AND EVERYONE WHO
SUPPLIED INFORMATION THROUGHOUT THE 2000-2001 SEASON.

THANKS ALSO TO ALL THE CLUBS WHO KINDLY GRANTED PERMISSION IN ALLOWING THEIR OFFICIAL
CLUB CRESTS TO BE REPRODUCED IN THIS PUBLICATION

Photographs
JOHN AND MATTHEW PETERS/MANCHESTER UNITED FC
Design and editorial
DESIGNSECTION FROME

First published in 2001
10 9 8 7 6 5 4 3 2 1

Manufactured and distributed by
Carlton Books Limited
20 Mortimer Street
London W1T 3JW

ISBN
0-233-99952-3

Printed and bound in the UK by
BUTLER & TANNER LTD. FROME AND LONDON

CONTENTS

| CHAIRMAN | 5 |
| MANAGER | 6 |

THE SEASON

Month-by-month reviews for all
Manchester United matches
in the 2000-2001 season, including

PREMIERSHIP

WORTHINGTON CUP

UEFA CHAMPIONS LEAGUE

FA CUP

AUGUST	7
SEPTEMBER	15
OCTOBER	31
NOVEMBER	47
DECEMBER	63
JANUARY	79
FEBRUARY	93
MARCH	105
APRIL	117
MAY	131

| 2000-01 SEASON IN REVIEW | 139 |

| FIRST TEAM FRIENDLIES | 142 |

PLAYER PROFILES

| PROFESSIONALS | 146 |
| YOUNG PROFESSIONALS | 162 |

| TRAINEES AND DEPARTURES | 169 |

| RESERVES | 170 |
| JUNIORS | 180 |

| MEMBERSHIP AND TRAVEL INFORMATION | 216 |
| SUPPORTERS' CLUBS 2001-02 | 218 |

MANCHESTER UNITED
FOOTBALL CLUB PLC

Directors	Chief Executive
C.M. EDWARDS (Chairman)	P.F. KENYON
J.M. EDELSON	
SIR BOBBY CHARLTON CBE	Manager
E.M. WATKINS LI.M.	SIR ALEX FERGUSON CBE
R.L. OLIVE	Secretary
P.F. KENYON	KENNETH R. MERRETT
D.A. GILL	

Honours

EUROPEAN CHAMPION CLUBS' CUP – Winners: 1968 · 1999

EUROPEAN CUP WINNERS' CUP – Winners: 1991

FA PREMIER LEAGUE – Champions: 1993 · 1994 · 1996 · 1997 · 1999 · 2000 · 2001

FOOTBALL LEAGUE DIVISION ONE – Champions: 1908 · 1911 · 1952 · 1956 · 1957 · 1965 · 1967

FA CHALLENGE CUP – Winners: 1909 · 1948 · 1963 · 1977 · 1983 · 1985 · 1990 · 1994 · 1996 · 1999

FOOTBALL LEAGUE CUP – Winners: 1992

INTER-CONTINENTAL CUP – Winners: 1999

UEFA SUPER CUP – Winners: 1991

FA CHARITY SHIELD – Winners: 1908 · 1911 · 1952 · 1956 · 1957 · 1983 · 1993 · 1994 · 1996 · 1997
Joint Holders: 1965 · 1967 · 1977 · 1990

CLUB TELEPHONE NUMBERS

Main Switchboard	0161-868 8000
Textphone for Deaf/Impaired Hearing	0161-868 8668
Ticket and Match Information	0161-868 8020
Matchday Hospitality	0161-868 8220
Megastore	0161-868 8567
Mail Order Hotline	0161-868-7000
United Review Subscriptions	0870 602 6000
Magazine Subscriptions	01458 271132
Development Association	0161-868 8600
Membership and Supporters' Club	0161-868 8450
Conference and Catering	0161-868 8300
Museum and Tour Centre	0161-868 8631
United in the Community	0161-708 9451
United Radio (Matchdays Only)	0161-868 8888
Red Café	0161-868 8303
MUTV	0870 8486888
Website	www.ManUtd.com

CHAIRMAN'S MESSAGE

Whenever I settle down to write my annual message for the club's official yearbook my mind wanders back to the time when we decided to launch the first of what has become an established series. Remarkably, it is now 15 years later and I have to say that the *Manchester United Official Yearbook* continues to go from strength to strength. It has always been packed with statistics, match details and player profiles, but in the last couple of years match reports have been included to make the season's coverage even more comprehensive. And, what a great season we have just witnessed with the FA Premier League being won for a third year running and the seventh time since it was introduced in season 1992-93. It's a wonderful achievement.

The cup competitions failed to provide honours but there were numerous exciting matches to enjoy in all of them. Our third round match against Fulham at Craven Cottage was a FA Cup match in the richest traditions of the competition. Jean Tigana's team pushed us all the way and it was only Teddy Sheringham's goal late in the game that gave us victory.

Interest in the League Cup may have ceased after only two games but having beaten Watford at Vicarage Road we went close to recording a notable win at Sunderland. I thought our young players who played in those games did themselves and the club great credit.

In the Champions League we were eliminated at the quarter-final stage for the second successive year. I suppose it was almost inevitable that Bayern Munich would come out on top following victory over them in the 1999 final. Events have an uncanny knack of balancing themselves out in football. Travelling to Munich with a one goal deficit wasn't ideal and when the Germans scored twice in the first half we were really up against it. But we never threw in the towel and when Ryan Giggs scored just after the break you could feel a sense of unease around the Olympic Stadium. Another goal soon after and there could have been a completely different conclusion to the tie. In the end our vastly improved second half performance wasn't enough and it was the famous German team that moved forward to the semi-final.

As always I commend the *Manchester United Official Yearbook* to you all in the hope that you enjoy its contents and the memories they evoke.

C. Martin Edwards

MANAGER'S MESSAGE

The 2000-2001 season may not have been quite as exciting – by our own recent standards – as some of our previous campaigns, but I still look back on it with enormous pride and satisfaction. Winning the FA Premier League is always a marvellous achievement, but to claim it for a third successive season was indeed a moment to cherish. Let us not forget that only three other clubs in English football history have done the hat-trick and to join that exclusive group is something very special.

The Premiership remains one of the most arduous and demanding leagues in the world and winning it must not be taken lightly. The fact that the title was clinched so early is further testimony to the immense determination, self-belief and commitment of the players. I have said it before, and no doubt will again, that I have nothing but total admiration for the players in the way they remain motivated each season despite their continuing success. It would be easy for them to rest on their past glories and many achievements, but that just isn't their style. They continue to be totally dedicated, thoroughly professional young men who are always looking forward to the next challenge. Don't get me wrong, the lads enjoy and savour to the full each of their triumphs as if it were the first, but it isn't long before they are looking ahead to chase for further success.

Many people have said that they were largely disappointed with the season, particularly from Christmas onwards, even though we ended with the Premiership trophy on the sideboard. And, whilst I accept that the season did slow down for us to some degree after the title had been clinched, I thought we performed to good level for most of the time.

Like everyone else I was bitterly disappointed to go out of the FA Cup and UEFA Champions League, but I'm realistic enough to recognise that it just isn't possible to win every competition we enter. Losing at Old Trafford against Bayern Munich left us with huge task in the second leg and despite a terrific second half performance we were forced to concede defeat to Ottmar Hitzfeld's team. And against West Ham it was one of those days when you get the feeling that it just isn't going to happen.

I'm not going to dwell on the downside of the season because, as I said earlier, winning the Premiership again was a great achievement and we should enjoy the moment.

Sir Alex Ferguson

AUGUST

SUNDAY 20	v NEWCASTLE UNITED	H
TUESDAY 22	v IPSWICH TOWN	A
SATURDAY 26	v WEST HAM UNITED	A

MANCHESTER UNITED 2

1. Fabien BARTHEZ
2. Gary NEVILLE
12. Phil NEVILLE
16. Roy KEANE
5. Ronny JOHNSEN
6. Jaap STAM
7. David BECKHAM
18. Paul SCHOLES
9. Andy COLE
10. Teddy SHERINGHAM
11. Ryan GIGGS

SUBSTITUTES

17. Raimond VAN DER GOUW
19. Dwight YORKE (10) 76
20. Ole Gunnar SOLSKJAER (9) 76
22. Ronnie WALLWORK (5) 63
25. Quinton FORTUNE

JOHNSEN 20
COLE 69

MATCH REPORT

Manchester United began the defence of their title in commanding style. Indeed, their performance throughout a high-tempo first half echoed their domination of the previous campaign, and though they dazzled more intermittently after the break, the destination of the points was never in doubt.

In front of a record Premiership crowd, the Reds surged on to the offensive from the first whistle, and new goalkeeper Barthez nearly pierced the Magpies' rearguard with a soaring through-ball after some 40 seconds.

That was the signal for a prolonged period of United enterprise, their quickfire passing and non-stop movement off the ball a delight to the eye, with Cole especially outstanding.

However, when the breakthrough came it was as a result of slackness in the visitors' defence. The splendid Given had just pulled off an acrobatic save from Stam's fierce header, following a characteristically inviting Beckham delivery, when Johnsen was accorded total freedom to nod home the resultant corner via the keeper's left hand.

For the remainder of the half, United ran riot. Giggs and Cole set up Sheringham only for the former England man to sidefoot wide from ten yards;

Roy Keane congratulates Ronny Johnsen on scoring United's first goal of the season

0 NEWCASTLE UNITED

1. Shay GIVEN
2. Warren BARTON
3. Elena MARCELINO
34. Nikolaos DABIZAS
5. Alain GOMA
18. Aaron HUGHES
7. Rob LEE
17. Daniel CORDONE
9. Alan SHEARER
16. Carl CORT
11. Gary SPEED

SUBSTITUTES

4. Didier DOMI
8. Kieran DYER (5) h-t
13. Steve HARPER
15. Nolberto SOLANO (7) 59
37. Laurent CHARVET

Andy Cole forces his way between Dabizas and Lee

Goma grounded Giggs in the box but no penalty was awarded; the Welshman volleyed savagely against an upright from a Scholes cross; raspers from Sheringham and Keane fizzed just wide, and Given tipped a Scholes howitzer over the bar.

Bobby Robson used the interval to rethink and his introduction of Dyer helped to stem the Red tide, but still the hosts held sway, Given being forced to save brilliantly from Beckham and Dabizas almost heading into his own goal.

The clincher came when Cole executed a sweet passing interchange with Giggs before netting clinically from ten yards. It was a fittingly deft climax to a gloriously fluent team display.

IPSWICH TOWN 1

WILNIS 6

1. Richard WRIGHT
2. Fabian WILNIS
3. Jamie CLAPHAM
19. Titus BRAMBLE
32. Hermann HREIDARSSON
6. Mark VENUS
7 Jim MAGILTON
8. Matt HOLLAND
9. David JOHNSON
14. Jermaine WRIGHT
11. Marcus STEWART

SUBSTITUTES

4. John McGREAL
10. James SCOWCROFT (11) 85
16. Gary CROFT
21. Keith BRANAGAN
30. Martijn REUSER (8) 49

MATCH REPORT

The pre-match unveiling of a statue of Sir Alf Ramsey had left Portman Road in the mood to celebrate, and the thrilling, evenly balanced contest which followed was entirely in keeping with the carnival atmosphere.

In view of the 9-0 thrashing dispensed by United when the teams had last met, it would hardly have been surprising had newly promoted Ipswich adopted a cautious mode, but not a bit of it. Instead, they tore into the champions from the first whistle, and their progressive outlook yielded rapid reward when the enterprising Wilnis cut in from the right to climax a sweeping move by beating Barthez with a low drive.

Having thus startled their illustrious visitors, George Burley's men sought to press home their advantage and both Stewart and Clapham shot wide when well placed. United finally steadied themselves and mounted a wave of attacks which saw Scholes and Giggs test Wright, Hreidarsson clear off the line from the England midfielder and Solskjaer shoot over following precise work from Beckham.

The pressure seemed certain to tell, and it did when Beckham curled a 30-yard

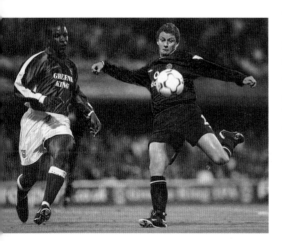

Ole Gunnar Solskjaer shoots over the crossbar

1 MANCHESTER UNITED

39 BECKHAM

1. Fabien BARTHEZ
2. Gary NEVILLE
12. Phil NEVILLE
16. Roy KEANE
22. Ronnie WALLWORK
6. Jaap STAM
7. David BECKHAM
18. Paul SCHOLES
20. Ole Gunnar SOLSKJAER
19. Dwight YORKE
11. Ryan GIGGS
SUBSTITUTES
9. Andy COLE (20) 63
10. Teddy SHERINGHAM (19) 79
17. Raimond VAN DER GOUW
25. Quinton FORTUNE
27. Mikael SILVESTRE (12) 76

David Beckham celebrates his goal in customary style

free-kick from the left, Wallwork jumped over the ball and it bounced into the far corner of the net.

Not even this could daunt Ipswich who responded in spectacular style when Magilton seized on a Barthez clearance and attempted a 50-yard floater, which the Frenchman cleared only at the painful cost of cannoning into an upright.

The second half saw United dominate possession but the hosts created clear-cut opportunities for Clapham, former Old Trafford starlet Johnson and Reuser, all of which were repelled expertly by the splendid Barthez. At the other end, Wright foiled Solskjaer (twice) and Beckham.

Ultimately a draw was a fair result, affording Ipswich a measure of sweet revenge for that previous annihilation.

WEST HAM UNITED 2

1. Shaka HISLOP

15. Rio FERDINAND

3. Stuart PEARCE

17. Nigel WINTERBURN

5. Igor STIMAC

30. Javier MARGAS

26. Joe COLE

21. Michael CARRICK

9. Davor SUKER

10. Paolo DI CANIO

11. Steve LOMAS

SUBSTITUTES

4. Steve POTTS

12. Paul KITSON (30) 87

23. Adam NEWTON

24. Christian BASSILA (15) 68

32. Stephen BYWATER

DI CANIO (penalty) 85
SUKER 89

MATCH REPORT

David Beckham gives United an early lead

So often Manchester United have demoralised hapless opponents with decisive late assaults, but this time it was the Red Devils who were mugged in the dying moments of a game they had all but won.

And, just to render the experience even more excruciating, after West Ham had netted twice in the last four minutes, the champions' outstanding player, David Beckham, twice rapped the Eastenders' woodwork but was not to add to his goal tally of one that afternoon.

2   MANCHESTER UNITED

6 BECKHAM
49 COLE

1. Fabien BARTHEZ
2. Gary NEVILLE
12. Phil NEVILLE
16. Roy KEANE
27. Mikael SILVESTRE
6. Jaap STAM
7. David BECKHAM
18. Paul SCHOLES
9. Andy COLE
10. Teddy SHERINGHAM
11. Ryan GIGGS

SUBSTITUTES

17. Raimond VAN DER GOUW
20. Ole Gunnar SOLSKJAER
21. Henning BERG (6) h-t

After surviving an early incursion by the brilliant di Canio, the visitors quickly took the lead when Stimac felled Sheringham and Beckham beat Hislop with a curling free-kick from 30 yards.

However, for the remainder of the half the hosts pushed forward with zest and invention. Given a free role, di Canio mesmerised as he roamed the park and one cross set up Carrick for a piledriver which brought an agile parry from Barthez. Both Suker and Joe Cole might have scored from free headers, di Canio lobbed wide of an empty net from 35 yards and more Barthez acrobatics were needed to repel a Lomas screamer.

The second period began in similar vein, with Stimac nodding narrowly wide from a corner, before United doubled their lead with a classic counter-attack. Beckham's glorious diagonal dispatch found Giggs, who touched on for Andy Cole to prod beyond the groping Hislop.

Thereafter an away victory seemed inevitable, but Joe Cole and di Canio had other ideas. First, the young Englishman was grounded by Berg and the veteran Italian netted from the spot. Then Cole found di Canio, whose cross was miskicked by Silvestre and headed home by Suker.

Too late the champions rallied and a looping Beckham free-kick bounced against the angle of West Ham's goalframe, then the England star cracked a low drive against the opposite post. Complacency? Perhaps, but riveting entertainment for all that.

Andy Cole tangles with West Ham's Igor Stimac

AUGUST IN REVIEW

SUNDAY 20	v NEWCASTLE UNITED	H	2-0
TUESDAY 22	v IPSWICH TOWN	A	1-1
SATURDAY 26	v WEST HAM UNITED	A	2-2

PLAYER IN THE FRAME

Fabien Barthez

The full dazzling glare of the Old Trafford spotlight was directed on the Red Devils' sole high-profile newcomer and, not unexpectedly to those who had followed the extrovert Frenchman's earlier exploits at club and international level, he revelled in it. The job of following the great Peter Schmeichel had proved beyond Mark Bosnich, but Fabien Barthez signalled his credibility with an early series of flamboyantly athletic displays which brooked no argument.

FA CARLING PREMIERSHIP

UP TO AND INCLUDING
SATURDAY 26 AUGUST 2000

	P	W	D	L	F	A	Pts
Arsenal	3	2	0	1	7	4	6
Leeds United	2	2	0	0	4	1	6
Newcastle United	3	2	0	1	5	4	6
Coventry City	3	2	0	1	5	5	6
MANCHESTER UNITED	3	1	2	0	5	3	5
Leicester City	3	1	2	0	1	0	5
Everton	3	1	1	1	5	4	4
Middlesbrough	3	1	1	1	5	4	4
Bradford City	3	1	1	1	2	1	4
Chelsea	3	1	1	1	5	5	4
Tottenham Hotspur	3	1	1	1	4	4	4
Liverpool	3	1	1	1	4	5	4
Ipswich Town	3	1	1	1	3	4	4
Charlton Athletic	3	1	0	2	7	8	3
Sunderland	3	1	0	2	3	5	3
Manchester City	3	1	0	2	5	8	3
Aston Villa	2	0	2	0	1	1	2
Derby County	3	0	2	1	6	7	2
Southampton	3	0	2	1	6	7	2
West Ham United	3	0	1	2	4	7	1

SEPTEMBER

TUESDAY 5	v BRADFORD CITY	H
SATURDAY 9	v SUNDERLAND	H
WEDNESDAY 13	v RSC ANDERLECHT	H
SATURDAY 16	v EVERTON	A
TUESDAY 19	v DYNAMO KIEV	A
SATURDAY 23	v CHELSEA	H
TUESDAY 26	v PSV EINDHOVEN	A

MANCHESTER UNITED 6

1. Fabien BARTHEZ
2. Gary NEVILLE
27. Mikael SILVESTRE
34. Jonathan GREENING
5. Ronny JOHNSEN
22. Ronnie WALLWORK
7. David BECKHAM
8. Nicky BUTT
9. Andy COLE
10. Teddy SHERINGHAM
25. Quinton FORTUNE

SUBSTITUTES

11. Ryan GIGGS
12. Phil NEVILLE (5) 66
17. Raimond VAN DER GOUW
18. Paul SCHOLES (8) 72
20. Ole Gunnar SOLSKJAER (9) 64

COLE 11
FORTUNE 23, 60
SHERINGHAM 71, 81
BECKHAM 85

MATCH REPORT

Andy Cole celebrates his stunning opener

Suitably chastised by Sir Alex Ferguson for squandering a two-goal lead at West Ham, the Red Devils responded precisely as their manager intended with the merciless destruction of Bradford City.

Despite giving youth a fling with rare starts for Wallwork, Greening and Fortune, and with a host of star absentees, United delivered a performance of shimmering fluency, leaving the plucky Bantams to toil unavailingly.

Teddy Sheringham scored his 199th and 200th League goals

0 **BRADFORD CITY**

13. Matthew CLARKE
2. Ian NOLAN
20. Peter ATHERTON
4. Stuart McCALL
5. David WETHERALL
6. Gareth WHALLEY
18. Gunnar HALLE
30. David HOPKIN
15. Dean WINDASS
10. Benito CARBONE
16. Lee SHARPE

SUBSTITUTES

3. Andy MYERS
9. Ashley WARD (16) 66
11. Peter BEAGRIE
17. Aidan DAVISON
22. Wayne JACOBS

Indeed, with Beckham and Butt assuming charge of centre field and with stand-in skipper Sheringham enjoying one of his most eye-catching outings in a red shirt, the result was hardly in doubt from the moment Cole opened the scoring with a first-time 20-yard chip which took a slight deflection off the boot of Atherton.

The lead was doubled when Beckham's cross eluded Cole but was met at the far post with a firm drive by the lively Fortune, who netted again on the hour with a spectacular dipping long-distance drive.

Soon after that Windass hit a post, thus confirming that nothing was going to fall right for the visitors, before Silvestre delivered a majestic raking crossfield pass into Sheringham's stride and the Londoner volleyed past Clarke from 15 yards.

That was Teddy's 199th League goal and his 200th was not long in following – a neat header to convert a lovely cross by Greening, who was injured when he crashed sickeningly into the hoardings in the act of dispatch.

Finally, with the match long since won and as if to emphasise the Reds' phenomenal work ethic, Beckham left two defenders leaden-footed before sweeping home a low 25-yarder which appeared to deceive Clarke with its wicked bounce. Before the season, Sir Alex had called for more goals from the England midfielder, and this was his third in consecutive Premiership outings.

Not to be outdone, David Beckham celebrates United's sixth

MANCHESTER UNITED 3

SCHOLES 14, 82
SHERINGHAM 76

1. Fabien BARTHEZ
2. Gary NEVILLE
27. Mikael SILVESTRE
18. Paul SCHOLES
5. Ronny JOHNSEN
6. Jaap STAM
7. David BECKHAM
8. Nicky BUTT
9. Andy COLE
10. Teddy SHERINGHAM
11. Ryan GIGGS
SUBSTITUTES
3. Denis IRWIN (6) h-t
12. Phil NEVILLE
17. Raimond VAN DER GOUW
20. Ole Gunnar SOLSKJAER (9) 80
22. Ronnie WALLWORK

MATCH REPORT

There were several passages of play during Manchester United's comprehensive dismissal of Sunderland that were as close to footballing perfection as it is possible to imagine. The opening goal from Scholes came after a team movement which was radiant in its brilliance, yet sublime in its sheer simplicity.

The ball travelled from Silvestre in defence and then to Scholes in midfield; it was ferried hither and thither in a bewildering blur of sweetly accurate passing, from Butt, to Sheringham, to Cole and back to Scholes, who stroked it out to Beckham on the right. The shaven-headed one took the dispatch in his stride, then delivered a typically exquisite arcing cross which was met by Scholes to nod it precisely into the far corner.

The visitors had no answer to that, or to other early sorties where the Red Devils strode through the Wearsiders' ranks to create chances which were missed by Butt, Cole and Scholes among others.

However, as the first half grew old, United's rhythm stuttered – might they yet pay for failing to make the most of their initial supremacy? Not so, though after 74 minutes Sunderland carved their best opportunity when a Thome header was glanced on by Quinn, only for Barthez to pull off a smart save.

Kevin Phillips struggled for goal-scoring form against a superior United as Ronny Johnsen stays on top of the game

0 SUNDERLAND

30. Jurgen MACHO

2. Chris MAKIN

3. Michael GRAY

4. Don HUTCHISON

36. Emerson THOME

17 Jody CRADDOCK

14. Darren HOLLOWAY

33. Julio ARCA

9. Niall QUINN

10. Kevin PHILLIPS

11. Kevin KILBANE

SUBSTITUTES

12. Danny DICHIO

13. Andrew MARRIOTT

18. Darren WILLIAMS

19. Eric ROY (14) h-t

28. John OSTER (33) 70

Ryan Giggs and Chris Makin go head to head in a game where the Reds, on almost every occasion, came out head and shoulders above their rivals

The escape stirred the Reds to action in the form of two more magnificent goals. First, Beckham's chip was nodded on by Cole for Sheringham to volley adroitly past Macho, then Scholes lashed in an unstoppable 20-yard howitzer.

MANCHESTER UNITED 5

1. Fabien BARTHEZ
2. Gary NEVILLE
3. Denis IRWIN
16. Roy KEANE
5. Ronny JOHNSEN
27. Mikael SILVESTRE
7. David BECKHAM
18. Paul SCHOLES
9. Andy COLE
10. Teddy SHERINGHAM
11. Ryan GIGGS

SUBSTITUTES

6. Jaap STAM
8. Nicky BUTT
12. Phil NEVILLE (3) 69
17. Raimond VAN DER GOUW
19. Dwight YORKE (9) 74
20. Ole Gunnar SOLSKJAER (11) 59
22. Ronnie WALLWORK

COLE 15, 50, 72
IRWIN (penalty) 31
SHERINGHAM 42

MATCH REPORT

Andy Cole looks delighted as he beats Denis Law's club record of 14 goals in the European Cup

On the night that Andy Cole outstripped 'The King', Manchester United began their latest Champions League adventure with a flamboyant five-goal flourish. The opening strike of an exuberant hat-trick by the Red Devils' England marksman was enough to take him past Denis Law's club record of 14 goals in the continent's premier club competition and, for good measure, to stretch United's tally to 300 in senior European games.

Anderlecht played neat if rather ordinary football, and in the colossal but deceptively skilful Koller they packed a

Veteran Denis Irwin strokes home United's 31st-minute penalty

1 RSC ANDERLECHT

55 KOLLER

1. Filip DE WILDE
16. Bertrand CRASSON
14. Patrick VAN DIEMEN
4. Yves VANDERHAEGHE
5. Glen DE BOECK
6. Lorenzo STAELENS
7. Bart GOOR
8. Jan KOLLER
9. Didier DHEEDENE
10. Walter BASEGGIO
13. Tomasz RADZINSKI
SUBSTITUTES
2. Aleksander ILIC (7) 59
3. Ddavy OYEN (14) h-t
11. Alin STOICA
22. Oleg IACHTCHOUK
23. Zvonko MILOSEVIC
26. Aruna DINDANE
28. Souleymane YOULA (13) 59

potentially deadly offensive weapon, but by half-time they were already a spent force.

Tormentor-in-chief of the Belgian champions was Ryan Giggs, whose darting runs from deep and quickfire passing interchanges with Cole and company wrought repeated havoc. Both Scholes and Giggs had already gone close before the Welshman engineered the breakthrough, scampering down the left and mesmerising several defenders before floating a cross for Cole to pass his milestone with a precise glancing header.

Radzinski and Van Diemen both had chances to equalise as United stuttered intermittently, but then Giggs scooted past four opponents before being felled in the box. Irwin made no mistake from the spot.

Beckham joined the show by picking out Sheringham whose first shot was saved brilliantly by De Wilde only for the veteran striker to net from close range at the second attempt.

Cole's second was a simple sidefoot into an empty net after a defensive mix-up, then Koller gained the reward his personal performance deserved when he rounded Barthez and squeezed home a spinning shot via a post. It was left to Cole to complete the rout with a looping header from Beckham's cross. If only it were always this easy.

David Beckham ghosts past the Anderlecht defence

FA CARLING PREMIERSHIP
Saturday 16 September, 2000

EVERTON 1

GRAVESEN 54

1. Paul GERRARD
2. Steve WATSON
15. Richard DUNNE
16. Thomas GRAVESEN
5. David WEIR
18. Paul GASCOIGNE
7. Niclas ALEXANDERSSON
8. Alex NYARKO
23. Mark HUGHES
10. Stephen HUGHES
14. Francis JEFFERS

SUBSTITUTES

6. David UNSWORTH (10) h-t
9. Kevin CAMPBELL (23) 70
13. Steve SIMONSEN
17. Scot GEMMILL (18) 70
19. Joe-Max MOORE

MATCH REPORT

Perhaps with their forthcoming expedition to the Ukraine in mind, United began this clinical demolition of Everton as if they wanted to put the result beyond reasonable doubt as quickly as possible. Despite being without the central spine of their team – Stam, Keane and Cole – that is exactly what they did in a performance of controlled brilliance.

First Sheringham sent in Solskjaer, whose left-foot strike was held by Gerrard. Then a sublime passing movement set up Scholes, whose drive was diverted away from goal by the hand of Watson, but no penalty was given.

Still the visitors flowed forward relentlessly, their persistence paying off when the elusive Solskjaer's curling cross was chested adroitly into Gerrard's net by the rampant, charging Butt.

Everton barely had time to draw breath before they were two adrift. A clearance by Brown, making his first appearance for more than a year following injury, was turned to Sheringham by Solskjaer. The acting captain skipped past Weir, Gerrard saved the shot but Giggs threaded home with perfect accuracy from 20 yards.

Dwight Yorke tangles with two Everton defenders

22   MANCHESTER UNITED OFFICIAL YEARBOOK 2000-01

3 MANCHESTER UNITED

26 BUTT
29 GIGGS
38 SOLSKJAER

1. Fabien BARTHEZ
2. Gary NEVILLE
3. Denis IRWIN
18. Paul SCHOLES
24. Wesley BROWN
27. Mikael SILVESTRE
7. David BECKHAM
8. Nicky BUTT
20. Ole Gunnar SOLSKJAER
10. Teddy SHERINGHAM
11. Ryan GIGGS
SUBSTITUTES
9. Andy COLE
12. Phil NEVILLE (18) 74
17. Raimond VAN DER GOUW (1) 79
19. Dwight YORKE (11) h-t
22. Ronnie WALLWORK

Ole Gunnar Solskjaer watches carefully but his effort goes wide of goal

Then Gerrard parried athletically from Solskjaer after Dunne had dallied and, at the other end, there was time for a volley from Mark Hughes, before the Reds scored the goal of the game. Silvestre delivered a long pass up the left, Beckham completed a devastating diagonal sprint, then controlled the ball silkily and laid it into the path of Solskjaer, who pounced and netted with alacrity.

Now annihilation seemed possible, but the Toffees retaliated defiantly when the gritty Gravesen shot under Barthez. Thereafter Yorke rapped a post and more chances went begging as United settled for restrained, but absolute, supremacy.

DYNAMO KIEV 0

1. Olexander SHOVKOVSKYI

2. Alixandr KHATSKEVITCH

26. Andrii NESMACHNYI

4. Olexander HOLOVKO

5. Vladyslav VASCHUK

6. Yurii DMYTRULIN

7. Kakha KALADZE

8. Valiantsin BIALKEVICH

14. Andrii HUSIN

10. Maksim SHATSKIKH

11. George DEMETRADZE

SUBSTITUTES

3. Alexey GERASIMENKO

12. Vyacheslav KERNOZENKO

15. Artem YASHKIN

16. Laszlo BODNAR (6) 83

17. Serhii FEDOROV (14) 87

23. Vladimir KUZMICHEV (11) 68

28. Serhii SEREBRENNIKOV

MATCH REPORT

On a dismally foggy, soggy Ukrainian night, Manchester United moved to the summit of their Champions League group, thanks to the width of the woodwork and the cat-like agility of Raimond van der Gouw.

After the Red Devils had enjoyed marginally the better of a first half which was always entertaining despite the sapping conditions, Dynamo surged back after the break to put their visitors under sustained pressure.

It was then that the powerful and mobile Shatskikh twice rattled the frame of the Dutchman's goal, first bursting through in the inside-right slot and crashing a savage shot against the crossbar from 15 yards, then dispatching a 25-yard thunderbolt

Andy Cole fails to find the net with this right-foot shot

0 MANCHESTER UNITED

17. Raimond VAN DER GOUW
2. Gary NEVILLE
3. Denis IRWIN
16. Roy KEANE
5. Ronny JOHNSEN
27. Mikael SILVESTRE
7. David BECKHAM
8. Nicky BUTT
9. Andy COLE
19. Dwight YORKE
11. Ryan GIGGS

SUBSTITUTES

6. Jaap STAM
10. Teddy SHERINGHAM (19) 67
12. Phil NEVILLE
13. Mark BOSNICH
18. Paul SCHOLES
20. Ole Gunnar SOLSKJAER (9) 78
22. Ronnie WALLWORK

which van der Gouw turned against a post at full stretch before clutching the rebound safely to his chest.

However, had Yorke taken either of two first-half opportunities, the second period might not have been quite so harrowing for the United contingent. First the Tobagan, surprisingly selected ahead of the in-form Sheringham, sliced wide with the outside of his right foot when sent in by Giggs, then he unleashed a scorcher which fizzed marginally the wrong side of Shovkovskyi's upright.

Thereafter, a Keane shot was saved and the Reds seemed ready to cruise, only for Dynamo – all of whose players had taken to the pitch with shaven heads, apparently to foster team spirit – mounted their impressive post-interval offensive.

Van der Gouw, deputising as impeccably for the sidelined Barthez as he was accustomed to do for Schmeichel, made several sharp saves, while Gary Neville continued his recent run of commanding form at the centre of defence in the absence of Stam.

Overall, while realising that they had been lucky, United could congratulate themselves on retaining their poise while picking up a precious away point on a tough ground where no English team has ever won.

Nicky Butt works hard to retain possession

MANCHESTER UNITED 3

- 17. Raimond VAN DER GOUW
- 2. Gary NEVILLE
- 3. Denis IRWIN
- 16. Roy KEANE
- 5. Ronny JOHNSEN
- 27. Mikael SILVESTRE
- 7. David BECKHAM
- 18. Paul SCHOLES
- 9. Andy COLE
- 10. Teddy SHERINGHAM
- 11. Ryan GIGGS

SUBSTITUTES

- 8. Nicky BUTT (10) 77
- 12. Phil NEVILLE
- 13. Mark BOSNICH
- 20. Ole Gunnar SOLSKJAER (9) 81
- 24. Wesley BROWN (3) 81

SCHOLES 14
SHERINGHAM 37
BECKHAM 39

MATCH REPORT

Chelsea came from two goals behind to earn a point, and the unpalatable truth for United was that the Blues deserved their share of the spoils.

Having recovered from conceding an early goal to lead 3-1 as they entered stoppage time at the end of the first half, the Red Devils were guilty of slackness at the back and they paid for it. That said, the midweek trip to the Ukraine must have taken its toll in terms of weariness, both physical and mental.

New Chelsea coach Claudio Ranieri could not have wished for a more auspicious start to his reign than the one provided by Hasselbaink's spectacular opening strike. Le Saux crossed from the left, Flo hooked it back to the edge of the box where it reached the Dutchman, who controlled it on his chest and adjusted his feet brilliantly before netting with a savage and unstoppable volley.

Not to be outdone, United replied in kind when Irwin's cross was directed by Sheringham to Scholes, who netted with a murderous half-volley from 20 yards.

Now the hosts began to flow and grabbed two goals in two minutes. First a long ball from Irwin was allowed to bounce by a succession of dithering defenders and Sheringham converted from eight yards; next the scorer sent in Cole,

Ryan Giggs was effervescent in United's superb first-half display

3 CHELSEA

8 HASSELBAINK
45, 70 FLO

23. Carlo CUDICINI
2. Christian PANUCCI
14. Graham LE SAUX
16. Roberto DI MATTEO
5. Frank LEBOEUF
6. Marcel DESAILLY
20. Jody MORRIS
19. Tore Andre FLO
9. Jimmy Floyd HASSELBAINK
25. Gianfranco ZOLA
24. Jon HARLEY

SUBSTITUTES

7. Winston BOGARDE (9) 87
13. Kevin HITCHCOCK
15. Mario MELCHIOT (34) h-t
18. Gabriel AMBROSETTI
24. Samuelle DALLA BONA (25) 84

Andy Cole works his way between Leboeuf and Di Matteo to shoot at goal

whose dink rebounded from a post for Beckham to stab into an unguarded net.

But the script went horribly awry as van der Gouw allowed Flo's brisk but hardly threatening header to squirm over his line. Then Le Saux rounded Beckham before crossing to Zola, the ball was transferred to Flo and the Norwegian curled in the equaliser.

United had other chances: at 3-2 a Cole shot was cleared off the line by Le Saux and Giggs scooped over when well placed. Thereafter, the Blues held firm and the shrewd Ranieri left Old Trafford a contented man.

PSV EINDHOVEN 3

23. Ronald WATERREUS
13. Chris VAN DER WEERDEN
21. Yuri NIKIFOROV
29. Kevin HOFLAND
5. Jan HEINTZE
6. Mark VAN BOMMEL
17. Bjorn VAN DER DOELEN
14. Johann VOGEL
9. Mateja KEZMAN
10. Arnold BRUGGINK
22. Wilfred BOUMA

SUBSTITUTES

2. Andre OOIJER
3. Jurgen DIRKX
11. Joonas KOLKKA (9) 84
15. John DE JONG
16. Theo LUCIUS (17) 77
19. Dennis ROMMEDAHL (22) 80
20. Patrick LODEWIJKS

BOUMA 17
VAN BOMMEL 43
KEZMAN 62

MATCH REPORT

For the third time in this fledgling season, Manchester United allowed a lead to slip away, but this was the first time they had been punished by defeat. True, they had started without eight players who might be deemed first choices, but while Barthez and Stam were injured, the absences of Beckham, Giggs, Cole, Sheringham, Johnsen and Irwin were all by managerial choice, with the imminent Premiership clash with Arsenal in mind.

The outcome was a reverse which was emphatic enough, but which might easily have attained embarrassing proportions, so thoroughly were the Red Devils outplayed.

The lively Jonathan Greening is forced to shoot wide by the close attention of the PSV defence

1 MANCHESTER UNITED

2 SCHOLES (penalty)

17. Raimond VAN DER GOUW
2. Gary NEVILLE
12. Phil NEVILLE
16. Roy KEANE
24. Wesley BROWN
27. Mikael SILVESTRE
34. Jonathan GREENING
8. Nicky BUTT
20. Ole Gunnar SOLSKJAER
19. Dwight YORKE
18. Paul SCHOLES

SUBSTITUTES

5. Ronny JOHNSEN
7. David BECKHAM (34) 70
9. Andy COLE
10. Teddy SHERINGHAM
11. Ryan GIGGS (18) 70
13. Mark BOSNICH
22. Ronnie WALLWORK (27) 70

Mancunian dismay was all the more acute as United had actually seized an early initiative with Scholes netting from the spot after the sprinting Solskjaer had his heels clipped by PSV keeper Waterreus. Soon after Butt crossed, Greening nodded down and Yorke failed to volley home from four yards.

After that it was all uphill for the visitors, who defended sloppily throughout. PSV equalised when Phil Neville was guilty of ball-watching and Bouma strode past him to score with a low left-footer from the edge of the box. They claimed a deserved lead when Van Bommel seized on to a perfect through-ball from Kezman and drove his shot through the legs of the United keeper.

After the interval Kezman continued to wreak havoc and he missed two opportunities before plundering a third goal by nipping past Silvestre and crashing a narrow-angled drive over the head of van der Gouw and into the net via the crossbar.

Later Bruggink missed a sitter and although the visitors revived somewhat with the introduction of Beckham and Giggs, the nearest they came to a tangible reply was a Butt header which was cleared off the line.

Even Roy Keane's exquisite skills were unable to ignite a lacklustre United

SEPTEMBER IN REVIEW

TUESDAY 5	v BRADFORD CITY	H	6-0
SATURDAY 9	v SUNDERLAND	H	3-0
WEDNESDAY 13	v RSC ANDERLECHT	H	5-1
SATURDAY 16	v EVERTON	A	3-1
TUESDAY 19	v DYNAMO KIEV	A	0-0
SATURDAY 23	v CHELSEA	H	3-3
TUESDAY 26	v PSV EINDHOVEN	A	1-3

PLAYER IN THE FRAME

Andy Cole

After his achievements of recent seasons Andy Cole had nothing left to prove, yet he managed to enhance his stock further by becoming the Reds' record scorer in Europe's premier club competition, outstripping no less a figure than Denis Law. Andy did it in style by plundering a hat-trick in the 5-1 demolition of Anderlecht, and his all-round sharpness hinted that his best may be yet to come.

FA CARLING PREMIERSHIP

UP TO AND INCLUDING
SATURDAY 30 SEPTEMBER 2000

	P	W	D	L	F	A	Pts
MANCHESTER UNITED	7	4	3	0	20	7	15
Leicester City	7	4	3	0	7	2	15
Newcastle United	8	4	1	3	8	7	13
Arsenal	7	3	3	1	13	9	12
Aston Villa	7	3	3	1	11	7	12
Liverpool	7	3	3	1	12	10	12
Charlton Athletic	8	3	3	2	14	13	12
Leeds United	7	3	2	2	11	9	11
Ipswich Town	8	3	2	3	11	10	11
Tottenham Hotspur	8	3	2	3	11	11	11
Middlesbrough	8	2	4	2	14	12	10
Southampton	8	2	3	3	11	12	9
Everton	8	2	2	4	11	15	8
Manchester City	8	2	2	4	10	14	8
Sunderland	7	2	2	3	7	11	8
Coventry City	8	2	2	4	8	14	8
West Ham United	8	1	4	3	10	11	7
Chelsea	7	1	4	2	10	12	7
Bradford City	8	1	3	4	4	12	6
Derby County	8	0	5	3	14	19	5

OCTOBER

SUNDAY 1	v ARSENAL	A
SATURDAY 14	v LEICESTER CITY	A
WEDNESDAY 18	v PSV EINDHOVEN	H
SATURDAY 21	v LEEDS UNITED	H
TUESDAY 24	v RSC ANDERLECHT	A
SATURDAY 28	v SOUTHAMPTON	H
TUESDAY 31	v WATFORD	A

ARSENAL   1

HENRY 30

1. David SEAMAN
22. Oleg LUZHNY
16. SILVINHO
18. Gilles GRIMANDI
5. Martin KEOWN
6. Tony ADAMS
15. Ray PARLOUR
8. Fredrik LJUNGBERG
25. KANU
10. Dennis BERGKAMP
14. Thierry HENRY

SUBSTITUTES

2. Lee DIXON
11. Sylvain WILTORD (10) 77
23. Nelson VIVAS (25) 57
24. John LUKIC
30. Paolo VERNAZZA

MATCH REPORT

Manchester United were beaten by a goal from Henry which was fit to win any match, and there can be no complaints about that.

Still, though, it was an intensely frustrating afternoon for the blue-shirted Reds, who suffered their first Premiership reverse since February despite playing the most fluent football, enjoying the most possession and making nearly three times as many goal attempts as their north London rivals.

Gallingly, on a day when the recently vulnerable defence looked firm and the midfield were in the ascendant, it was the hitherto prolific attack which faltered when faced with the formidable Gunners rearguard of the majestic Adams and Keown.

United enjoyed the better of the opening half-hour, with Arsenal always straining to cope with their visitors' briskly precise passing, and Scholes (twice), Cole and Keane all went close to forcing a breakthrough.

But then came Henry's masterpiece. Though surrounded by defenders, he accepted Grimandi's pass with his back to goal, flicked the ball up, then turned and dispatched a sublime looping volley from 20 yards which left Barthez helpless. No one was at fault: it was just a ravishingly brilliant strike. Before the interval Bergkamp might have

Fabien Barthez organised the United defence superbly

0 MANCHESTER UNITED

1. Fabien BARTHEZ

2. Gary NEVILLE

3. Denis IRWIN

16. Roy KEANE

5. Ronny JOHNSEN

27. Mikael SILVESTRE

7. David BECKHAM

18. Paul SCHOLES

9. Andy COLE

10. Teddy SHERINGHAM

11. Ryan GIGGS

SUBSTITUTES

8. Nicky BUTT

13. Mark BOSNICH

19. Dwight YORKE (10) 68

20. Ole Gunnar SOLSKJAER (11) 85

24. Wesley BROWN

Mikael Silvestre works hard to keep Kanu at bay

doubled the lead but he scuffed his shot, then Cole nearly equalised with a fierce left-footer. The second half was a story of steady United pressure and stalwart Arsenal resistance. Seaman saved from Giggs and blocked Scholes, Keane volleyed wide, Sheringham shot over, Cole headed wide.

In reply there was a mazy Silvinho dribble which took him round four opponents before the ball was scrambled away, and Barthez had to race from his area to tackle Henry near the end. When the final whistle sounded Highbury exploded in relief and United fans were left to contemplate a fourth game without a win.

LEICESTER CITY   0

1. Tim FLOWERS
2. Gary ROWETT
15. Phil GILCHRIST
24. Andrew IMPEY
18. Matt ELLIOT
6. Mustafa IZZET
7. Neil LENNON
8. Robbie SAVAGE
9. Darren EADIE
22. Ade AKINBIYI
14. Callum DAVIDSON

SUBSTITUTES

3. Frank SINCLAIR (6) 72
11. Steve GUPPY (22) 59
12. Simon ROYCE
17. Stefan OAKES
23. Richard CRESSWELL (24) 59

MATCH REPORT

After recent setbacks, United's clash with table-topping Leicester assumed a loftier profile than tends usually to be reserved for visits to Filbert Street and this comfortable victory, achieved without many first-team notables, was especially sweet.

For all that, the Foxes had begun with typical feistiness. Two penetrating early runs by Eadie set up Davidson's powerful shot, and Akinbiyi's header, both of which Barthez scrambled away. Then Lennon's chipped free-kick was allowed to reach the visitors' far post but Rowett sidefooted inaccurately.

Teddy Sheringham heads United's first on 37 minutes

3 MANCHESTER UNITED

37, 54 SHERINGHAM
90 SOLSKJAER

1. Fabien BARTHEZ
27. Mikael SILVESTRE
3. Denis IRWIN
16. Roy KEANE
5. Ronny JOHNSEN
24. Wesley BROWN
20. Ole Gunnar SOLSKJAER
8. Nicky BUTT
19. Dwight YORKE
10. Teddy SHERINGHAM
25. Quinton FORTUNE

SUBSTITUTES

11. Ryan GIGGS (10) 72
12. Phil NEVILLE
13. Mark BOSNICH
18. Paul SCHOLES
22. Ronnie WALLWORK

That was to prove a costly miss as United went ahead soon afterwards when Irwin crossed from the right and Sheringham's glancing header beat Flowers via a post. Thereafter the Red Devils became dominant, with Fortune and Butt both going close to doubling the lead before the interval.

However, Leicester showed their resilience early in the second period, and both Rowett and Eadie had spurned fleeting chances before Brown's rash lunge flattened Savage who demanded a penalty. But his plea fell on deaf ears and, from the resultant corner, City squandered possession.

Fortune counter-attacked briskly, Irwin's shot was parried by Flowers and man-of-the-match Sheringham swooped to pop in the rebound, and his second, from close range. Now United assumed absolute control.

A third goal appeared inevitable and duly it arrived in stoppage time when Solskjaer exchanged crisp passes with Yorke before dispatching a low, typically clinical, left-footed cross-shot past Flowers. The on-form custodian had been beaten more times in one afternoon than in all the rest of Leicester's League games put together, and United reclaimed their position at the Premiership's pinnacle.

Nicky Butt shrugs off Leicester's Cresswell

MANCHESTER UNITED 3

1. Fabien BARTHEZ
2. Gary NEVILLE
3. Denis IRWIN
16. Roy KEANE
5. Ronny JOHNSEN
27. Mikael SILVESTRE
7. David BECKHAM
18. Paul SCHOLES
9. Andy COLE
10. Teddy SHERINGHAM
11. Ryan GIGGS

SUBSTITUTES

8. Nicky BUTT (7) 88
12. Phil NEVILLE
13. Mark BOSNICH
19. Dwight YORKE (10) 74
20. Ole Gunnar SOLSKJAER
24. Wesley BROWN (3) 80
25. Quinton FORTUNE

SHERINGHAM 8
SCHOLES 82
YORKE 87

MATCH REPORT

Teddy Sheringham celebrates after heading United into the lead

After making one of their most purposefully incisive starts to a European encounter in recent years, United surrendered the initiative so alarmingly that, with only 15 minutes to play, two sorely-needed points were in danger of slipping away. However, the Reds rallied to earn a deservedly emphatic victory.

The Mancunians were bristling with resolution as they faced the team which had bested them comprehensively in Holland, PSV being stretched to the limit in repelling an early succession

1 PSV EINDHOVEN

76 VAN BOMMEL

23. Ronald WATERREUS	
13. Chris VAN DER WEERDEN	
29. Kevin HOFLAND	
21. Yuri NIKIFOROV	
5. Jan HEINTZE	
6. Mark VAN BOMMEL	
7. Adil RAMZI	
17. Bjorn VAN DER DOELEN	
9. Mateja KEZMAN	
10. Arnold BRUGGINK	
14. Johann VOGEL	

SUBSTITUTES

2. Andre OOIJER	
3. Jurgen DIRKX	
11. Joonas KOLKKA (7) 65	
15. John DE JONG (17) 73	
16. Theo LUCIUS (10) 29	
19. Dennis ROMMEDAHL	
20. Patrick LODEWIJKS	

of high-tempo assaults before Sheringham drew first blood with a thunderous header from a Beckham corner.

With left-winger Ramzi looking particularly menacing, the visitors responded positively before the Reds resumed control. The first of several Beckham free-kicks was punched away by Waterreus, then Johnsen miscued, and Sheringham blazed over an empty net in first-half stoppage time when the Dutch keeper parried a cross from the endlessly inventive Giggs into his path.

The second period began in similar vein, with Beckham going close before Johnsen twanged the Eindhoven crossbar with a header. But a second goal refused to materialise and PSV equalised with a slick 18-yard half-volley from Van Bommel.

A crisis? Not a bit of it. Now the Reds regained their early authority and were rewarded when Silvestre's deep cross was turned back by Yorke, Cole let it run and Scholes dinked it up before volleying sweetly beyond Waterreus.

Finally, the scoreline started to look realistic when Scholes' pass was touched on by Giggs to Yorke, who ran 40 yards pursued by the PSV defence before netting his first goal of the season.

Dwight Yorke slides the ball into the net after a glorious 40-yard run

MANCHESTER UNITED 3

1. Fabien BARTHEZ
2. Gary NEVILLE
12. Phil NEVILLE
16. Roy KEANE
5. Ronny JOHNSEN
27. Mikael SILVESTRE
18. Paul SCHOLES
8. Nicky BUTT
20. Ole Gunnar SOLSKJAER
19. Dwight YORKE
25. Quinton FORTUNE

SUBSTITUTES

7. David BECKHAM (16) 31
9. Andy COLE
11. Ryan GIGGS
13. Mark BOSNICH
24. Wesley BROWN (5) h-t

YORKE 40
BECKHAM 50
JONES (o.g.) 82

MATCH REPORT

David Beckham strokes home United's second goal

From the moment the team sheets were submitted, there appeared scant prospect of the titanic contest traditionally served up by these bitter rivals. While the Reds were missing a handful of stars Leeds were decimated by injuries and predictions that they would be outclassed proved correct.

Eventually, that is. For half an hour the Yorkshiremen, while spending most of their time on the back foot, maintained at least a semblance of equality. Enter David Beckham, who rose from the bench to replace hamstring victim Roy Keane and proceeded to dictate the pattern of the game with imperious grace.

A delighted Dwight Yorke celebrates his second goal in four days

0 LEEDS UNITED

| 13. Paul ROBINSON |
| 2. Gary KELLY |
| 21. Dominic MATTEO |
| 14. Steven McPHAIL |
| 24. Danny HAY |
| 6. Jonathan WOODGATE |
| 20. Matthew JONES |
| 25. Jacob BURNS |
| 9. Mark VIDUKA |
| 17. Alan SMITH |
| 11. Lee BOWYER |

SUBSTITUTES

| 12. Darren HUCKERBY (17) 77 |
| 26. Danny MILOSEVIC |
| 30. Robert MOLENAAR |
| 31. Gareth EVANS |
| 38. Tony HACKWORTH |

His only conceivable rival for the man-of-the-match accolade was Leeds' rookie keeper Paul Robinson, whose athleticism and courage prevented a rout. Indeed, the game's first notable action was a flying save by Robinson to deflect a Fortune drive, after which the visitors mounted their one truly menacing move of the morning, a sweeping counter-attack which climaxed with Smith's cross eluding Bowyer's lunging boot by a hair's breadth.

Thereafter, the hosts poured forward, a swirling Butt shot producing an acrobatic Robinson parry, then Yorke shooting over from the resultant corner.

But United did not hit their customary sweet-passing stride until the arrival of Beckham, who was at the heart of the delicious move which culminated in Yorke stooping to nod home Solskjaer's curving centre shortly before the break.

Both of the Reds' second-half strikes owed something to luck, although Leeds could blame their irresolute defensive wall for letting in Beckham's deflected free-kick, and Jones was under severe pressure when he turned the ball into his own net.

On another day, United might have doubled their tally but Robinson pulled off a succession of stunning saves and Leeds' dignity, at least, was preserved.

David Beckham is rightly happy with a superb personal display

RSC ANDERLECHT 2

RADZINSKI 15, 34

1. Filip DE WILDE
16. Bertrand CRASSON
13. Tomasz RADZINSKI
4. Yves VANDERHAEGHE
5. Glen DE BOECK
6. Lorenzo STAELENS
7. Bart GOOR
8. Jan KOLLER
9. Didier DHEEDENE
10. Walter BASSEGIO
11. Alin STOICA

ŠUBSTITUTES

2. Aleksander ILIC
3. Davy OYEN (11) 81
12. Olivier DOLL
23. Zvonko MILOSEVIC
26. Aruna DINDANE (13) 90
28. Souleymane YOULA
36. MBEMBA

MATCH REPORT

A combination of abysmal defending by Manchester United and superb attacking by Anderlecht left the Red Devils straddling a qualification knife-edge. In the first half the visitors' back four were befuddled time and again by the dazzling work of the giant Koller and the pacy Radzinski, and but for the acrobatics of Barthez they would have been swamped.

There had already been warnings aplenty before the rearguard was breached for the first time, Silvestre failing to police Radzinski, who sprinted on to a Baseggio chip before netting with an emphatic left-foot shot.

Nicky Butt works hard to keep United moving

1 MANCHESTER UNITED

36 IRWIN (penalty)

1. Fabien BARTHEZ
2. Gary NEVILLE
3. Denis IRWIN
18. Paul SCHOLES
5. Ronny JOHNSEN
27. Mikael SILVESTRE
7. David BECKHAM
8. Nicky BUTT
9. Andy COLE
19. Dwight YORKE
11. Ryan GIGGS

SUBSTITUTES

12. Phil NEVILLE
17. Raimond VAN DER GOUW
20. Ole Gunnar SOLSKJAER (3) 78
22. Ronnie WALLWORK
24. Wesley BROWN (27) 63
25. Quinton FORTUNE
34. Jonathan GREENING

Wisely, the Belgians were not content to rest on their laurels and continued to embarrass the Reds. First Radzinski crossed to Koller, whose savage drive from a narrow angle brought a brilliant block from Barthez. Radzinski then seized on a loose ball and prompted another blinding save from the Frenchman.

A second goal seemed inevitable and duly it materialised when Koller's clever cross was met with a low 16-yarder from the ubiquitous Radzinski, the Canadian international's finish a study in exquisite technique and unerring accuracy.

Two minutes later United lifted the siege when Cole completed a smart one-two interchange with Yorke before being fouled in the box, and Irwin reduced the arrears with a scuffed penalty kick.

There seemed plenty of time for Sir Alex Ferguson's men to regain lost ground and, after the interval, they dominated possession, but their resultant pressure created only a succession of unconverted half-chances.

In truth, Anderlecht thoroughly deserved their victory, and to complete a miserable night for United, Scholes was booked for the third time in the competition, ruling him out of the decisive confrontation with Dynamo Kiev.

Mikael Silvestre is dispossessed by Anderlecht's Vanderhaeghe

MANCHESTER UNITED 5

COLE 9, 73
SHERINGHAM 45, 51, 55

1. Fabien BARTHEZ
2. Gary NEVILLE
3. Denis IRWIN
18. Paul SCHOLES
24. Wesley BROWN
12. Phil NEVILLE
7. David BECKHAM
8. Nicky BUTT
9. Andy COLE
10. Teddy SHERINGHAM
11. Ryan GIGGS

SUBSTITUTES
17. Raimond VAN DER GOUW
19. Dwight YORKE (10) 75
20. Ole Gunnar SOLSKJAER (9) 75
30. Ronnie WALLWORK (2) 59
27. Mikael SILVESTRE

MATCH REPORT

Teddy Sheringham receives the congratulations for his superb hat-trick

Hapless Southampton fell victim to a predictably devastating backlash following United's Anderlecht reverse, as veteran marksman Teddy Sheringham offered comprehensive vindication of his summer decision to remain in Manchester, and of his recent England recall, with a sumptuous hat-trick.

For all that, the Saints had begun brightly, with Kachloul chipping narrowly high as Barthez was stranded, and they fell behind only through a goalkeeping howler when Jones allowed a 25-yarder from Cole to squirm between his legs.

0 SOUTHAMPTON

Barthez was lucky when his attempted clearance hit Tessem and rebounded into his arms, and it was not until Sheringham's first strike, shortly before the break, that the Reds assumed dominance. It was the pick of his three, a sublime left-footed floater from the edge of the box, and thereafter the visitors were gunned down with clinical ruthlessness.

First Scholes won a tackle in midfield before feeding Beckham, whose cross found Sheringham in acres of space some 12 yards out, leaving the Londoner to sweep the ball majestically into the corner of Jones' net.

Then Butt charged through the inside-left channel, and although Cole might have mis-controlled the subsequent pass – or was it a perfect touch-back? – Sheringham sidefooted unerringly inside the post from 15 yards.

Duly a fifth breakthrough materialised, thanks to the tenacity of Cole in earning a corner. Beckham took the kick, Scholes nodded on and Cole rose between three defenders to head home at the far post.

Thereafter Beattie should have spoiled the hosts' clean sheet but was blocked by Barthez. By then, though, United were coasting.

Ryan Giggs drives forward in search of number six

WATFORD   0

1. Alec CHAMBERLAIN
2. Neil COX
3. Paul ROBINSON
4. Robert PAGE
5. Steve PALMER
23. Darrren WARD
14. Nordin WOOTER
28. Allan NIELSEN
9. Tommy MOONEY
17. Tommy SMITH
15. Gifton NOEL-WILLIAMS

SUBSTITUTES

13. Chris DAY
16. Nigel GIBBS
18. Heidar HELGUSON (15) 64
19. Clint EASTON (14) h-t
21. Dominic FOLEY (3) 64

MATCH REPORT

Fielding a stronger side than has been their custom in the Worthington Cup, but still markedly under-strength, the Premiership leaders disposed of the First Division pace-setters with consummate ease.

Particularly encouraging from the United viewpoint was the poise and enterprise of rookies such as centre-half O'Shea and right-winger Chadwick, while the more experienced but still youthful likes of Brown and Wallwork impressed mightily.

For all that, though, it was the familiar, dead-eyed marksmanship of star strikers Solskjaer and Yorke which ensured the Red Devils' progress into the next round.

The Hornets, thus far unbeaten in the League, opened brightly enough with Mooney (twice) and Nielsen making brisk attempts on goal, but it was United who seized the early initiative.

Ronnie Wallwork, giving a passable imitation of Roy Keane in midfield, won a crunching tackle and fed Chadwick on the right. The England under-21 international's shot was blocked by Chamberlain but only to the lethal right foot of Solskjaer, who crashed the ball home from eight yards.

A spectacular volley gave Ole Gunnar Solskjaer his second goal of the night

3 MANCHESTER UNITED

12, 81 SOLSKJAER
54 YORKE

17. Raimond VAN DER GOUW
23. Michael CLEGG
12. Phil NEVILLE
22. Ronnie WALLWORK
24. Wesley BROWN
30. John O'SHEA
36. Luke CHADWICK
34. Jonathan GREENING
20. Ole Gunnar SOLSKJAER
19. Dwight YORKE
25. Quinton FORTUNE
SUBSTITUTES
28. Michael STEWART (22) 71
29. Alex NOTMAN
32. Bojan DJORDJIC
33. Paul RACHUBKA (25) 86
35. David HEALY

Scottish teenager Michael Stewart makes his senior debut

Watford retaliated gamely, with Smith and Mooney prominent, though shortly before the break Cox had to clear off the line from Yorke. The Tobagan was not to be denied, however, and he doubled the visitors' lead with a deflected shot from 12 yards after exchanging passes with the excellent Chadwick.

United's third goal was of the route-one variety, Solskjaer latching on to van der Gouw's booming clearance before volleying spectacularly beyond the leaping Chamberlain.

Still there was time for a whiff of drama when the Dutch keeper was adjudged to have felled Helguson in the box and was red-carded. On came Rachubka to face the resultant spot-kick, which was walloped high over the crossbar by Mooney.

A routine victory, then, but a memorable night for teenaged Scottish redhead Michael Stewart, who made his senior debut.

OCTOBER IN REVIEW

SUNDAY 1	v ARSENAL	A	0-1
SATURDAY 14	v LEICESTER CITY	A	3-0
WEDNESDAY 18	v PSV EINDHOVEN	H	3-1
SATURDAY 21	v LEEDS UNITED	H	3-0
TUESDAY 24	v RSC ANDERLECHT	A	1-2
SATURDAY 28	v SOUTHAMPTON	H	5-0
TUESDAY 31	v WATFORD	A	3-0

PLAYER IN THE FRAME

Teddy Sheringham

His critics thought it was all over for Teddy Sheringham a long time ago, but since then he has made them gobble their words. Never, though, has he performed more majestically than in the autumn of 2000, making and taking goals with delicious assurance. Stand-out moments in October included the hat-trick which stunned Southampton.

FA CARLING PREMIERSHIP

UP TO AND INCLUDING
TUESDAY 31 OCTOBER 2000

	P	W	D	L	F	A	Pts
MANCHESTER UNITED	11	7	3	1	31	8	24
Arsenal	11	7	3	1	22	10	24
Liverpool	11	6	3	2	20	14	21
Leicester City	11	5	4	2	9	7	19
Ipswich Town	11	5	3	3	16	12	18
Chelsea	11	4	4	3	22	14	16
Aston Villa	10	4	4	2	13	9	16
Newcastle United	11	5	1	5	11	10	16
Sunderland	11	4	4	3	9	11	16
Leeds United	10	4	3	3	15	14	15
Charlton Athletic	11	4	3	4	17	18	15
Tottenham Hotspur	11	4	2	5	15	17	14
Manchester City	11	4	2	5	14	19	14
Everton	11	3	3	5	14	19	12
West Ham United	11	2	5	4	13	14	11
Coventry City	11	3	2	6	11	22	11
Middlesbrough	11	2	4	5	16	18	10
Southampton	11	2	4	5	12	20	10
Bradford City	11	1	4	6	5	17	7
Derby County	11	0	5	6	16	28	5

NOVEMBER

SATURDAY 4	v COVENTRY CITY	A
WEDNESDAY 8	v DYNAMO KIEV	H
SATURDAY 11	v MIDDLESBROUGH	H
SATURDAY 18	v MANCHESTER CITY	A
TUESDAY 21	v PANATHINAIKOS	H
SATURDAY 25	v DERBY COUNTY	A
TUESDAY 28	v SUNDERLAND	A

COVENTRY CITY 1

ZUNIGA 65

13. Chris KIRKLAND

2. Marc EDWORTHY

19. Ivan GUERRERO

4. Paul WILLIAMS

17. Gary BREEN

6. Richard SHAW

7. David THOMPSON

8. Youssef CHIPPO

28. Jay BOTHROYD

10. Moustapha HADJI

22. Barry QUINN

SUBSTITUTES

5. Colin HENDRY

11. Ysrael ZUNIGA (28) h-t

12. Paul TELFER (7) 57

15. John EUSTACE (22) 57

34. Alan MILLER

MATCH REPORT

The slender margin of Manchester United's victory over injury-stricken Coventry City failed utterly to reflect the chasm that yawned between the two sides.

The Red Devils could and should have won by more, yet there was always a feeling that, had the need been pressing, they could have lifted their game to a more exalted plane.

Though Coventry began purposefully, with Thompson prominent in midfield, it was the calm, almost serene visitors who always carried the most potent threat.

There might have been an early breakthrough when Scholes was grounded by Shaw and Beckham's free-kick was touched around a post by the diving Kirkland, then Edworthy almost turned a raking delivery from Beckham into his own net.

When a goal materialised, it was stunning in its combination of pure simplicity and crushing authority. Irwin chipped out of defence, Sheringham's first-time lay-off was perfect and Scholes volleyed majestically into the path of Beckham, who was racing down the right flank.

Disdaining the need for a controlling touch, the England star crossed instantly to Cole, who eluded Shaw and clipped home clinically at the near post. Beautiful to behold, impossible to stop, it was a master-class in fluent counter-attacking.

Thereafter a second strike was not long in coming. An adroit turn from Cole prompted a probing run by Giggs, who was

David Beckham strikes a familiar pose as he scores United's second ...

2 MANCHESTER UNITED

27 COLE
37 BECKHAM

1. Fabien BARTHEZ
2. Gary NEVILLE
3. Denis IRWIN
16. Roy KEANE
24. Wesley BROWN
12. Phil NEVILLE
7. David BECKHAM
18. Paul SCHOLES
9. Andy COLE
10. Teddy SHERINGHAM
11. Ryan GIGGS
SUBSTITUTES
17. Raimond VAN DER GOUW
19. Dwight YORKE (10) 72
20. Ole Gunnar SOLSKJAER (18) 50
27. Mikael SILVESTRE
36. Luke CHADWICK

fouled on the edge of the box. Beckham stepped up to curl a low free-kick through a disintegrating defensive wall, the hapless Kirkland being deceived by a wicked bounce.

In the second half Coventry were rather more competitive, and Zuniga reduced the arrears when he touched in Breen's towering header from a corner. But Yorke, who cracked the foot of a post with a searing drive, Keane, Sheringham and Cole all might have made the scoreline more commensurate with the balance of play.

... Ryan Giggs, Roy Keane and Wes Brown are delighted

MANCHESTER UNITED 1

SHERINGHAM 18

1. Fabien BARTHEZ
2. Gary NEVILLE
3. Denis IRWIN
16. Roy KEANE
24. Wesley BROWN
12. Phil NEVILLE
7. David BECKHAM
8. Nicky BUTT
9. Andy COLE
10. Teddy SHERINGHAM
11. Ryan GIGGS

SUBSTITUTES

17. Raimond VAN DER GOUW
19. Dwight YORKE (10) 74
20. Ole Gunnar SOLSKJAER
22. Ronnie WALLWORK
25. Quinton FORTUNE (11) 35
27. Mikael SILVESTRE (25) 88
34. Jonathan GREENING

MATCH REPORT

On a night of nerve-shredding tension at an anxiety-wracked Old Trafford, Manchester United squeezed into the second stage of the Champions League. They had to win to progress, and they did so courtesy of a first-half goal created and dispatched by the magnificent Sheringham, yet with five minutes remaining they might have fallen to a simple tap-in.

Patience and discipline were the Red Devils' watchwords as Dynamo set out to defend in depth and threaten their hosts on the break. With the stakes so high for both teams – the visitors needed victory to qualify for the UEFA Cup and reportedly their players were offered huge bonuses to succeed – the opening was understandably edgy, but the contest burst into life after a Beckham free-kick had been saved smartly by Shovkovskyi.

Gaining possession deep inside his own half, Sheringham dispatched a long-distance crossfield pass towards Cole, then pounded off in pursuit. At first Cole miscontrolled the ball before linking slickly with Giggs, then slipping a pass to Sheringham who found Keane with an adroit clip. The skipper's shot was parried by Shovkovskyi and Teddy turned home the rebound. This signalled a brief period

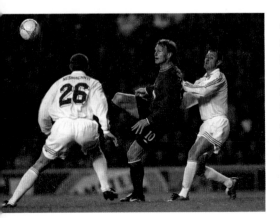

Teddy Sheringham's delicate approach work set himself up for United's winner

0 DYNAMO KIEV

1. Olexander SHOVKOVSKYI
2. Aliaxandr KHATSKEVITCH
3. Alexev GERASIMENKO
4. Olexander HOLOVKO
5. Vladyslav VASCHUK
16. Laszllo BODNAR
7. Kakha KALADZE
8. Valiantsin BIALKEVICH
29. Vitalii LYSYTSKYY
10. Maksim SHATSKIKH
26. Andrii NESMACHNYI

SUBSTITUTES

11. George DEMETRADZE (10) 67
12. Vyacheslav KERNOZENKO
15. Artem YASHKIN
17. Serhii FERDOROV (4) 76
18. Vassyl KARDASH
23. Vladimir KUZMICHEV (3) 62
28. serhii SEREBRENNIKOV

Skipper Roy Keane is delighted with the goalscorer ...

of concerted pressure by the Reds, but Kiev survived and retaliated with shots from Kaladze and Bodnar before the break.

In the second period Beckham responded with two spectacular long-range efforts, one saved by Shovkovskyi and the other shaving a post, but gradually the Ukrainians gained more territory and looked ever-more menacing. Then came Demetradze's astonishing bungle, stabbing wide from four yards following a cross from the right, and Old Trafford practically sobbed with relief.

United – for whom Brown and Gary Neville had been outstanding in central defence – were through by a whisker.

... and he tries to repeat the dose himself

MANCHESTER UNITED 2

1. Fabien BARTHEZ
2. Gary NEVILLE
27. Mikael SILVESTRE
16. Roy KEANE
24. Wesley BROWN
12. Phil NEVILLE
7. David BECKHAM
8. Nicky BUTT
20. Ole Gunnar SOLSKJAER
19. Dwight YORKE
18. Paul SCHOLES

SUBSTITUTES

3. Denis IRWIN
10. Teddy SHERINGHAM (20) 40
17. Raimond VAN DER GOUW
22. Ronnie WALLWORK (24) h-t
36. Luke CHADWICK (19) 90

BUTT 62
SHERINGHAM 65

MATCH REPORT

A plague of profligate finishing threatened to cost the Red Devils dearly against the last opponents to leave Old Trafford with three Premiership points. On the balance of play it would have been a travesty if Middlesbrough had repeated their success of 23 months earlier, yet they led for a third of the contest and the home fans – perhaps even Roy Keane's prawn-eaters – were consumed by anxiety before their nerves were settled by two goals inside three second-half minutes.

United began at a high tempo and should have surged into an unassailable early lead as their sweet passing movements cut a swathe through the Teessiders' rearguard. First Keane rampaged unstoppably down the left before finding Yorke, whose sharp effort from 16 yards was thwarted acrobatically by Schwarzer. Then the Tobagan misfired twice more, first shooting tamely after being set up by the skipper and Scholes, then turning the ball over the bar from close range following yet another Keane dispatch.

Suddenly, after all that attacking, the Reds found themselves on the back foot when Karembeu dispossessed Butt, played a neat one-two with Ricard and lobbed deftly over fellow French international Barthez from ten yards.

The hosts continued to pour forward, but still a breakthrough proved elusive. Before the break Silvestre

United's winner came from Teddy Sheringham's left boot

1 MIDDLESBROUGH

31 KAREMBEU

A jinking Dwight Yorke is thwarted by the determined Schwarzer

1. Mark SCHWARZER
2. Curtis FLEMING
28. Colin COOPER
4. Steve VICKERS
22. Mark SUMMERBELL
6. Gary PALLISTER
24. Phil STAMP
8. Christian KAREMBEU
19. Hamilton RICARD
10. Brian DEANE
18. Andy CAMPBELL
SUBSTITUTES
3. Dean GORDON (28) h-t
5. Gianluca FESTA
11. Alan BOKSIC (18) 63
23. Carlos MARINELLI (19) 78
25. Mark CROSSLEY

was unlucky with a header and a Beckham free-kick skimmed the bar. Early in the second period the usually accurate Scholes squandered a sitter at the far post before rising unmarked to head wide from Beckham's cross.

At the other end Campbell miscued with a half-volley when he might have put the match beyond United but, at last, relief was imminent. The equaliser arrived when Butt nudged home Keane's precise pull-back, then Sheringham latched on to a loose ball to supply the winner with a flashing left-foot drive from 12 yards.

MANCHESTER CITY 0

1. Nicky WEAVER
31. Laurent CHARVET
19. Danny TIATTO
4. Gerard WIEKENS
24. Steve HOWEY
15. Alf-Inge HAALAND
7. Spencer PRIOR
18. Jeff WHITLEY
9. Paul DICKOV
10. Shaun WRIGHT-PHILLIPS
34. Mark KENNEDY

SUBSTITUTES

8. Ian BISHOP (34) h-t
10. Shaun GOATER (4) h-t
13. Tommy WRIGHT
22. Richard DUNNE
23. Paolo WANCHOPE

MATCH REPORT

A David Beckham special after only 90 seconds signalled the resumption of the Manchester 'Derby' in sensational style and, though there were no more goals, the breakneck tempo of this compelling encounter did not relent until the final whistle.

Toiling like men possessed, City enjoyed lengthy spells of possession and spurned a handful of half-chances, but United repeatedly shredded the home defence with a series of scything

A David Beckham free-kick gives United a 2nd-minute lead

1 MANCHESTER UNITED

2 BECKHAM

1. Fabien BARTHEZ
2. Gary NEVILLE
3. Denis IRWIN
16. Roy KEANE
24. Wesley BROWN
12. Phil NEVILLE
7. David BECKHAM
8. Nicky BUTT
19. Dwight YORKE
10. Teddy SHERINGHAM
18. Paul SCHOLES

SUBSTITUTES

11. Ryan GIGGS (10) 76
22. Ronnie WALLWORK
27. Mikael SILVESTRE
33. Paul RACHUBKA
36. Luke CHADWICK

counter-attacks and created enough clear opportunities to have triumphed by a comfortable margin.

The drama commenced after only a minute when the combative Haaland felled Scholes some 30 yards from goal. Inexplicably, the Blues disdained to construct a full wall and the new England captain stepped up to dispatch an exquisite bender past the despairing Weaver.

City responded briskly and Phil Neville cleared from in front of the Reds' posts after a frantic scramble and Wright-Phillips volleyed narrowly over, but the Reds might have increased their advantage after 23 minutes when Scholes sent Yorke through on the keeper, who brought off a smart block.

City, prompted by the intelligent Bishop, threw more men forward and enjoyed their most penetrative period, only for Howey and Charvet to head inaccurately when well placed, while the majestic Brown hacked a Haaland effort off the line.

As the hosts became ever more stretched, United lacerated them on the break, but several openings went begging and the visitors were not sorry when the referee called time.

Roy Keane joins him in celebration

MANCHESTER UNITED 3

SHERINGHAM 48
SCHOLES 81, 90

1. Fabien BARTHEZ
2. Gary NEVILLE
27. Mikael SILVESTRE
16. Roy KEANE
24. Wesley BROWN
12. Phil NEVILLE
7. David BECKHAM
8. Nicky BUTT
19. Dwight YORKE
10. Teddy SHERINGHAM
18. Paul SCHOLES

SUBSTITUTES

3. Denis IRWIN
5. Ronny JOHNSEN
17. Raimond VAN DER GOUW
22. Ronnie WALLWORK
25. Quinton FORTUNE
34. Jonathan GREENING
35. David HEALY

MATCH REPORT

Two late flashes of typical opportunism from Paul Scholes enabled the Reds to preserve their 100 per cent home record during this European campaign, but not before their defence was repeatedly cut to ribbons by a polished Panathinaikos.

Though United were enjoying imperious ascendancy by the final whistle, they owed a vast debt to Barthez who kept them in the contest during a first half in which the conquerors of Juventus fashioned a succession of scoring opportunities. During this traumatic interlude, the Frenchman blocked three goal-bound efforts from Liberopoulos and one from Warzycha, while the visitors were off target on several other occasions.

United's most telling response came from the excellent Sheringham who forced Nikopolidis to save a fierce shot after fine work from Phil Neville, then nodded over the bar from a Beckham cross.

However, the second period brought almost instant relief for tense home supporters when a booming Barthez clearance was glanced on by Yorke to Sheringham who volleyed in from 12 yards. Panathinaikos refused to panic, though, and gained a deserved equaliser with a clever 30-yard floater from Karagounis following a short free-kick.

The setback appeared to lift United, who attacked with increasing fluency and regained the

Teddy Sheringham's goal turned the tide for United

1 PANATHINAIKOS

64 KARAGOUNIS

1. Antonis NIKOPOLIDIS
2. Rene HENRIKSEN
30. Panagiotis FYSSAS
20. Agelos BASINAS
5. Fernando Edgar GALETTO
14. Leonidas VOKOLOS
26. Giorgios KARAGOUNIS
8. Ioannis GOUMAS
9. Krzysztof WARZYCHA
21. Nikolaos LIBEROPOULOS
13. Igor SYPNIEWSKI
SUBSTITUTES
3. PERCY OLIVARES (13) 79
7. Goran VLAOVIC (26) 67
12. Stefanos KOTSOLIS
17. Giorgios NASIOPOULOS
18. Evangelos KOUTSOURES
19. Blendar KOLA
31. Konstantinos KIASSOS (9) 75

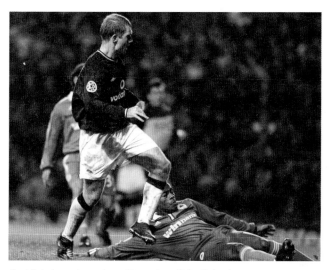

Paul Scholes nets a rebound to restore United's lead...

lead when Silvestre played a slick one-two with Sheringham before surging between two defenders and unleashing a savage left-foot drive. Nikopolidis parried brilliantly but the rebound fell to the predatory Scholes, who made no mistake.

Scholes removed the final shreds of anxiety by chipping home deliciously from the edge of the box which climaxed a sumptuous 32-pass move. It was a goal of utter splendour which shouldn't be allowed to gloss over entirely those worrying first-half wobbles.

...then grabs his second to complete the scoring

DERBY COUNTY 0

1. Mart POOM
2. Horacio CARBONARI
3. Brian O'NEIL
4. Darryl POWELL
5. Rory DELAP
34. Taribo WEST
7. Seth JOHNSON
16. Lilian MARTIN
12. Martin CHRISTIE
10. Giorgi KINKLADZE
21. Chris RIGGOTT

SUBSTITUTES

8. Dean STURRIDGE (2) 68
11. Lee MORRIS (3) h-t
15. Danny HIGGINBOTHAM
20. Stefano ERANIO (16) 68
24. Andy OAKES

MATCH REPORT

It took Manchester United more than an hour to pick the padlock on Derby's obdurate rearguard, which began in buoyant mood after recording four successive clean sheets, but when the breakthrough materialised it was utterly emphatic.

First came an enchanting eight-man move, involving a delectable flick from Sheringham to Gary Neville, who sent Scholes scampering down the right. An adroit cutback returned the ball into the veteran marksman's path and he applied an impudent final touch with the outside of his right foot from ten yards, claiming his 15th goal of the campaign.

Next there was a Beckhamesque 25-yard curler from Butt, who had been set up by Yorke, and then Sheringham dinked into the box, where Yorke juggled the ball on his knee before swivelling to crash a fierce shot past the valiant Poom.

Derby had barely mounted a serious attack on the Red Devils' goal, their most menacing effort being a free-kick from Kinkladze – conceded by Keane following an isolated charge forward by West – which skewed to safety off the wall.

Such was the visitors' dominance that Barthez was a virtual spectator almost all

Nicky Butt holds off a challenge from Derby's O'Neil

3 MANCHESTER UNITED

61 SHERINGHAM
69 BUTT
76 YORKE

1. Fabien BARTHEZ
2. Gary NEVILLE
3. Denis IRWIN
16. Roy KEANE
24. Wesley BROWN
27. Mikael SILVESTRE
36. Luke CHADWICK
8. Nicky BUTT
19. Dwight YORKE
10. Teddy SHERINGHAM
18. Paul SCHOLES

SUBSTITUTES

5. Ronny JOHNSEN
17. Raimond VAN DER GOUW (1) 81
20. Ole Gunnar SOLSKJAER (36) 74
25. Quinton FORTUNE
34. Jonathan GREENING

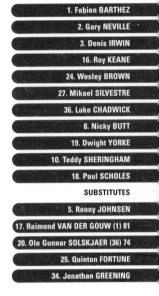

afternoon and, with the match won and the under-employed Frenchman shivering in the raw conditions, he was withdrawn to seek warmth some 12 minutes from time.

United's supremacy emanated from all areas of the pitch, but Scholes and Butt deserved particular praise for their uplifting combination of zest and precision, while Chadwick – patrolling the right flank in place of the rested Beckham – sparkled on his full Premiership debut. On several occasions he danced past hefty challenges, once leaving Johnson and West trailing in his wake before shooting narrowly high. The former Arsenal schoolboy is an emerging talent worth monitoring.

Dwight Yorke claims the congratulations of his teammates after scoring

SUNDERLAND 2

1. Thomas SORENSEN
2. Chris MAKIN
3. Michael GRAY
4. Don HUTCHISON
36. Emerson THOME
17. Jody CRADDOCK
16. Alex RAE
18. Darren WILLIAMS
12. Daniele DICHIO
10. Kevin PHILLIPS
33. Julio ARCA

SUBSTITUTES

8. Gavin McCANN (2) h-t
9. Niall QUINN
20. Stefan SCHWARZ
30. Jurgen MACHO (1) 91
32. Stanislav VARGA (36) 87

ARCA 75
PHILLIPS (penalty) 101

MATCH REPORT

On an evening of melodrama in front of the Stadium of Light's record attendance, a largely inexperienced Manchester United side were edged out of the Worthington Cup.

Sadly, the visitors' satisfaction with the spirited performances of several rookie Reds – notably Greening, Wallwork and Fortune – was tarnished by the dismissal of Yorke for a reckless lunge at the Brazilian defender, Thome.

There was no hint of controversy to come as United stroked the ball around neatly for the first half-hour and they took the lead when Yorke and Craddock chased Solskjaer's deft flick and

Ole Gunnar Solskjaer harasses the Sunderland defence to no avail

1 MANCHESTER UNITED

after extra time

31 YORKE

17. Raimond VAN DER GOUW
23. Michael CLEGG
12. Phil NEVILLE
22. Ronnie WALLWORK
5. Ronny JOHNSEN
30. John O'SHEA
36. Luke CHADWICK
34. Jonathan GREENING
19. Dwight YORKE
20. Ole Gunnar SOLSKJAER
25. Quinton FORTUNE
SUBSTITUTES
28. Michael STEWART (5) 85
32. Bojan DJORDJIC
33. Paul RACHUBKA
35. David HEALY (36) 95
37. Danny WEBBER (22) 109

the ball broke to Greening, whose pass was driven home by the Tobagan via the crossbar.

Sunderland retaliated, Phillips rapping the foot of the post before the interval and twice going close after it. However, the Reds appeared to have ridden the storm when the otherwise excellent Clegg allowed Arca to nod an equaliser.

United hit back and a penalty seemed inevitable when Sorensen upended Greening, but the referee demurred, and then the sending off of Yorke tilted the balance of power.

The Wearsiders seized the initiative during extra time when O'Shea was adjudged to have tugged Phillips' shirt and the England striker netted from the spot, but even then United's gallant youngsters – the average age of the nine remaining outfielders was a mere 21 following substitutions – refused to wilt.

First one of the newcomers, Healy, clipped the bar with a snap-shot, then Macho turned a reflex header from debutant Webber against the same length of wood following a Fortune cross.

The final whistle signalled defeat, but it was gratifyingly clear that Old Trafford's conveyor belt of fresh talent shows no sign of faltering.

Greening is upended by keeper Sorensen but was not awarded a penalty for his trouble

NOVEMBER IN REVIEW

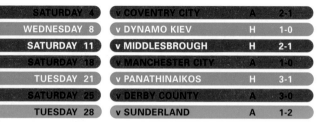

SATURDAY 4	v COVENTRY CITY	A	2-1
WEDNESDAY 8	v DYNAMO KIEV	H	1-0
SATURDAY 11	v MIDDLESBROUGH	H	2-1
SATURDAY 18	v MANCHESTER CITY	A	1-0
TUESDAY 21	v PANATHINAIKOS	H	3-1
SATURDAY 25	v DERBY COUNTY	A	3-0
TUESDAY 28	v SUNDERLAND	A	1-2

PLAYER IN THE FRAME

David Beckham

In match after match Beckham's distribution was destructively grand, never more so than at Coventry, where his instant dispatch to Andy Cole provided the penultimate component of an unstoppably flowing move. Best of all for most fans was that wickedly curling free-kick which unhinged Manchester City at Maine Road.

FA CARLING PREMIERSHIP

		P	W	D	L	F	A	Pts
UP TO AND INCLUDING	MANCHESTER UNITED	15	11	3	1	39	10	36
THURSDAY 30 NOVEMBER 2000	Arsenal	15	8	4	3	23	13	28
	Ipswich Town	15	8	3	4	23	16	27
	Leicester City	15	7	5	3	14	11	26
	Liverpool	15	7	3	5	29	23	24
	Aston Villa	14	6	5	3	17	12	23
	Newcastle United	15	7	2	6	17	15	23
	Tottenham Hotspur	15	7	2	6	22	21	23
	Sunderland	15	6	5	4	15	16	23
	Leeds United	14	6	4	4	21	19	22
	West Ham United	15	5	6	4	21	17	21
	Charlton Athletic	15	6	3	6	21	21	21
	Everton	15	6	3	6	19	21	21
	Chelsea	15	4	5	6	26	22	17
	Southampton	15	4	5	6	21	27	17
	Manchester City	15	4	2	9	17	28	14
	Coventry City	15	3	5	9	14	30	12
	Middlesbrough	15	2	5	8	19	26	11
	Derby County	15	1	7	7	18	31	10
	Bradford City	15	1	5	9	7	24	8

DECEMBER

SATURDAY 2	v TOTTENHAM HOTSPUR	H
WEDNESDAY 6	v SK STURM GRAZ	A
SATURDAY 9	v CHARLTON ATHLETIC	A
SUNDAY 17	v LIVERPOOL	H
SATURDAY 23	v IPSWICH TOWN	H
TUESDAY 26	v ASTON VILLA	A
SATURDAY 30	v NEWCASTLE UNITED	A

MANCHESTER UNITED 2

SCHOLES 40
SOLSKJAER 84

1. Fabien BARTHEZ
2. Gary NEVILLE
27. Mikael SILVESTRE
16. Roy KEANE
24. Wesley BROWN
12. Phil NEVILLE
7. David BECKHAM
8. Nicky BUTT
19. Dwight YORKE
10. Teddy SHERINGHAM
18. Paul SCHOLES

SUBSTITUTES

3. Denis IRWIN
11. Ryan GIGGS (8) 74
17. Raimond VAN DER GOUW
20. Ole Gunnar SOLSKJAER
34. Jonathan GREENING

MATCH REPORT

Nicky Butt battles for the ball with Tottenham's Campbell and Carr

Manchester United brushed aside a woefully unadventurous Spurs side in consummately competent fashion, yet the margin of their victory should have been far more comfortable.

Though the visitors defended resolutely, their rearguard was cut open repeatedly by the Reds' incisive passing. Butt alone might have more than doubled the score but imprecise finishing kept alive Tottenham's hopes and they gave their dominant hosts a tense ten minutes before Solskjaer's late clincher.

George Graham's men ran on to the pitch weighed down by the season's worst away record in the Premiership, and they seemed bent on doubling their tally of points collected on their travels by grinding out a goalless draw.

0 TOTTENHAM HOTSPUR

13. Neil SULLIVAN
2. Steve CARR
25. Stephen CLEMENCE
31. Alton THELWELL
5. Sol CAMPBELL
6. Chris PERRY
7. Darren ANDERTON
8. Tim SHERWOOD
9. Les FERDINAND
16. Chris ARMSTRONG
26. Ledley KING
SUBSTITUTES
1. Ian WALKER
4. Steffen FREUND
15. Willem KORSTEN (16) 63
29. Simon DAVIES
34. Ramon VEGA

United's response was measured, all dashing movement and patient distribution, interspersed with sudden explosive assaults on goal. Typical was a cute angled through-ball from Beckham, which sent Keane charging through for the skipper to drive marginally wide. A rasping Scholes volley, following a slick interchange with Butt, was saved splendidly by Sullivan.

However, the red-headed England star was not to be denied, putting United ahead when he chested down a lofted delivery from Sheringham, then side-stepping Carr before curling a delightful cross-shot into the far corner of the net from ten yards.

After the break Sheringham, Beckham and Yorke all set up opportunities which Butt could not quite convert before Spurs, sensing the Reds' mounting frustration, became more purposeful and enjoyed a spell of unlikely supremacy.

But justice was done when Scholes poked the ball beyond a square Tottenham back line and Solskjaer slipped it past Sullivan with characteristic efficiency. Thus the champions recorded their eighth consecutive League triumph and maintained their eight-point advantage at the Premiership summit.

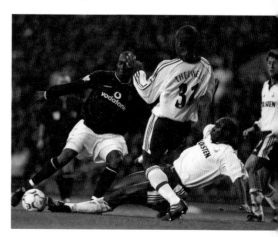

There's no way through a packed Spurs defence for Dwight Yorke

SK STURM GRAZ 0

1. Kamimierz SIDORCZUK
15. Ramiz MAMEDOV
3. Gunther NEUKIRCHNER
12. Gilbert PRILASNIG
24. Ranko POPOVIC
20. Mehrdad MINAVAND
18. Markus SCHOPP
30. Andres Jose FLEURQUIN
21. Tomislav KOCIJAN
10. Ivica VASTIC
11. Gyorgy KORSOS

SUBSTITUTES

5. Franco FODA
6. Roman MAHLICH (15) 85
7. Gerald STRAFNER (3) 82
9. Hannes REINMAYR (11) 70
16. Ferdinand FELDHOFER
19. Imre SZABICS
25. Alexander KNEZEVIC

MATCH REPORT

The scoreline looked comfortable in the end, and United fully deserved the first away win of their European campaign, but before Giggs' late clincher the Reds underwent a penetrating second-half examination by the feisty Austrian champions.

The first period was a different story, with Graz apparently overawed by the visitors, who dictated play with barely credible ease, retaining possession calmly while waiting for scoring chances to materialise.

Yorke, giving perhaps his most assured performance of the season to date, nearly achieved an early breakthrough but ballooned his shot over the bar after wrong-footing a defender.

Soon, though, the Tobagan made amends with a through-ball to Sheringham, whose deliciously subtle flick rolled into the path of Scholes. His run was timed perfectly although it seemed that the predatory redhead had been driven too wide, but he applied the most clinical of angled clips to pass Sidorczuk.

Now United assumed total domination, the only first-half threat from the hosts being a Vastic free-kick which Barthez dived smartly to deflect.

But after the break Graz thrust forward enterprisingly and made a game

Paul Scholes beats Sidorczuk from a narrow angle

2 MANCHESTER UNITED

18 SCHOLES
89 GIGGS

1. Fabien BARTHEZ
2. Gary NEVILLE
3. Denis IRWIN
16. Roy KEANE
24. Wesley BROWN
27. Mikael SILVESTRE
7. David BECKHAM
8. Nicky BUTT
19. Dwight YORKE
10. Teddy SHERINGHAM
18. Paul SCHOLES
SUBSTITUTES
11. Ryan GIGGS (8) 80
12. Phil NEVILLE (3) 89
17. Raimond VAN DER GOUW
20. Ole Gunnar SOLSKJAER (19) 89
25. Quinton FORTUNE
30. John O'SHEA
34. Jonathan GREENING

of it. Though volleys from Scholes and Sheringham brought the best out Sidorczuk, the Reds' supremacy was threatened by efforts from Mamedov and Vastic, who was denied a penalty after falling in the box and, most tellingly, by Kocijan, whose 25-yard howitzer cannoned to safety off the crossbar.

United responded with a sweeping attack which ended with Sheringham netting, only for Keane to be judged offside, but then Barthez was forced into a brilliant reflex save after a Keane deflection. Finally, Beckham fed Yorke, who freed Giggs to score with a near-post drive, thus ensuring that the Austrians' run of six successive European home victories was at an end.

Ryan Giggs drives home the clincher to seal the fate of the plucky Austrians

CHARLTON ATHLETIC 3

1. Dean KIELY
2. Radostin KISHISHEV
3. Chris POWELL
4. Graham STUART
5. Richard RUFUS
36. Mark FISH
20. Claus JENSEN
8. Mark KINSELLA
21. Jonatan JOHANSSON
37. Shaun BARTLETT
28. John SALAKO

SUBSTITUTES

11. John ROBINSON (28) 69
12. Steve BROWN
18. Paul KONCHESKY (2) 89
26. Mathias SVENSSON (37) 87
35. Tony CAIG

BARTLETT 10, 79
ROBINSON 85

MATCH REPORT

Charlton rallied valiantly to snatch a point after being 3-1 down, and for that Alan Curbishley's men can claim colossal credit. But Manchester United left The Valley kicking themselves for allowing a two-goal lead to be wiped out for the third time during the current Premiership campaign. Lack of concentration in the dying stages of contests which had seemed to be won was becoming an ominous habit.

In truth, the rampaging Addicks could have been five to the good before United registered. The visitors' rearguard was undone aerially with embarrassing ease as Powell crossed and van der Gouw made a flying save from Johansson's nod, then the Dane's dispatch from the same left flank was headed firmly against the inside of an upright by Bartlett. The South African debutant was not to be denied, though, and he dived to net at the near post from Stuart's centre.

It could have been worse: Johansson beat the offside trap but shot narrowly wide and a Jensen free-kick needed acrobatics from van der Gouw.

Though lucky still to be in contention, United responded devastatingly, gradually building pressure before hitting their hosts with two goals inside a minute just before the break. First Giggs curled home calmly from 20 yards after being supplied by Solskjaer, then returned the favour in

Ryan Giggs strokes home United's opener

3 MANCHESTER UNITED

42 GIGGS
43 SOLSKJAER
66 KEANE

17. Raimond VAN DER GOUW	
2. Gary NEVILLE	
27. Mikael SILVESTRE	
16. Roy KEANE	
24. Wesley BROWN	
12. Phil NEVILLE	
7. David BECKHAM	
8. Nicky BUTT	
20. Ole Gunnar SOLSKJAER	
36. Luke CHADWICK	
11. Ryan GIGGS	
SUBSTITUTES	
3. Denis IRWIN	
10. Teddy SHERINGHAM (7) 75	
18. Paul SCHOLES (36) 60	
33. Paul RACHUBKA	
34. Jonathan GREENING (16) 71	

Ole Gunnar Solskjaer volleys number two

spectacular fashion, hooking a bouncing ball from the centre circle on to Kiely's crossbar, enabling the alert Norwegian to volley in the rebound.

Now United created a succession of chances and when Keane's 18-yard toe-poke entered the net via Kiely's palm it seemed the game was up for Charlton. But after a wondrous run by Giggs was climaxed with a shot against a post, parity was regained through another Bartlett header and a Robinson cross-shot. At the end of a stirring match, Athletic's share of the spoils was richly deserved.

Roy Keane pokes in a third and it looks like three points...

MANCHESTER UNITED 0

1. Fabien BARTHEZ
2. Gary NEVILLE
3. Denis IRWIN
16. Roy KEANE
24. Wesley BROWN
27. Mikael SILVESTRE
7. David BECKHAM
8. Nicky BUTT
20. Ole Gunnar SOLSKJAER
18. Paul SCHOLES
11. Ryan GIGGS

SUBSTITUTES

12. Phil NEVILLE
17. Raimond VAN DER GOUW
30. John O'SHEA
34. Jonathan GREENING (8) 71
36. Luke CHADWICK (3) 80

MATCH REPORT

On a day of momentous milestones, Liverpool pulled off a thoroughly deserved victory, their first at Old Trafford for a decade. Though United enjoyed by far the most possession and applied virtually ceaseless pressure, they lacked their customary penetration. Indeed, it was telling that, despite spending lengthy periods besieged in their own half, the Merseysiders mustered more goal attempts than their arch rivals.

Ryan Giggs and co. found it hard to penetrate a resolute Merseyside defence

1 LIVERPOOL

43 MURPHY

1. Sander WESTERVELD
2. Stephane HENCHOZ
23. Jamie CARRAGHER
17. Steven GERRARD
12. Sami HYYPIA
6. Markus BABBEL
25. Igor BISCAN
8. Emile HESKEY
20. Nick BARMBY
10. Michael OWEN
13. Danny MURPHY

SUBSTITUTES

7. Vladimir SMICER (10) 75
8. Robbie FOWLER
21. Gary McALLISTER (13) 89
26. Jorgen NIELSEN
30. Djimi TRAORE

The result marked the Red Devils' century of League defeats under Sir Alex Ferguson – albeit their first at home for two years – while Gerard Houllier was celebrating his one hundredth senior game in sole charge of Liverpool.

But the statistic which truly mattered was the game's only goal, a curling, 22-yard free-kick, beautifully executed by Murphy after a needless handball by Neville shortly before the interval. A decidedly lop-sided defensive wall offered Barthez no protection as the ball scraped inside a post.

The game had begun at a furiously high tempo with the home side pouring forward relentlessly. But with Sheringham, Yorke and Cole all unavailable, United had no cutting edge and it was Liverpool who looked most menacing through periodic counter-attacks.

The Red Devils' best effort was a header from Keane, which was held comfortably by Westerveld, but more meaningful action unfolded at the other end when Barthez saved Murphy's 30-yarder, then Scholes headed off the line from Heskey's nod.

That was the prelude to the decisive free-kick, and the lead might have been doubled early in the second half when Owen's shot clipped the crossbar after Babbel had beaten Butt.

Thereafter, the champions huffed and puffed, but they offered little more than two low shots by Solskjaer, both of which were saved smartly by Westerveld. Later, Chadwick was sent off for fouling Smicer when the Czech was through on goal, thus rounding off a sorry afternoon for Ferguson's men.

MANCHESTER UNITED 2

SOLSKJAER 20, 32

- 1. Fabien BARTHEZ
- 2. Gary NEVILLE
- 27. Mikael SILVESTRE
- 16. Roy KEANE
- 24. Wesley BROWN
- 12. Phil NEVILLE
- 7. David BECKHAM
- 18. Paul SCHOLES
- 20. Ole Gunnar SOLSKJAER
- 25. Quinton FORTUNE
- 11. Ryan GIGGS

SUBSTITUTES

- 3. Denis IRWIN
- 17. Raimond VAN DER GOUW
- 22. Ronnie WALLWORK (16) 82
- 34. Jonathan GREENING (7) 82
- 35. David HEALY (11) 59

MATCH REPORT

Ole Gunnar Solskjaer skips round a helpless Wright for the opener...

Placing recent aberrations firmly behind them, Manchester United romped back to their most irresistible form, overcoming third-placed Ipswich Town in emphatic manner. Sir Alex Ferguson's men began as if they had a point to prove and soon Scholes was scampering through the East Anglians' defence before wrong-footing Wright with a 20-yard effort which was narrowly off target.

Next, Giggs, who sparkled as Solskjaer's front-running partner, backheeled to Beckham. The England skipper's shot

0 IPSWICH TOWN

was blocked but the ball rebounded to Scholes, whose 25-yard left-footer just cleared the angle of post and bar.

As the pressure mounted, Wright did well to keep out a low shot from Solskjaer, who was about to stamp his presence on proceedings in conclusive fashion. First Beckham planted the ball forward, the Norwegian and Giggs unhinged Town's rearguard with a quicksilver exchange of passes, and Ole waltzed around Wright to score. A second breakthrough seemed inevitable and Beckham delivered another precision dispatch which Solskjaer controlled immaculately then volleyed home.

After the break, the visitors fought back, and Armstrong brought the best out of Barthez with a thunderous goalbound drive, then Brown almost sliced a harmless cross into his own net.

United continued to enchant, albeit more intermittently, and one move was inches away from utter perfection. Scholes hit a delicious crossfield pass to Beckham, whose inviting centre was met with a bullet header from Healy, the ball cannoning to safety off an upright. Disappointing for the young Irishman but his ebullient display suggested that United had added another viable striking option to their formidable armoury.

... and crashes in his second 12 minutes later

ASTON VILLA   0

1. David JAMES
16. ALPAY Ozalan
3. Alan WRIGHT
4. Gareth SOUTHGATE
15. Gareth BARRY
6. George BOATENG
18. Steve STONE
17. Lee HENDRIE
25. Gilles DE BILDE
10. Paul MERSON
14. David GINOLA

SUBSTITUTES

2. Mark DELANEY (16) 38
9. Dion DUBLIN (25) 67
11. Steve STAUNTON
22. Darius VASSELL (15) 87
39. Peter ENCKELMAN

MATCH REPORT

For 85 minutes the Red Devils in general, and Ole Gunnar Solskjaer in particular, suffered serial frustration at the fortress that was Villa Park, where the Midlanders had not lost a League encounter all season.

Despite exerting overwhelming dominance, especially in the first half, United squandered chance after chance, with the normally unerring Norwegian the chief culprit.

Then, as time ebbed away and with Villa increasingly menacing on the counter-attack, the champions conjured a happy ending. Beckham, whose crossing had been uncharacteristically wayward, finally got his range right and Solskjaer pounced with a venomous near-post header which the athletic James reached but could not repel.

Such a dramatic finale should not have been necessary. Solskjaer himself might have started a rout in the fourth minute when Barthez launched a searching high ball which the Norwegian controlled beautifully but then, with a clear shooting opportunity, he shaved the wrong side of an upright.

That was the prelude to a siege. Giggs went close, James left his area to head clear from Solskjaer, a Keane shot was deflected narrowly wide, James parried a Giggs scorcher and an

Mikael Silvestre denies Villa's Lee Hendrie

1 MANCHESTER UNITED

85 SOLSKJAER

1. Fabien BARTHEZ
2. Gary NEVILLE
3. Denis IRWIN
16. Roy KEANE
24. Wesley BROWN
27. Mikael SILVESTRE
7. David BECKHAM
8. Nicky BUTT
20. Ole Gunnar SOLSKJAER
18. Paul SCHOLES
11. Ryan GIGGS

SUBSTITUTES

12. Phil NEVILLE (27) h-t
17. Raimond VAN DER GOUW
22. Ronnie WALLWORK (3) 60
34. Jonathan GREENING
36. Luke CHADWICK

Nicky Butt battles with Villa's crowded midfield

unmarked Solskjaer nodded over from six yards. Then James made the most stunning of many exceptional saves, a point-blank block from a Scholes header, and Solskjaer miskicked when well-placed before Villa began to show signs of life after an hour. Finally, they fashioned a genuine opening when Ginola's centre was met with a flying De Bilde header which brought a superb save from Barthez.

United's desire never faltered, though, and still they poured forward inexorably, only for lovely moves to be marred by inaccurate finishes by Scholes (twice) and Butt.

Thus it was left for Solskjaer to settle matters, ensuring that the Mancunians did not suffer their first Boxing Day reverse since 1989, when they lost at . . . Villa Park.

NEWCASTLE UNITED 1

GLASS 82

13. Steve HARPER

2. Warren BARTON

12. Andrew GRIFFIN

18. Aaron HUGHES

5. Alan GOMA

6. Clarence ACUNA

15. Nolberto SOLANO

8. Kieron DYER

23. Shola AMEOBI

10. Christian BASSEDAS

11. Gary SPEED

SUBSTITUTES

1. Shay GIVEN

17. Daniel CORDONE (23) 75

19. Stephen GLASS (6) 75

20. Lomana LUA LUA (10) 75

30. Steve CALDWELL

MATCH REPORT

The Red Devils might have won this rip-roaring encounter in the bleak north-east by several goals but, then again, so might the injury-ravaged Magpies. Thus, come the final whistle, a draw seemed like a fair result, even though Sir Alex Ferguson must have been a touch perturbed by the concession of another late equaliser.

David Beckham accepts the congratulations after his rare penalty goal

1 MANCHESTER UNITED

25 BECKHAM (penalty)

1. Fabien BARTHEZ
2. Gary NEVILLE
27. Mikael SILVESTRE
16. Roy KEANE
24. Wesley BROWN
12. Phil NEVILLE
7. David BECKHAM
8. Nicky BUTT
20. Ole Gunnar SOLSKJAER
19. Dwight YORKE
11. Ryan GIGGS
SUBSTITUTES
17. Raimond VAN DER GOUW
18. Paul SCHOLES (20) 71
22. Ronnie WALLWORK (27) 62
34. Jonathan GREENING
36. Luke CHADWICK (8) 89

Newcastle tore into their visitors from the off, but United soaked up the early pressure and retaliated with a spell of precision football during which Giggs sent in Yorke, only for Harper to block inelegantly but effectively with his body.

Bobby Robson's men were undaunted, though, and twice Ameobi might have given them the lead, first heading a corner against the foot of a post, then skying a Dyer cross over an empty net from two yards.

Five minutes later the Magpies paid for the young Nigerian's profligacy when Giggs was nudged by Griffin and, in the absence of regular penalty specialists Irwin and Scholes, up stepped Beckham to convert from the spot.

If that award appeared harsh, the Reds had a seemingly more obvious penalty claim denied when Butt's heels were clipped, but they had only themselves to blame for not sealing victory during a period of dominance early in the second half.

First, Yorke broke free on the right before finding Giggs, who volleyed tamely wide. Next, Beckham and Butt combined sweetly to set up Solskjaer, only for Harper to save the Norwegian's first effort and Goma to smother his second.

Soon Solskjaer went close again, but then Robson made a triple substitution which reaped instant dividends. The perpetually excellent Dyer found newcomer one (Cordone) on the right, his cross was sliced by newcomer two (Lua Lua) to newcomer three (Glass), who swept the ball home. It was galling for the champions, but justice was done.

DECEMBER IN REVIEW

SATURDAY 2	v TOTTENHAM HOTSPUR	H	2-0
WEDNESDAY 6	v SK STURM GRAZ	A	2-0
SATURDAY 9	v CHARLTON ATHLETIC	A	3-3
SUNDAY 17	v LIVERPOOL	H	0-1
SATURDAY 23	v IPSWICH TOWN	H	2-0
TUESDAY 26	v ASTON VILLA	A	1-0
SATURDAY 30	v NEWCASTLE UNITED	A	1-1

PLAYER IN THE FRAME

Paul Scholes

The thoroughbred nature of Scholes' football continued to be showcased with individual moments buttressed by his usual high level of consistency. In the 2-0 victory over Tottenham he contributed a goal of sweet precision and created another. Then came the exquisite chip against Sturm Graz – yet again Scholesy had made the difference.

FA CARLING PREMIERSHIP

		P	W	D	L	F	A	Pts
UP TO AND INCLUDING	**MANCHESTER UNITED**	21	14	5	2	48	15	47
SUNDAY 31 DECEMBER 2000	Arsenal	21	11	6	4	38	21	39
	Ipswich Town	21	11	4	6	32	22	37
	Sunderland	21	10	6	5	25	21	36
	Leicester City	20	10	5	5	23	21	35
	Liverpool	20	10	3	7	37	25	33
	Newcastle United	21	9	4	8	23	26	31
	West Ham United	20	7	8	5	30	21	29
	Aston Villa	19	7	8	4	23	18	29
	Charlton Athletic	21	8	4	9	30	36	28
	Chelsea	20	7	6	7	37	27	27
	Southampton	21	7	6	8	27	32	27
	Tottenham Hotspur	21	7	5	9	26	32	26
	Leeds United	19	7	4	8	26	28	25
	Everton	20	6	4	10	21	32	22
	Derby County	21	4	8	9	23	36	20
	Coventry City	21	5	5	11	20	36	20
	Middlesbrough	21	4	7	10	22	29	19
	Manchester City	21	5	4	12	26	37	19
	Bradford City	20	2	6	12	14	37	12

JANUARY

MONDAY 1	v WEST HAM UNITED	H
SUNDAY 7	v FULHAM	A
SATURDAY 13	v BRADFORD CITY	A
SATURDAY 20	v ASTON VILLA	H
SUNDAY 28	v WEST HAM UNITED	H
WEDNESDAY 31	v SUNDERLAND	A

MANCHESTER UNITED 3

- 1. Fabien BARTHEZ
- 2. Gary NEVILLE
- 27. Mikael SILVESTRE
- 16. Roy KEANE
- 24. Wesley BROWN
- 12. Phil NEVILLE
- 7. David BECKHAM
- 18. Paul SCHOLES
- 20. Ole Gunnar SOLSKJAER
- 19. Dwight YORKE
- 11. Ryan GIGGS

SUBSTITUTES

- 8. Nicky BUTT (18) 79
- 17. Raimond VAN DER GOUW
- 22. Ronnie WALLWORK (16) 61
- 23. Michael CLEGG
- 34. Jonathan GREENING (11) 61

SOLSKJAER 3
PEARCE (o.g.) 33
YORKE 57

MATCH REPORT

Ole Gunnar Solskjaer punished the Hammers with a typically predatory goal after only three minutes

Manchester United gave an awe-inspiring performance to surge 11 points clear at the top of the Premiership table, yet Sir Alex Ferguson was too canny to join in premature celebrations, warning that 'No one wins the title on New Year's Day.'

For all that, the task facing the chasing pack assumed overwhelming proportions as the Red Devils' football verged on perfection for prolonged periods, particularly in the first half.

1 WEST HAM UNITED

72 KANOUTE

1. Shaka HISLOP
17. Nigel WINTERBURN
3. Stuart PEARCE
21. Michael CARRICK
15. Rigobert SONG
16. John MONCUR
18. Frank LAMPARD
8. Trevor SINCLAIR
14. Frederic KANOUTE
29. Titi CAMARA
11. Steve LOMAS

SUBSTITUTES

4. Steve POTTS
22. Craig FORREST
25. Kaba DIAWARA
26. Joe COLE (16) h-t
28. Hannu TIHINEN (29) h-t

West Ham got off to a desperate start when Song dallied twice on the edge of his penalty box. The first time he was dispossessed by Solskjaer but the ball ran free; on the second occasion he was robbed again by the predatory Norwegian who punished the Cameroonian by drilling home a 12-yard cross-shot.

Thereafter United purred delectably, the precision of their passing matched by their prodigious work rate as chance followed chance: Yorke drove inches wide, Hislop plucked a Beckham free-kick from the air, then tipped over a curling rasper from the England captain. Song cleared a Yorke header off his line, Hislop deflected a sizzler from the rampant Giggs, all before the Reds doubled their lead when Pearce deflected in a cross from Phil Neville.

When Kanoute mustered the Hammers' first goal attempt after 38 minutes, United had already managed 17, and although the visitors regrouped in the second half there was no stopping the third strike, a brilliant diving header from Yorke.

However, Kanoute was excellent and deserved his consolation goal. Later Lampard went close to setting up a tense finish, but that would have been a travesty on a night when the Reds were majestic, even by their own exalted standards.

*Ole Gunnar Solskjaer congratulates Dwight Yorke
on his thumping diving header*

FULHAM 1

FERNANDES 24

1. Maik TAYLOR
2. Steve FINNAN
3. Rufus BREVETT
4. Andy MELVILLE
22. Luis BOA MORTE
6. Kit SYMONS
19. Bjarne GOLDBAEK
8. Lee CLARK
9. Nicolas SAHNOUN
20. Louis SAHA
25. Fabrice FERNANDES

SUBSTITUTES

7. Paul TROLLOPE
12. Marcus HAHNEMANN
16. Alan NEILSEN
31. Eddie LEWIS
40. Andre STOLCERS (22) 71

MATCH REPORT

Teddy Sheringham had missed United's Christmas programme through injury, but there were no signs of rustiness when he returned towards the end of a gripping encounter with runaway Division One leaders Fulham.

With the final whistle imminent, Sheringham's fellow substitute, Chadwick, duped a defender adroitly before switching the ball to the veteran marksman, whose low, 20-yard left-footer scorched past Fulham keeper Taylor to settle the tie.

It was an imperious strike worthy of winning any contest, but the sweet-passing Londoners were a tad unfortunate not to earn a replay after giving their visitors a torrid examination throughout most of the first half.

All this was after the Red Devils, playing their first FA Cup tie since beating Newcastle at Wembley in 1999, had eased into an early lead when Beckham harried Clark into a mistake and Solskjaer had pounced on the loose ball, passing into the net with typical precision from the edge of the box.

Soon afterwards the Norwegian nearly doubled his goal tally following a dazzling Giggs dribble only for Brevett to clear off his line, but then Fulham grabbed the upper hand with Saha and Boa Morte stretching United's defence with their quicksilver interchanges.

Ole Gunnar Solskjaer strikes after only eight minutes...

2 MANCHESTER UNITED

8 SOLSKJAER
89 SHERINGHAM

17. Raimond VAN DER GOUW
2. Gary NEVILLE
27. Mikael SILVESTRE
16. Roy KEANE
24. Wesley BROWN
12. Phil NEVILLE
7. David BECKHAM
8. Nicky BUTT
20. Ole Gunnar SOLSKJAER
19. Dwight YORKE
11. Ryan GIGGS
SUBSTITUTES
3. Denis IRWIN
10. Teddy SHERINGHAM
22. Ronnie WALLWORK (8) 29
33. Paul RACHUBKA
36. Luke CHADWICK (7) 84

... and earns the congratulations of his teammates

Jean Tigana's side equalised with a breathtaking Beckham-style free-kick from Fernandes and should have gone ahead when the Frenchman's corner was deflected by Yorke into the path of Symons, who headed wide when unmarked.

Thereafter, Fulham put United under more pressure than most Premiership opponents, but Brown, the Nevilles, Silvestre and van der Gouw – who replaced flu victim Barthez and shone on his FA Cup debut – held firm. Having weathered the storm by the midway point of the second period, the champions began to regain the upper hand. A replay seemed inevitable until Sheringham obliged with his 25th goal in 41 FA Cup outings.

Not to be outdone, Teddy Sheringham grabs the winner a minute from time

BRADFORD CITY 0

1. Gary WALSH
14. Andrew O'BRIEN
20. Peter ATHERTON
4. Stuart McCALL
12. Robert MOLENAAR
27. Billy McKINLAY
29. Eoin JESS
8. Robbie BLAKE
9. Ashley WARD
15. Dean WINDASS
22. Wayne JACOBS

SUBSTITUTES

3. Andy MYERS
7. Jamie LAWRENCE
11. Peter BEAGRIE
17. Aidan DAVISON
21. Dean SAUNDERS (8) 66

MATCH REPORT

The scoreline appears emphatic enough, but until former United keeper Gary Walsh gifted the Red Devils their breakthrough goal by dropping the most colossal of clangers deep inside the game's final quarter, the points were hanging in the balance.

True, the champions had looked the most cohesive combination, as might be expected of table-toppers facing the bottom side, but despite scintillating work by Giggs and Beckham, in particular, they had failed to break down the Bantams' stubborn and well-organised rearguard.

In fact, the most eye-catching incident all afternoon had almost furnished City with a shock first-half lead, when Windass dispatched a sudden drive from some 40 yards and Barthez needed all his agility to turn the crazily swirling effort over the bar.

But then came the moment which will probably haunt poor Walsh into retirement and beyond. O'Brien delivered a routine back-pass and, under no pressure, the Bradford custodian shaped to punt downfield. However, he kicked air with his left foot as the ball bobbled evilly, then ran several yards into the path of the dumbfounded Sheringham, who sidefooted into an empty net.

Demoralised by this freak setback, the hosts crumbled. First Giggs grabbed the goal his sparkling performance had deserved, controlling a chip from Silvestre with impudent ease, then bamboozling the right flank of the City rearguard for the umpteenth time before scoring with a fierce shot off the near post.

Thank you very much – Teddy Sheringham tucks away a gift from keeper Walsh

3 MANCHESTER UNITED

72 SHERINGHAM
75 GIGGS
87 CHADWICK

1. Fabien BARTHEZ
2. Gary NEVILLE
3. Denis IRWIN
16. Roy KEANE
27. Mikael SILVESTRE
6. Jaap STAM
7. David BECKHAM
12. Phil NEVILLE
20. Ole Gunnar SOLSKJAER
10. Teddy SHERINGHAM
11. Ryan GIGGS
SUBSTITUTES
9. Andy COLE (20) 76
17. Raimond VAN DER GOUW
24. Wesley BROWN (6) 66
34. Jonathan GREENING
36. Luke CHADWICK (12) 66

Ryan Giggs outpaces Bradford's Robert Molenaar

Then Beckham threaded a deliciously weighted through-ball to the lively Chadwick, who ran on and netted with aplomb from 15 yards.

Earlier, Sheringham, Giggs, Keane and Solskjaer had all missed beautifully crafted openings and Walsh had made a brilliant flying save from a Beckham piledriver. Sadly for the unfortunate net-minder, that would not be the memory most observers would take with them when they filed out of Valley Parade on a day when the Yorkshiremen were well outclassed.

Luke Chadwick rounded off a great afternoon with United's third

MANCHESTER UNITED 2

1. Fabien BARTHEZ
2. Gary NEVILLE
3. Denis IRWIN
16. Roy KEANE
12. Phil NEVILLE
6. Jaap STAM
34. Jonathan GREENING
8. Nicky BUTT
20. Ole Gunnar SOLSKJAER
10. Teddy SHERINGHAM
11. Ryan GIGGS

SUBSTITUTES

9. Andy COLE (20) 63
17. Raimond VAN DER GOUW
19. Dwight YORKE
24. Wesley BROWN
36. Luke CHADWICK (34) 63

G. NEVILLE 57
SHERINGHAM 87

MATCH REPORT

After dominating the first half but failing to score, Manchester United were forced to endure a torrid spell during which Villa might have registered several times immediately after the interval. However, once Gary Neville nudged the Red Devils ahead with a deft backheel – only the third senior goal of his Old Trafford career – they resumed command and moved 14 points clear at the head of the Premiership with only 14 games remaining.

Prompted by Giggs, whose teasing runs down the left flank and through the centre repeatedly disturbed the Midlanders'

Gary Neville celebrates only his third senior goal for United...

0 ASTON VILLA

rearguard, the hosts fashioned several early scoring opportunities but James was in top form.

Other half-chances were either spurned or blocked by last-ditch tackles, then the contest threatened to swivel on its axis as Villa emerged for the second period as a team transformed.

First, debutant Angel, their £9.5 million Colombian import, crossed to Dublin but the former Old Trafford marksman pulled his shot wide. Then Merson freed Hendrie, who rounded Barthez and was on the point of netting when the French keeper recovered brilliantly to fingertip the ball to safety. Still John Gregory's men pressed and Barry's goal-bound 12-yarder had to be cleared off the line by Greening before play swung to the other end and James denied Sheringham.

Soon it transpired that Villa had shot their bolt. Keane was fouled on the left flank and took the kick himself, his curving delivery enabling Neville to outwit James at his near post.

That steadied United and now, with Butt at his most tigerish, they re-asserted their authority. The points were clinched when Cole skinned Staunton and centred, the leaping James parried to Sheringham, and the veteran marksman sidefooted home. After the match the Reds' title odds were quoted at 100-1 on.

... while brother Phil tries to get in on the act

MANCHESTER UNITED 0

1. Fabien BARTHEZ
2. Gary NEVILLE
3. Denis IRWIN
16. Roy KEANE
27. Mikael SILVESTRE
6. Jaap STAM
7. David BECKHAM
8. Nicky BUTT
9. Andy COLE
10. Teddy SHERINGHAM
11. Ryan GIGGS

SUBSTITUTES

12. Phil NEVILLE
17. Raimond VAN DER GOUW
19. Dwight YORKE (8) 79
20. Ole Gunnar SOLSKJAER (3) 79
36. Luke CHADWICK

MATCH REPORT

West Ham ended a sequence of 11 straight defeats at Old Trafford by ejecting Manchester United from the FA Cup in a contest sprinkled with moments of sheer artistry from both sides.

The Red Devils attacked with their customary verve but it was di Canio who provided the decisive breakthrough when he latched on to a free-kick from Kanoute, then flicked the ball nonchalantly past Barthez, whose attention seemed to be divided between the advancing Italian and an appeal for offside.

The hosts might have been awarded two penalties, when Dailly handled in the first half and Winterburn appeared to get

All hands to the pump as West Ham keep Andy Cole at bay

1 WEST HAM UNITED

76 DI CANIO

both hands to the ball near the end, and they missed a few chances, notably when Sheringham ballooned over an empty net after Hislop had parried Andy Cole's shot. But the Hammers deserved immense praise. They boasted plenty of man-of-the-match candidates – Hislop, Tihinen, Carrick, Joe Cole and Kanoute – and their organisation and resolution was impeccable.

Not that the Reds played badly. Stam was majestic and at times Giggs looked capable of winning the match on his own with his electrifying pace and mesmeric footwork, including one magical double-dragback which left defenders lunging at air.

The tone for an afternoon of high entertainment was set in the opening minute when Barthez raced from his goal to deliver an outrageous backheel to enable Stam to clear. Thereafter, United enjoyed the lion's share of possession and Giggs, Keane and Beckham all went close before the interval. After the break West Ham increased their tempo, but still there were opportunities for Andy Cole, Giggs and Sheringham, who saw one narrow-angled effort cleared off the line.

After di Canio's goal, there was serial pinball inside the Hammers' box as the Reds poured forward frenetically, but it was all to no avail.

1. Shaka HISLOP
17. Nigel WINTERBURN
3. Stuart PEARCE
4. Michael CARRICK
28. Hannu TIHINEN
30. Sebastian SCHEMMEL
7. Christian DAILLY
18. Frank LAMPARD
16. Frederic KANOUTE
10. Paolo DI CANIO
26. Joe COLE
SUBSTITUTES
4. Steve POTTS
16. John MONCUR
19. Ian PEARCE (26) 90
22. Craig FORREST
36. Ragnvald SOMA(10) 89

Ryan Giggs had several chances during the match but was unable to turn them into goals

SUNDERLAND 0

1. Thomas SORENSEN

18. Darren WILLIAMS

3. Michael GRAY

4. Don HUTCHISON

32. Stanislav VARGA

17. Jody CRADDOCK

16. Alex RAE

8. Gavin McCANN

9. Niall QUINN

10. Kevin PHILLIPS

20. Stefan SCHWARZ

SUBSTITUTES

2. Chris MAKIN (36) 58

11. Kevin KILBANE (9) 29

28. John OSTER

36. Emerson THOME (20) 52

40. Michael INGHAM

MATCH REPORT

Andy Cole lifts the ball over Thomas Sorensen to score the only goal of a tense and fraught encounter

On a passionate and chaotic night at a seething Stadium of Light, three players were sent off amid a blaze of controversy and, more significantly, Manchester United stretched their Premiership advantage to 15 points. In the end, the valiant nine men of Sunderland might have snatched a draw but the ten Red Devils stood firm against a frantic late assault.

The Wearsiders had begun with a wave of early attacks during which Phillips volleyed over, Quinn failed narrowly to connect with a Gray cross and Rae attempted to catch Barthez off his line with a speculative 35-yarder.

1 MANCHESTER UNITED

46 COLE

1. Fabien BARTHEZ
2. Gary NEVILLE
27. Mikael SILVESTRE
16. Roy KEANE
24. Wesley BROWN
6. Jaap STAM
7. David BECKHAM
18. Paul SCHOLES
9. Andy COLE
10. Teddy SHERINGHAM
11. Ryan GIGGS

SUBSTITUTES

8. Nicky BUTT (18) 77
12. Phil NEVILLE (27) 86
17. Raimond VAN DER GOUW
19. Dwight YORKE
20. Ole Gunnar SOLSKJAER (10) 67

But United soaked up the pressure before finishing the first half the stronger side, Sheringham climaxing a flowing move with a near-post flick which shaved the far post and Sorensen almost spilling a Beckham free-kick at the feet of Cole.

But it was some 25 seconds after the restart that the game caught fire. Keane nodded forward to Cole, Craddock miskicked and the United marksman lifted the ball neatly beyond Sorensen and into the net.

Incensed by an apparent handball during the build-up, Sunderland skipper Gray was dismissed for abusing the referee. Then Sheringham and Keane went close while Hutchison bent a free-kick inches past at the other end before Cole and Rae became embroiled in a scuffle. The two men, looking distinctly comical, pressed their foreheads together and were sent off for violent conduct.

Outraged but unbowed, Sunderland retaliated, and Barthez was forced to save at the feet of Kilbane. Thereafter, the visitors began to stretch their hosts, but still the courageous Wearsiders were not done.

Indeed, during a hectic finale Phillips shot wide, then Varga's free-kick precipitated a goalmouth scramble which almost yielded an equaliser. Had it done so, United could not have complained.

The United players are delighted with the goal sensing that it might be enough to settle the match

JANUARY IN REVIEW

MONDAY 1	v WEST HAM UNITED	H	3-1
SUNDAY 7	v FULHAM	A	2-1
SATURDAY 13	v BRADFORD CITY	A	3-0
SATURDAY 20	v ASTON VILLA	H	2-0
SUNDAY 28	v WEST HAM UNITED	H	0-1
	v SUNDERLAND	A	1-0

PLAYER IN THE FRAME

Ryan Giggs

Throughout January Giggs' pace and trickery provided penetration to the Red Devils' attack, usually on the left flank but also wandering to delightful effect in central positions. Ryan was irresistible at Bradford, capping a thrilling individual display with a splendid goal; he ran amok at home to Villa and posed United's most potent threat in the disappointing FA Cup encounter with West Ham.

FA CARLING PREMIERSHIP

UP TO AND INCLUDING
WEDNESDAY 31 JANUARY 2001

	P	W	D	L	F	A	Pts
MANCHESTER UNITED	25	18	5	2	57	16	59
Arsenal	25	12	8	5	41	23	44
Sunderland	25	12	7	6	31	23	43
Liverpool	24	12	5	7	43	27	41
Ipswich Town	24	12	4	8	36	30	40
Chelsea	24	10	7	7	46	30	37
Newcastle United	25	11	4	10	32	35	37
Leicester City	24	10	6	8	24	26	36
Charlton Athletic	25	10	6	9	34	38	36
Leeds United	24	10	5	9	35	32	35
Tottenham Hotspur	25	8	8	9	30	34	32
Southampton	25	8	8	9	29	34	32
West Ham United	24	7	10	7	32	27	31
Aston Villa	23	7	8	8	24	26	29
Everton	24	7	6	11	26	36	27
Middlesbrough	25	5	10	10	29	32	25
Derby County	25	5	9	11	26	43	24
Manchester City	25	5	7	13	29	44	22
Coventry City	25	5	6	14	23	44	21
Bradford City	24	3	7	14	16	43	16

FEBRUARY

SATURDAY 3	v EVERTON	H
SATURDAY 10	v CHELSEA	A
WEDNESDAY 14	v VALENCIA CF	A
TUESDAY 20	v VALENCIA CF	H
SUNDAY 25	v ARSENAL	H

MANCHESTER UNITED 1

WATSON (o.g.) 52

1. Fabien BARTHEZ
27. Mikael SILVESTRE
3. Denis IRWIN
12. Phil NEVILLE
24. Wesley BROWN
6. Jaap STAM
7. David BECKHAM
18. Paul SCHOLES
9. Andy COLE
19. Dwight YORKE
36. Luke CHADWICK

SUBSTITUTES

10. Teddy SHERINGHAM (36) 80
11. Ryan GIGGS (18) h-t
17. Raimond VAN DER GOUW
20. Ole Gunnar SOLSKJAER
22. Ronnie WALLWORK (7) 72

MATCH REPORT

Despite high expectations amongst the huge crowd the Red Devils gave their scrappiest performance of the season to date – and they got away with it. The only goal of the game arrived via an extravagant deflection from United's sole shot on target, while the relegation-haunted Merseysiders created several inviting opportunities, all of which were spurned.

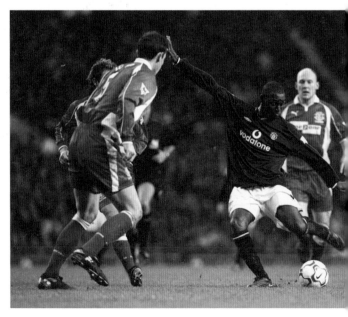

Andy Cole's low shot found the Everton net via a crazy deflection

0 EVERTON

1. Paul GERRARD
2. Steve WATSON
15. Gary NAYSMITH
4. Richard GOUGH
5. David WEIR
12. Michael BALL
19. Joe-Max MOORE
17. Scot GEMMILL
9. Kevin CAMPBELL
16. Thomas GRAVESEN
33. Idan TAL

SUBSTITUTES

6. David UNSWORTH (15) 72
13. Steve SIMONSEN
21. Danny CADAMARTERI (19) 77
26. Phil JEVONS (33) 84
30. Peter CLARKE

Before kick-off Sir Alex Ferguson's squad rotation policy was the principal topic of discussion by the Old Trafford faithful, who found that Keane and Gary Neville were rested, while Giggs and Sheringham were to occupy the bench.

Still, there were ten full internationals in the starting line-up and a largely lethargic opening passage of play was gruesomely anti-climactic. Gradually, though, Everton emerged from their shell and threatened United's serenity. Moore set up Gravesen but the Dane fired weakly wide from 18 yards, then the American marksman lifted his effort over the bar from eight yards after enterprising work from Naysmith.

However, it was the Reds who registered when a Barthez clearance was nodded by Giggs to Yorke, who turned it on to Cole. The England man shot low and powerfully, the ball cannoning off Watson before ballooning in a crazy arc over the stranded Gerrard and into the net.

Thus stung, Everton retaliated with vigour and twice they might have equalised but for Stam. First the Dutch man-mountain banged clear a menacing cross from Gravesen, then Moore's shot rebounded off his knee before squirming inches over the bar, with Barthez beaten.

Thereafter Walter Smith's men continued to threaten intermittently, but the champions played out time with practised calm. Hardly a match to remember, then, but the Reds could gird their loins for a hectic spring with their 15-point Premiership lead intact.

CHELSEA 1

HASSELBAINK 24

23. Carlo CUDICINI
17. Albert FERRER
3. Celestine BABAYARO
26. John TERRY
5. Frank LEBOEUF
6. Marcel DESAILLY
30. Jesper GRONKJAER
24. Samuelle DALLA BONA
9. Jimmy Floyd HASSELBAINK
25. Gianfranco ZOLA
11. Dennis WISE

SUBSTITUTES

1. Ed DE GOEY
10. Slavisa JOKANOVIC (30) 69
12. Mario STANIC
21. Bernard LAMBOURDE (17) 87
22. Eidar GUDJOHNSEN (25) 90

MATCH REPORT

Playing their most potent football for weeks, Manchester United dominated most of the action, yet couldn't muster a winner against a Chelsea side which became increasingly beleaguered as their initially shaky visitors recovered their customary fluency.

In truth, though, Claudio Ranieri's men deserved their share of the spoils for an exhilarating first-half display, for several breathtaking breakaways after the interval, and for providing the game's outstanding individual in the eye-catching Gronkjaer.

Indeed, had fortune favoured the Blues they might have taken all three points after going ahead through an uncharacteristic error by Scholes, whose ill-judged attempt to head the ball to van der Gouw was seized upon by Hasselbaink, who glanced it into the net from close range.

United retaliated, with the dynamic Keane prominent, but Chelsea might have doubled their advantage when Gronkjaer ran past Neville and Brown before forcing van der Gouw to parry a fierce shot.

After the interval the elusive Dane struck again, this time waltzing through the left flank of the Reds' rearguard before setting up Hasselbaink for a seemingly certain goal, only for the Dutchman to dither, and Silvestre to make a saving tackle.

Next, although United were getting on top, Chelsea found the net again when Zola dispossessed van der Gouw, who had gone walkabout near the corner flag. The Italian curled home exquisitely, only for the strike to be disallowed because the ball

1   MANCHESTER UNITED

69 COLE

Andy Cole pounces to earn United a well-deserved draw after a tense battle

17. Raimond VAN DER GOUW	
2. Gary NEVILLE	
27. Mikael SILVESTRE	
16. Roy KEANE	
24. Wesley BROWN	
6. Jaap STAM	
7. David BECKHAM	
18. Paul SCHOLES	
9. Andy COLE	
20. Ole Gunnar SOLSKJAER	
11. Ryan GIGGS	
SUBSTITUTES	
8. Nicky BUTT	
10. Teddy SHERINGHAM	
12. Phil NEVILLE	
19. Dwight YORKE	
33. Paul RACHUBKA	

had gone out of play. Thus reprieved, the Reds attacked relentlessly and Beckham, Cole and Giggs all went close before Giggs set up Cole who equalised with a deft near-post finish.

Thereafter, both sides fashioned chances but most fell to United, the pick of which was created by Neville's cross to Scholes, who failed to connect with a free header from six yards. Overall, the little redhead had contributed mightily, but his two aerial errors had proved costly.

Andy Cole and Ole Gunnar Solskjaer share their delight at United's second-half equaliser

VALENCIA CF   0

1. Santiago CANIZARES Ruiz
2. Mauricio PELLEGRINO
15. Amedeo CARBONI
20. Jocelyn ANGLOMA
12. Robero Fabian AYALA
6. Gaizca MENDIETA
7. John CAREW
18. Kily GONZALEZ
19. Ruben BARAJA
10. Miguel Angel ANGULO
22. Pablo Cesar AIMAR

SUBSTITUTES

4. Didier DESCHAMPS
5. Miroslav DJUKIC
9. DIEGO Martin ALONSO (7) 75
14. VICENTE Rodriguez Guillen
17. Juan SANCHEZ
23. David ALBELDA
25. Andres PALOP

MATCH REPORT

The scoreline was blank but the action was enthralling as Valencia and the Reds turned on the quality beneath the steepling, intimidating decks of the seething Mestalla.

After an even first half, the Spaniards – for whom midfielders Mendieta and the young Argentinian debutant, Aimar, were outstanding – turned up the heat and placed their visitors under concerted pressure. But United, for whom Brown and Stam were at their most majestic, held firm and even threatened to plunder all three points with a succession of late counter-attacks.

The pitch was sodden, throwing up splashes of water with every bounce of the ball, yet both sides contrived to produce flowing, progressive football of superb technical quality.

Before the interval, this was typified by a beautiful passing interchange between Sheringham and Giggs which was halted only by a last-ditch Pellegrino clearance, and a tantalising cross from Giggs which Beckham narrowly failed to reach.

At the other end Angulo netted but was judged offside, then the inventive Mendieta bore down on Barthez, but delayed his shot and was blocked by Brown.

Roy Keane almost stole the points for United at the death

0   MANCHESTER UNITED

1. Fabien BARTHEZ
2. Gary NEVILLE
27. Mikael SILVESTRE
16. Roy KEANE
24. Wesley BROWN
6. Jaap STAM
7. David BECKHAM
18. Paul SCHOLES
9. Andy COLE
10. Teddy SHERINGHAM
11. Ryan GIGGS
SUBSTITUTES
3. Denis IRWIN
8. Nicky BUTT (7) 75
12. Phil NEVILLE
17. Raimond VAN DER GOUW
19. Dwight YORKE
20. Ole Gunnar SOLSKJAER (9) 85
36. Luke CHADWICK

Ryan Giggs' usual inventiveness failed to pierce a resolute Spanish defence

After the break, the cultured Spaniards began to dictate, pinning United back for lengthy periods. Barthez was equal to the examination, though, producing two vintage moments of audacity when he flicked the ball away from Angloma and Kily Gonzalez, then saving admirably from both Kily and Mendieta.

As Valencia began to turn the screw ever more ominously, Butt replaced Beckham, thus forming a tighter screen in front of the back four, and the Reds began to mount their own threat.

Indeed, they might have won when Solskjaer's centre was almost turned in by Keane, but in the end United were content to settle for an honourable draw which saw them retain a two-point advantage at the top of their group.

MANCHESTER UNITED 1

COLE 12

1. Fabien BARTHEZ
2. Gary NEVILLE
27. Mikael SILVESTRE
16. Roy KEANE
24. Wesley BROWN
6. Jaap STAM
7. David BECKHAM
18. Paul SCHOLES
9. Andy COLE
10. Teddy SHERINGHAM
11. Ryan GIGGS

SUBSTITUTES

3. Denis IRWIN
8. Nicky BUTT (11) 18
12. Phil NEVILLE
19. Dwight YORKE
20. Ole Gunnar SOLSKJAER (10) 63
33. Paul RACHUBKA
36. Luke CHADWICK

MATCH REPORT

A cruelly late own goal by the otherwise impeccable Wes Brown deprived United of early qualification for the Champions League quarter-finals but, in all honesty, Valencia deserved their draw.

For most of a disappointing game, on a pudding of a pitch, the Spaniards had played the more enterprising football, enjoying more possession than their hosts and passing with more conviction. Yet the Red Devils had created what seemed a platform for likely victory with a beautiful early goal.

After pouncing eagerly on a fortunate rebound, Giggs played a slick one-two with Cole before pulling the ball back for the United marksman to sidefoot past Canizares with delicious precision from 14 yards.

Sadly, the Welshman was forced to withdraw almost immediately with a hamstring strain, thus unbalancing the Reds attack, which seemed out of sorts for the remainder of the evening.

Still, the lead might have been doubled when Sheringham located Cole with a curling, long-range delivery, but the United scorer shot straight at Canizares from 20 yards. Thereafter, Valencia performed with beguiling fluency and Mendieta sent Aimar in on Barthez, only for the gifted young Argentinian to pull his shot wide of the goal.

Ryan Giggs danced around the Spaniards with dazzling skills before a hamstring strain forced his early departure

1 VALENCIA CF

87 BROWN (o.g.)

1. Santiago CANIZARES Ruiz
2. Mauricio PELLEGRINO
15. Amedeo CARBONI
20. Jocelyn ANGLOMA
12. Robero Fabian AYALA
6. Gaizca MENDIETA
7. John CAREW
19. Ruben BARAJA
35. Pablo Cesar AIMAR
10. Miguel Angel ANGULO
18. Kily GONZALEZ

SUBSTITUTES

4. Didier DESCHAMPS
5. Miroslav DJUKIC
9. DIEGO Martin ALONSO
14. VICENTE Rodriguez Guillen (18) 76
17. Juan SANCHEZ (10) 65
23. David ALBELDA (35) 89
25. Andres PALOP

A snappy one-two with Ryan Giggs and into the net from Andy Cole

After the interval the pattern remained unchanged and Aimar set up Kily Gonzalez for a fierce cross-shot which was blocked by Barthez.

However, for all Valencia's poise, the most influential man afield was the United skipper, Keane, and he was the rock on which so much of the Spaniards' smooth approach work foundered time and time again.

As the end approached, the visitors stepped up the pressure, and Scholes was forced to clear a powerful header from Baraja off his line. Alas, that narrow escape was merely the prelude to Brown's traumatic finale. Lively substitute Vicente crossed low and hard from the left, the England man stuck out a leg and the ball bounced agonisingly inside the near post. It was a desparate way for the match to end for the talented youngster.

Andy Cole salutes Ryan Giggs for his part in the goal

MANCHESTER UNITED 6

1. Fabien BARTHEZ
2. Gary NEVILLE
27. Mikael SILVESTRE
16. Roy KEANE
24. Wesley BROWN
6. Jaap STAM
7. David BECKHAM
8. Nicky BUTT
20. Ole Gunnar SOLSKJAER
19. Dwight YORKE
18. Paul SCHOLES

SUBSTITUTES

3. Denis IRWIN
10. Teddy SHERINGHAM (19) 75
12. Phil NEVILLE
33. Paul RACHUBKA
36. Luke CHADWICK (16) 75

YORKE 3, 18, 22
KEANE 26
SOLSKJAER 38
SHERINGHAM 90

MATCH REPORT

Six goals against the Gunners, a 19-minute Dwight Yorke hat-trick, a 16-point lead at the top of the Premiership – it was one of those perfect days at a sun-drenched Old Trafford.

There were moments when United's football was awesome, and even if they didn't replicate the consistent fluency produced against, say, West Ham on New Year's Day, it was enough to provide United with their biggest home win over the north London club in many a long day.

The rout began when a Scholes dummy set up a scintillating one-two with Yorke, which culminated with the Tobagan bundling home with his thigh. Arsenal didn't lie down, though, and crafted a magnificent equaliser, a sweeping move involving Luzhny, Pires and Wiltord and a clinical finish from Henry.

United might have wobbled here but instead set about inflicting Wenger's heaviest defeat in English football.

First, a through-ball from the omnipotent Keane sprang the Arsenal offside trap and Yorke raced on to slot into the corner. Then Seaman was forced to save smartly from Yorke's header, before being beaten for a third time by the Tobagan, who had been set up by

Dwight Yorke's shot wrongfoots Arsenal's hapless David Seaman

1 ARSENAL

15 HENRY

1. David SEAMAN
22. Oleg LUZHNY
3. Igor STEPANOVS
4. Patrick VIEIRA
18. Gilles GRIMANDI
29. Ashley COLE
7. Robert PIRES
15. Ray PARLOUR
14. Thierry HENRY
16. SILVINHO
11. Sylvain WILTORD
SUBSTITUTES
8. Fredrik LJUNGBERG (29) 46
10. Dennis BERGKAMP
13. Alex MANNINGER
23. Nelson VIVAS (15) 69
25. KANU

Roy Keane joins the rout by banging in number four

Beckham following a neat dribble past Silvinho and a trademark crossfield dispatch.

Yorke then turned provider, crossing for Keane to volley the fourth, then Butt broke clear cleverly to cross for Solskjaer to contribute the fifth with a classic near-post sidefoot.

The second half was a formality with United controlling and Arsenal toiling dispiritedly. Vieira and Ljungberg might have reduced the arrears, but Beckham, Stam, Sheringham and Solskjaer all went close for the hosts before Sheringham rounded off proceedings by sweeping home from ten yards.

Before the game the Reds had been accused of not beating enough top-quality opponents – an eloquent response.

Ole Gunnar Solskjaer adds number five just before half-time

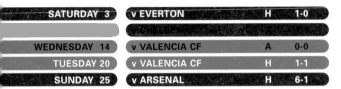

FEBRUARY IN REVIEW

SATURDAY 3	v EVERTON	H	1-0
WEDNESDAY 14	v VALENCIA CF	A	0-0
TUESDAY 20	v VALENCIA CF	H	1-1
SUNDAY 25	v ARSENAL	H	6-1

PLAYER IN THE FRAME

Wesley Brown

That mortifying moment at home to Valencia, when Wes deflected a cross past Barthez with only three minutes to go, can be forgotten. Both in Spain and in the Old Trafford return, the young Mancunian performed with the authority of a veteran against world-class opposition. Having impressed mightily alongside Gary Neville in central defence earlier in the season, during February Wes struck up a majestic partnership with fit-again Jaap Stam.

FA CARLING PREMIERSHIP

UP TO AND INCLUDING
WEDNESDAY 28 FEBRUARY 2001

	P	W	D	L	F	A	Pts
MANCHESTER UNITED	28	20	6	2	65	18	66
Arsenal	28	14	8	6	44	29	50
Liverpool	26	13	6	7	47	28	45
Sunderland	28	12	8	8	32	27	44
Ipswich Town	27	13	4	10	39	33	43
Leeds United	28	12	7	9	41	36	43
Leicester City	27	12	6	9	29	29	42
Charlton Athletic	28	11	8	9	38	40	41
Chelsea	26	10	8	8	48	33	38
Southampton	27	10	8	9	32	34	38
Newcastle United	27	11	4	12	32	38	37
Tottenham Hotspur	28	9	9	10	32	36	36
West Ham United	27	8	11	8	35	32	35
Aston Villa	26	8	9	9	28	28	33
Everton	28	8	7	13	30	42	31
Derby County	28	7	10	11	28	43	31
Middlesbrough	28	5	12	11	31	35	27
Manchester City	28	6	8	14	31	46	26
Coventry City	28	5	8	15	26	48	23
Bradford City	27	3	7	17	17	50	16

MARCH

SATURDAY 3	v LEEDS UNITED	A
WEDNESDAY 7	v PANATHINAIKOS	A
TUESDAY 13	v SK STURM GRAZ	H
SATURDAY 17	v LEICESTER CITY	H
SATURDAY 31	v LIVERPOOL	A

LEEDS UNITED 1

VIDUKA 84

1. Nigel MARTYN
18. Danny MILLS
3. Ian HARTE
4. Olivier DACOURT
5. Lucas RADEBE
29. Rio FERDINAND
7. Robbie KEANE
23. David BATTY
9. Mark VIDUKA
21. Dominic MATTEO
11. Lee BOWYER

SUBSTITUTES

2. Gary KELLY
10. Harry KEWELL (21) 46
13. Paul ROBINSON
17. Alan SMITH (7) 46
19. Eirik BAKKE

MATCH REPORT

Fabien Barthez saves Harte's spotkick just before half-time

The Red Devils carved out a point with a colossal defensive display at Elland Road, and came within a few minutes of escaping with all three. But they almost left empty-handed too, so their share of the spoils was nothing to be sniffed at.

Sir Alex Ferguson's men weathered a match-long battering from their bitter Yorkshire rivals, surviving a penalty – both conceded and saved by Barthez – before taking the lead following their first goal attempt, which did not materialise until after the hour mark.

Just six days on from their exhilarating demolition of Arsenal, United showed a sharply contrasting side to their character. Marshalled by the majestic Stam, who was skipper in

1   MANCHESTER UNITED

64 CHADWICK

1. Fabien BARTHEZ
2. Gary NEVILLE
3. Denis IRWIN
12. Phil NEVILLE
24. Wesley BROWN
6. Jaap STAM
7. David BECKHAM
8. Nicky BUTT
20. Ole Gunnar SOLSKJAER
10. Teddy SHERINGHAM
18. Paul SCHOLES
SUBSTITUTES
4. David MAY
19. Dwight YORKE
33. Paul RACHUBKA
34. Jonathan GREENING
36. Luke CHADWICK (8) 46

the absence of the injured Keane, they soaked up wave after wave of Leeds attacks in a first half of one-way traffic.

However, for all the industrious Yorkshiremen's possession, they created no clear-cut chances until Barthez tripped Harte in stoppage time before the break. The Irishman took the kick but the Frenchman sprang athletically to his right to parry brilliantly.

After the interval it was a tad more even but still against the run of play when Scholes found Solskjaer with a peach of a pass and the Norwegian's low shot was fumbled by Martyn, allowing the sprinting Chadwick to net gleefully from close range.

Thereafter, Leeds resumed the offensive, but when Barthez had saved smartly from Smith and Kewell, an away victory seemed likely. Then Mills charged past Irwin and crossed, Bowyer glanced the ball on and Viduka headed home emphatically.

Still there was drama to come. First Scholes uncharacteristically misheaded in front of an empty net, then Brown turned a last-minute Bowyer cross into his own goal but was reprieved when the referee gave a marginal offside decision against Viduka. It was the hardest earned point of United's season.

Luke Chadwick is congratulated
after giving United the lead

PANATHINAIKOS 1

SEITARIDIS 25

1. Antonis NIKOPOLIDIS
2. Rene HENRIKSEN
3. PERCY OLIVARES
20. Agelos BASINAS
16. Georgios SEITARIDIS
30. Panagiotis FYSSAS
7. Goran VLAOVIC
8. Ioannis GOUMAS
26. Georgios KARAGOUNIS
21. Nikolaos LIBEROPOULOS
24. Derek BOATENG

SUBSTITUTES

5. Fernando GALETTO (7) 59
9. Krzysztof WARZYCHA (21) 66
10. Karl-Heinz PFLIPSEN (20) 85
11. Helgi SIGURDSON
17. Georgios NASIOPOULOS
22. Konstantinos CHALKIAS
27. Andreas KOUTELIERES

MATCH REPORT

A goal by Paul Scholes, some two minutes into stoppage time, saw Manchester United escape with an undeserved point from a contest in which they'd been outplayed for long periods.

Five times Barthez was required to be inspired as the uncharacteristically ragged Reds rearguard was cut to ribbons with almost embarrassing ease by a Panathinaikos side that had already been eliminated. The Greeks were more enterprising, their passing more fluent and accurate, even their touch on the ball was more reliable than a poor United side.

Even Jaap Stam was troubled by the enterprising Greek side

1 MANCHESTER UNITED

90 SCHOLES

1. Fabien BARTHEZ
2. Gary NEVILLE
27. Mikael SILVESTRE
16. Roy KEANE
24. Wesley BROWN
6. Jaap STAM
7. David BECKHAM
18. Paul SCHOLES
9. Andy COLE
19. Dwight YORKE
12. Phil NEVILLE
SUBSTITUTES
3. Denis IRWIN
4. David MAY
10. Teddy SHERINGHAM (12) 78
20. Ole Gunnar SOLSKJAER (9) 78
33. Paul RACHUBKA
34. Jonathan GREENING
36. Luke CHADWICK (27) 64

Barthez apart, the visitors' most imposing player was Scholes, who offered his customary creative threat but lacked support from his mysteriously wan team-mates. Even Keane was giving the ball away carelessly.

The game began untidily, but promise of better things was carried by narrowly off-target efforts by Vlaovic at one end and Scholes at the other before Barthez and Gary Neville became entangled and almost gifted the Greeks an opener.

That breakthrough was not long delayed, though, arriving in the form of a waspish 25-yard cross-shot from the debutant Seitaridis after a free-kick had been inadequately cleared.

United improved slightly during the second period, but still it was Panathinaikos who held sway and Barthez was called on to foil Karagounis, the brilliant young Boateng and Basinas before Scholes' late saver in extra time, a sublime swivel and shot following an off-beam drive from Chadwick.

After that the irrepressible redhead almost won the game with a snap volley, but that would have been highway robbery against the brave Greeks.

Paul Scholes is delighted after his last-minute equaliser

MANCHESTER UNITED 3

1. Fabien BARTHEZ	
2. Gary NEVILLE	BUTT 5
3. Denis IRWIN	SHERINGHAM 20
16. Roy KEANE	KEANE 86
27. Mikael SILVESTRE	
6. Jaap STAM	
18. Paul SCHOLES	
8. Nicky BUTT	
20. Ole Gunnar SOLSKJAER	
10. Teddy SHERINGHAM	
36. Luke CHADWICK	
SUBSTITUTES	
7. David BECKHAM	
9. Andy COLE	
12. Phil NEVILLE	
19. Dwight YORKE	
24. Wesley BROWN	
33. Paul RACHUBKA	
34. Jonathan GREENING (18) 74	

MATCH REPORT

A return to authority after recent fluctuations in form assured the Red Devils of their place in the Champions League quarter-finals for the fifth successive season.

Admittedly, Sturm Graz were poor but that was due in no small measure to the iron control exuded by Butt and Keane in United's central midfield, and to a convincingly commanding display by Gary Neville and Stam at the heart of the defence. Certainly Sir Alex Ferguson's decision to freshen up the side through the omission of Beckham, Cole, Yorke and Brown was vindicated handsomely.

All the Reds needed to qualify for the last eight was to avoid a three-goal defeat, and that issue was settled with only minimal delay. In the opening minutes a close-range header from Solskjaer was blocked by Sidorczuk, but the Austrians' reprieve was to be brief.

After clever interplay by Chadwick and Solskjaer on the right, the ball broke to Butt, who crashed home a fierce, low cross-shot from 25 yards. Now the Reds poured forward relentlessly and soon they went further ahead when the persistence of Butt earned possession on the left. The workaholic man of the match crossed to Solskjaer, whose adroit square pass was swept precisely into the far corner of the net by the left foot of Sheringham.

Luke Chadwick congratulates Nicky Butt on the opener

0 SK STURM GRAZ

1. Kazimerz SIDORCZUK
23. Robert IBERTSBERGER
3. Gunther NEUKIRCHNER
30. Andres FLEURQUIN
20. Mehrdad MINAVAND
6. Roman MAHLICH
18. Markus SCHOPP
8. Markus SCHUPP
31. Mario HAAS
10. Ivica VASTIC
11. Gyorgy KORSOS

SUBSTITUTES

2. Petr HLINKA (6) 46
5. Franco FODA
7. Gerald STRAFNER
14. Jan-Pieter MARTENS (8) 65
19. Imre SZABICS (20) 46
22. Josef SCHICKLGRUBER
27. Georgios KOUTSOUPIAS

Teddy Sheringham sweeps in number two

Come the second half, understandably, United displayed less urgency while Sturm rallied enough to make several goal attempts, Vastic forcing Barthez into one fabulous plunging save from a 22-yard free-kick.

But the Austrians' flurry of activity stung their hosts into retaliation, and after Sidorczuk had acrobatically repelled a 30-yarder from Scholes, the Reds rounded off proceedings with a beautifully worked third goal.

Chadwick tricked a marker and surged unstoppably down the left, his cross was met by the deftest of flicks from Solskjaer, and Keane drilled in emphatically from 12 yards to see the United through to the quarter-finals in style.

Ole Gunnar Solskjaer sets up Keane for number three

MANCHESTER UNITED 2

33. Paul RACHUBKA
2. Gary NEVILLE
3. Denis IRWIN
16. Roy KEANE
12. Phil NEVILLE
6. Jaap STAM
34. Jonathan GREENING
8. Nicky BUTT
20. Ole Gunnar SOLSKJAER
10. Teddy SHERINGHAM
18. Paul SCHOLES

SUBSTITUTES

19. Dwight YORKE (34) 46
24. Wes BROWN
26. Mark WILSON
27. Mikael SILVESTRE (12) 80
36. Luke CHADWICK (8) 68

YORKE 88
SILVESTRE 90

MATCH REPORT

They came to nullify and frustrate and catch United with a surprise counter-punch, and only a freakish late breakthrough prevented the injury-ravaged Foxes from returning home with a point.

As it was, with only three minutes remaining, a Solskjaer shot from outside the box was deflected past the wrong-footed Royce by Yorke to give the Red Devils the points their comprehensive domination had deserved. To compound the woes of a devastated Leicester, Silvestre netted his first goal for United with a low cross-shot from the left flank.

The afternoon had begun on an uplifting note with the celebration of Denis Irwin's 500th senior appearance for the

A Dwight Yorke deflection puts United ahead two minutes from time

0 LEICESTER CITY

12. Simon ROYCE	
2. Gary ROWETT	
24. Andrew IMPEY	
29. Damien DELANEY	
18. Matt ELLIOT	
15. Phil GILCHRIST	
7. Matthew JONES	
25. Junior LEWIS	
9. Darren EADIE	
21. Dean STURRIDGE	
22. Ade AKINBIYI	

SUBSTITUTES

1. Tim FLOWERS	
11. Steve GUPPY (7) 89	
17. Stefan OAKES	
20. Trevor BENJAMIN (22) 70	
35. Kevin ELLISON (21) 84	

Mikael Silvestre's first ever goal for United came on 90 minutes

Reds, appropriately enough on St Patrick's Day, and to mark the occasion he replaced his fellow Irishman, Roy Keane, as captain.

Little was demanded of Irwin as United poured forward from the off to be confronted by two walls of blue shirts – a five-strong barrier at the back being protected by a four-man unit only marginally further forward.

At least the circumstances offered a comfortable League baptism for Paul Rachubka, plunged into the Premiership fray after Barthez had strained a thigh muscle during the warm-up. Indeed, the Californian-born rookie was a virtual spectator for the whole afternoon, strolling off at the end virtually untested.

That said, such was Leicester's defensive efficiency that the Reds, for all their territorial advantage, didn't carve too many clear-cut scoring opportunities. As so often before, though, United asserted themselves convincingly at the death.

Californian Paul Rachubka had an easy afternoon on his Premiership debut

LIVERPOOL 2

1. Sander WESTERVELD	**GERRARD 16**
2. Stephane HENCHOZ	**FOWLER 40**
23. Jamie CARRAGHER	
16. Dietmar HAMANN	
12. Sami HYYPIA	
6. Marcus BABBEL	
17. Steven GERRARD	
8. Emile HESKEY	
9. Robbie FOWLER	
13. Danny MURPHY	
15. Patrik BERGER	

SUBSTITUTES

10. Michael OWEN (17) 88
19. Pegguy ARPHEXAD
20. Nick BARMBY (15) 70
21. Gary McALLISTER (9) 70
30. Djimi TRAORE

MATCH REPORT

Teddy Sheringham tries to chip the Liverpool defence

Sluggish Manchester United fell victim to their first League double defeat by Liverpool in nearly a quarter of a century.

The defeat against the Red Devils' fiercest rivals was comprehensive, utterly deserved and, for mortified supporters, there was no consolation in the theory that their side's collective mind might have been on European battles to come.

Nor did it help that United remained in the so-called 'comfort zone' in the Premiership. The images that remained vivid after

0 MANCHESTER UNITED

1. Fabien BARTHEZ
2. Gary NEVILLE
3. Denis IRWIN
16. Roy KEANE
24. Wesley BROWN
12. Phil NEVILLE
7. David BECKHAM
8. Nicky BUTT
19. Dwight YORKE
10. Teddy SHERINGHAM
11. Ryan GIGGS

SUBSTITUTES

14. Andy GORAM
18. Paul SCHOLES (8) 76
25. Quinton FORTUNE
27. Mikael SILVESTRE (3) 72
36. Luke CHADWICK (10) 72

this emphatic reverse was of two brilliant Liverpool goals and a series of near misses by a sharp and hungry team.

United started competently enough and there were escapes at either end before a stunning strike by Gerrard changed the game decisively. After being fed by Fowler, the England midfielder, finding himself in yards of space, 30 yards from goal, unleashed a drive of awesome velocity. Barthez had no chance.

Soon afterwards, Keane, by far the visitors' most effective performer, might have equalised but his shot struck Westerveld's foot and then Liverpool assumed control. Fowler slipped when offered a free header from a Gerrard cross, but then he controlled a clever clip from the man of the match before half-volleying home unstoppably.

Thereafter, a Heskey shot scraped a post, though United were unlucky midway through the second half when Yorke netted from a Phil Neville cross only to be judged marginally offside.

A minute later Murphy was sent off for his second bookable offence and the Red Devils poured forward, but the nearest they came to reducing the deficit was when a Yorke effort was blocked bravely by Westerveld. This was a performance to erase from the United memory bank.

Dwight Yorke surrenders as Liverpool do the double over United

March in Review

SATURDAY 3	v LEEDS UNITED	A	1-1
WEDNESDAY 7	v PANATHINAIKOS	A	1-1
TUESDAY 13	v SK STURM GRAZ	H	3-0
SATURDAY 17	v LEICESTER CITY	H	2-0
SATURDAY 31	v LIVERPOOL	A	0-2

PLAYER IN THE FRAME

Luke Chadwick

One day Luke Chadwick might look back on March 2001 and reflect that it was the month when, in a footballing sense, he started to come of age. At Elland Road, where the Reds' attack had been frustratingly ineffective, he rose from the bench to give his side an exciting new dimension with his fearless forward runs, and his goal came close to securing all three points. Luke then played a full part in the crucial win over Sturm Graz, thus underlining his vast potential.

FA Carling Premiership

UP TO AND INCLUDING
SATURDAY 31 MARCH 2001

	P	W	D	L	F	A	Pts
MANCHESTER UNITED	31	21	7	3	68	21	70
Arsenal	31	16	9	6	49	29	57
Leeds United	31	14	8	9	46	38	50
Liverpool	29	14	7	8	50	31	49
Ipswich Town	30	15	4	11	44	36	49
Sunderland	31	13	9	9	37	32	48
Chelsea	30	12	9	9	54	38	45
Leicester City	29	13	6	10	31	31	45
Southampton	29	12	8	9	34	34	44
Charlton Athletic	30	11	9	10	39	42	42
Aston Villa	30	10	11	9	34	31	41
Tottenham Hotspur	31	10	9	12	36	40	39
Newcastle United	30	11	6	13	36	43	39
West Ham United	31	8	11	12	35	40	35
Everton	31	9	8	14	33	44	35
Derby County	31	8	11	12	31	47	35
Middlesbrough	31	6	13	12	34	38	31
Manchester City	31	6	9	16	34	52	27
Coventry City	31	6	9	16	28	51	27
Bradford City	30	3	9	18	22	57	18

APRIL

TUESDAY 3	v FC BAYERN MUNICH	H
TUESDAY 10	v CHARLTON ATHLETIC	H
SATURDAY 14	v COVENTRY CITY	H
WEDNESDAY 18	v FC BAYERN MUNICH	A
SATURDAY 21	v MANCHESTER CITY	H
SATURDAY 28	v MIDDLESBROUGH	A

MANCHESTER UNITED 0

1. Fabien BARTHEZ
2. Gary NEVILLE
27. Mikael SILVESTRE
16. Roy KEANE
24. Wesley BROWN
6. Jaap STAM
7. David BECKHAM
18. Paul SCHOLES
9. Andy COLE
20. Ole Gunnar SOLSKJAER
11. Ryan GIGGS

SUBSTITUTES

3. Denis IRWIN
8. Nicky BUTT
10. Teddy SHERINGHAM
12. Phil NEVILLE
17. Raimond VAN DER GOUW
19. Dwight YORKE (7) 86
36. Luke CHADWICK

MATCH REPORT

The irony was inescapable. Bayern Munich were the opponents, there was a late winner and it came from the boot of a substitute. But there the similarities with that unforgettable night in Barcelona ended; this time the chant might have been 'Who put the ball in United's net?'

The answer to that painful question was the Brazilian, Paulo Sergio, who turned the ball past Barthez from six yards after Linke had touched on a chip from the influential Effenberg with only four minutes of normal time remaining. Coming four days after the gruesome debacle at Anfield, it was a savage blow to the Reds' hopes of renewed European glory.

In broad terms, Sir Alex Ferguson's men shaded the first half-hour of a tense, cagey contest, then gradually Bayern established parity before finishing on top.

Early on United played some neat, cohesive football, but Cole shot wide twice after being set up by Beckham and Solskjaer, a free-kick by England's captain was gathered comfortably by Kahn and a Keane drive was deflected for a corner. At the other end Scholes cleared off the line following an Andersson header and Barthez fielded a shot from Jancker.

Bayern's midfield keeps a tight rein on Andy Cole

1 FC BAYERN MUNICH

86 PAULO SERGIO

1. Olivier KAHN

20. Hasan SALIHAMIDZIC

3. Bixente LIZARAZU

4. Samuel KUFFOUR

5. Patrik ANDERSSON

25. Thomas LINKE

7. Mehmet SCHOLL

16. Jens JEREMIES

9. Giovane ELBER

19. Carsten JANCKER

11. Stefan EFFENBERG

SUBSTITUTES

2. Willy SAGNOL

6. Michael WIESINGER

13. PAULO SERGIO (7) 77

18. Michael TARNAT

21. Alexander ZICKLER (19) 69

22. Bernd DREHER

24. Roque SANTA CRUZ

Ryan Giggs forces his way past Jeremies

After the break, though, the Red Devils were reduced mainly to long-range efforts, while Munich came close to breaking the deadlock when an Effenberg free-kick landed on top of the net.

As the visitors gained the ascendancy, Barthez saved athletically from Elber and Jeremies (twice), and United had a reprieve when Zickler volleyed against the bar after an Effenberg cross. But then came the goal, and it might have been worse subsequently as Zickler missed from close range.

Bookings meant that Beckham, Salihamidzic and Lizarazu would all miss the second leg, in which United would need a gargantuan effort to progress.

FA CARLING PREMIERSHIP
Tuesday 10 April, 2001

MANCHESTER UNITED   2

1. Fabien BARTHEZ
2. Gary NEVILLE
3. Denis IRWIN
16. Roy KEANE
24. Wesley BROWN
27. Mikael SILVESTRE
18. Paul SCHOLES
8. Nicky BUTT
9. Andy COLE
19. Dwight YORKE
11. Ryan GIGGS

SUBSTITUTES

7. David BECKHAM
10. Teddy SHERINGHAM (10) 77
12. Phil NEVILLE (3) 90
14. Andy GORAM
20. Ole Gunnar SOLSKJAER (19) 77

COLE 45
SOLSKJAER 82

MATCH REPORT

In one sense, this was a close-run contest, with United owing their narrow victory to a bizarre accidental one-two between Cole and the referee, and a late strike by Solskjaer.

But the reality was that the Red Devils mounted a match-long onslaught on their gutsy visitors, mustering no less than 28 shots and rapping the woodwork four times. True, the Addicks defended stoutly and looked menacing on the counter-attack, but any outcome other than three points for the champions would have been a travesty.

Lining up with Scholes on the right and Beckham on the bench, United poured forward from the off, creating a succession of chances, and Yorke might easily have claimed a first-half hat-trick.

As it was, Charlton came closest to opening the scoring against the run of play when Parker chipped against the bar in the 28th minute, then a Jensen rasper warmed the hands of Barthez.

Overall, though, United continued to dominate yet their breakthrough was to materialise in almost surreal fashion. When Cole cut in from the left he was tackled by Kishishev, the ball broke free and rebounded off the heel of referee Mark Halsey into the path of the England marksman, who netted with a low shot.

Andy Cole celebrates his strike on the stroke of half-time

1 CHARLTON ATHLETIC

63 FISH

13. Sasa ILIC
2. Radostin KISHISHEV
3. Chris POWELL
4. Graham STUART
5. Richard RUFUS
36. Mark FISH
17. Scot PARKER
19. Andy TODD
37. Shaun BARTLETT
21. Jonatan JOHANSSON
20. Claus JENSEN
SUBSTITUTES
8. Mark KINSELLA (4) 59
11. John ROBINSON (20) 59
18. Paul KONCHESKY (2) 73
26. Mathias SVENSSON
35. Tony CAIG

Mikael Silvestre works hard to break up a Charlton attack

Soon after the break Keane shot against an upright, but Charlton refused to capitulate and equalised when Neville enabled Fish to score from close range.

Thereafter United resumed their barrage, with first a Neville cross and then a Scholes shot slapping the goal frame. Strive as they might, it seemed that the Reds might be doomed to frustration, but Solskjaer, that substitute sublime, was having none of it and he secured the points with a typical finish.

Still there was time for Sheringham to head against the post before the inadvertent creator of United's opener signalled an end to proceedings.

Ole Gunnar Solskjaer wraps up the points eight minutes from time

MANCHESTER UNITED 4

14. Andy GORAM

2. Gary NEVILLE

27. Mikael SILVESTRE

16. Roy KEANE

24. Wesley BROWN

6. Jaap STAM

18. Paul SCHOLES

8. Nicky BUTT

9. Andy COLE

19. Dwight YORKE

11. Ryan GIGGS

SUBSTITUTES

7. David BECKHAM (8) 69

10. Teddy SHERINGHAM

12. Phil NEVILLE

17. Raimond VAN DER GOUW (14) 67

20. Ole Gunnar SOLSKJAER (9) 82

YORKE 13, 28
GIGGS 81
SCHOLES 87

MATCH REPORT

Dwight Yorke drives the ball past the outstanding Kirkland

Champagne corks were popping by teatime at Old Trafford – thanks to Arsenal's shock collapse at Highbury – but the Red Devils were not treated to a carefree stroll in the Premiership comfort zone by a bold Coventry side who matched their hosts valiantly throughout a thrilling first half.

Indeed, it was Gordon Strachan's men, looking anything but prospective relegation fodder, who snatched the lead when a Telfer cross was controlled exquisitely by Hartson, who saw his first shot blocked by Goram before netting the rebound.

United's response was devastating. First Coventry conceded possession in midfield, then failed to tackle the advancing Yorke, who rifled an unstoppable low drive from 25 yards.

2 COVENTRY CITY

11, 33 HARTSON

13. Chris KIRKLAND
22. Barry QUINN
24. Marcus HALL
17. Gary BREEN
5. John HARTSON
6. Richard SHAW
7. David THOMPSON
15. John EUSTACE
12. Paul TELFER
32. Lee CARSLEY
18. Craig BELLAMY
SUBSTITUTES
1. Magnus HEDMAN
2. Marc EDWORTHY
4. Paul DICHIO (15) 78
8. Youssef CHIPPO (12) 63
28. Jay BOTHROYD

Soon the game appeared to be up when the superlative Keane crossed from the left for Yorke to control deftly before beating the helpless Kirkland's lunge. However, Coventry continued to press and harry, and it was no less than they deserved when the combative Hartson outjumped Brown to equalise with an explosive header from another Telfer dispatch.

Almost immediately the Reds might have retaliated when a perfect cross from Cole was turned over a gaping net by Yorke, then Scholes mishit his shot following a scintillating run by Giggs.

Predictably, the second half produced wave upon wave of United pressure, but Kirkland was in marvellous form, saving superbly from Neville, Cole and Keane, the Reds' skipper also nodding a Giggs delivery against the base of a post.

Finally, in what has become a familiar scenario to denizens of Old Trafford, the pressure paid off just as time appeared to be running out. First Giggs scored with a majestic, looping, 17-yard header from a lofted Neville cross, then Beckham set up Scholes for a trademark 25-yard sizzler. Three hours later and the Red Devils were champions yet again.

Something to smile about – Ryan Giggs scores with a super header

FC BAYERN MUNICH 2

1. Olivier KAHN

2. Willy SAGNOL

18. Michael TARNAT

4. Samuel KUFFOUR

5. Patrik ANDERSSON

25. Thomas LINKE

7. Mehmet SCHOLL

16. Jens JEREMIES

9. Giovane ELBER

19. Carsten JANCKER

11. Stefan EFFENBERG

SUBSTITUTES

6. Michael WIESINGER

13. PAULO SERGIO (7) 88

21. Alexander ZICKLER (19) 35

22. Bernd DREHER

23. Owen HARGREAVES

24. Roque SANTA CRUZ (9) 64

31. Stephan KLING

ELBER 5
SCHOLL 40

MATCH REPORT

This time there was no miracle. As in Barcelona two years earlier, two late goals were required to beat Bayern, and Sheringham and Solskjaer had been summoned from the bench.

But now the Germans, marshalled by the superb Effenberg and inspired by the lion-hearted Kahn, resisted the Red Devils' late charge and reached the semi-finals. In truth, United had been undone by woeful first-half defending which had seen their opponents snatch two crucial goals.

Roy Keane battles for the ball in a crowded midfield

1 MANCHESTER UNITED

49 GIGGS

1. Fabien BARTHEZ
2. Gary NEVILLE
27. Mikael SILVESTRE
16. Roy KEANE
24. Wesley BROWN
6. Jaap STAM
18. Paul SCHOLES
8. Nicky BUTT
9. Andy COLE
19. Dwight YORKE
11. Ryan GIGGS

SUBSTITUTES

5. Ronny JOHNSEN
10. Teddy SHERINGHAM (19) 66
12. Phil NEVILLE
17. Raimond VAN DER GOUW
20. Ole Gunnar SOLSKJAER (8) 78
22. Ronnie WALLWORK
36. Luke CHADWICK (24) 85

Elber had opened the scoring from close range after the unattended Tarnat had dispatched a low cross from the left. Three minutes later, with the Reds' rearguard in tatters again, Jancker drove against Barthez's bar, then miskicked instead of capitalising on a horribly loose header from Brown.

With United lacking either creativity or conviction, their pre-interval retaliation was limited to a Giggs cross almost turned in by Cole before Scholl cleared off the line, a wide volley from Scholes and a Kahn fumble from a Cole placement.

The game seemed up when Jeremies broke down the right and his cross was ferried by Elber and Zickler to the unmarked Scholl, who shot home from 14 yards.

However, the second period heralded a United fightback which began when Giggs met a delightful dink from Scholes and lobbed delicately over Kahn and into the net. For a time things looked brighter for United and there were several moments when they might have struck again. A swerving Giggs volley was repelled acrobatically by Kahn, who later turned a shot from Scholes over his bar. Twice Sheringham shot narrowly wide and the wiles of Chadwick threatened late on, but it was not to be. In the end, Bayern Munich won at a canter and an old score had been settled.

Kuffour heads clear from Andy Cole's challenge

MANCHESTER UNITED 1

1. Fabien BARTHEZ
2. Gary NEVILLE
12. Phil NEVILLE
16. Roy KEANE
24. Wesley BROWN
6. Jaap STAM
7. David BECKHAM
18. Paul SCHOLES
20. Ole Gunnar SOLSKJAER
10. Teddy SHERINGHAM
36. Luke CHADWICK

SUBSTITUTES

8. Nicky BUTT (18) 76
11. Ryan GIGGS (36) 61
17. Raimond VAN DER GOUW
25. Quinton FORTUNE
27. Mikael SILVESTRE (24) 69

SHERINGHAM (penalty) 71

MATCH REPORT

United take the lead from the second penalty of the day

United fans expecting a feast of goals against their relegation-haunted rivals left Old Trafford disillusioned after the Manchester 'Derby' lurched to a less than ideal ending.

Despite dominating territorially, the Red Devils were in disjointed mode and after conceding a scrappy late equaliser they saw skipper Roy Keane sent off for a foul on his opposite number, Alf-Inge Haaland.

Doubtlessly still smarting from their European exit, United started slugglishly and could not have complained had they

1 MANCHESTER CITY

84 HOWEY

20. Carlo NASH
15. Alf-Inge HAALAND
36. Danny GRANVILLE
4. Gerard WIEKENS
24. Steve HOWEY
22. Richard DUNNE
37. Laurent CHARVET
28. Tony GRANT
9. Paul DICKOV
23. Paulo WANCHOPE
18. Jeff WHITLEY

SUBSTITUTES

1. Nick WEAVER
7. Spencer PRIOR (4) 69
10. Shaun GOATER (12) 85
12. Andrei KANCHELSKIS (28) 46
34. Mark KENNEDY

been two goals adrift in the first eight minutes. First Brown's weak clearance was met by a Wiekens drive which the England defender deflected against his own crossbar, then Wanchope rounded Barthez only for Stam to clear his shot off the line.

Scholes responded with a 25-yard skimmer which was well held by Nash, but then Dickov went close with a low effort on the turn. The Reds upped the pace, laying siege to the City goal for 20 minutes before the break, but all to no avail as Beckham volleyed over and Solskjaer was foiled by Nash.

The deadlock should have been broken on the hour when Dickov fouled Brown and a penalty was awarded, only for Scholes to scuff it wide. Now the Blues' goal led a charmed life until Dunne tripped Solskjaer and newly-elected Footballer of the Year Teddy Sheringham netted, rather edgily via the hand of Nash, from the spot.

That seemed likely to be that, but not so. Dickov curled in a City corner, Butt got the merest touch as he attempted to clear and Howey turned the ball in at the far post.

All that remained was for Keane's over-vigorous challenge on Haaland to be punished by a red card. Suddenly what should have been a day of celebration had turned distinctly sour.

Jaap Stam calmly stems the City tide

MIDDLESBROUGH 0

1. Mark SCHWARZER
29. Jason GAVIN
28. Colin COOPER
4. Steve VICKERS
17. Ugo EHIOGU
14. Paul OKON
24. Phil STAMP
20. Dean WINDASS
9. Paul INCE
19. Hamilton RICARD
11. Alen BOKSIC

SUBSTITUTES

3. Dean GORDON (28) 84
7. Robbie MUSTOE (19) 84
10. Brian DEANE
23. Carlos MARINELLI (24) 67
25. Mark CROSSLEY

MATCH REPORT

It emanated from an unlikely source but such was the ferocity of Phil Neville's early piledriver that it would not have disgraced Bobby Charlton in his prime.

It began with Beckham, whose crossfield pass travelled the length of the halfway line before reaching the charging full-back, who was allowed to progress unchallenged until, some 30 yards out, he unleashed the howitzer which produced only his third goal in more than 200 senior outings.

Middlesbrough, still not safe from relegation, were visibly jolted and Teddy Sheringham might have pressed home the Reds' advantage after 15 minutes but could only direct a free header tamely into Schwarzer's arms.

Thereafter, despite Windass (twice) and Ricard going close, the champions maintained general command for the remainder of the first half and Schwarzer was called on to make an agile save from Solskjaer shortly before the break.

But when the Norwegian failed to convert an inviting opportunity after 63 minutes it signalled a Boro resurgence which might have produced an equaliser. The nearest they came was when a Marinelli free-kick – moved to a menacing position only 12 yards from goal following dissent – was blocked by van der Gouw, then rebounded to Gavin

Ole Gunnar Solskjaer tested Boro's defence without scoring

2 MANCHESTER UNITED

4 P. NEVILLE
84 BECKHAM

17. Raimond VAN DER GOUW
24. Wesley BROWN
12. Phil NEVILLE
28. Michael STEWART
5. Ronny JOHNSEN
6. Jaap STAM
7. David BECKHAM
8. Nicky BUTT
20. Ole Gunnar SOLSKJAER
10. Teddy SHERINGHAM
25. Quinton FORTUNE
SUBSTITUTES
9. Andy COLE (20) 75
11. Ryan GIGGS (25) 73
19. Dwight YORKE
33. Paul RACHUBKA
36. Luke CHADWICK (28) 84

David Beckham set up the first goal before scoring United's second himself

whose thunderous shot hit a post before being walked into the net by the offside Ehiogu. The effort was ruled out, possibly erroneously, as the Dutch keeper may have got a touch to Gavin's scorcher, thus playing Ehiogu onside.

Whatever, on 78 minutes the England defender headed over when well placed, then United killed the game off when Giggs opened the Boro defence on the left before finding Beckham, who swivelled to dispatch a low shot from the edge of the box.

In the absence of Keane and Scholes, the England captain appeared to relish his free role, while Premiership debutant Stewart caught the eye in central midfield. The conveyor belt of talent at Old Trafford rolls on and on.

APRIL IN REVIEW

TUESDAY 3	v FC BAYERN MUNICH	H	0-1
TUESDAY 10	v CHARLTON ATHLETIC	H	2-1
SATURDAY 14	v COVENTRY CITY	H	4-2
WEDNESDAY 18	v FC BAYERN MUNICH	A	1-2
SATURDAY 21	v MANCHESTER CITY	H	1-1
SATURDAY 28	v MIDDLESBROUGH	A	2-0

PLAYER IN THE FRAME

Roy Keane

There should be no gainsaying that the infamous misdeed against Manchester City was to be deplored. Equally, though, there is no doubt that the footballing contribution of Roy Keane was consistently awesome throughout April. The Irishman was a box-to-box inspiration, a majestic, gifted performer and a born motivator coveted by almost every manager in Europe.

FA CARLING PREMIERSHIP

UP TO AND INCLUDING
MONDAY 30TH APRIL 2001

	P	W	D	L	F	A	Pts
MANCHESTER UNITED	35	24	8	3	77	25	80
Arsenal	35	19	9	7	59	34	66
Leeds United	35	18	8	9	54	39	62
Ipswich Town	36	19	5	12	54	40	62
Liverpool	34	17	8	9	60	37	59
Chelsea	35	15	9	11	62	41	54
Sunderland	36	14	11	11	41	37	53
Charlton Athletic	36	14	10	12	48	50	52
Aston Villa	36	12	15	9	43	38	51
Newcastle United	34	13	7	14	40	46	46
Tottenham Hotspur	36	12	10	14	42	49	46
Southampton	34	12	9	13	34	41	45
Leicester City	36	13	6	17	34	46	45
Everton	36	11	8	17	42	55	41
West Ham United	36	9	12	15	41	48	39
Middlesbrough	36	8	14	14	41	42	38
Derby County	36	9	11	16	35	58	38
Manchester City	36	8	10	18	39	61	34
Coventry City	36	8	9	19	34	60	33
Bradford City	34	5	9	20	28	61	24

MAY

SATURDAY 5	v DERBY COUNTY	H
SUNDAY 13	v SOUTHAMPTON	A
SATURDAY 19	v TOTTENHAM HOTSPUR	A

MANCHESTER UNITED   0

1. Fabien BARTHEZ
12. Phil NEVILLE
3. Denis IRWIN
28. Michael STEWART
5. Ronny JOHNSEN
22. Ronnie WALLWORK
7. David BECKHAM
8. Nicky BUTT
9. Andy COLE
10. Teddy SHERINGHAM
36. Luke CHADWICK

SUBSTITUTES

6. Jaap STAM
11. Ryan GIGGS (28) 65
17. Raimond VAN DER GOUW (1) 87
19. Dwight YORKE
27. Mikael SILVESTRE (12) 77

MATCH REPORT

Ronny Johnsen takes no chances in clearing this Derby attack

The champagne flowed and the fireworks fizzed as United celebrated yet another title triumph, but the only prize at stake on the day went to Derby County.

By inflicting on the Reds their second home League defeat of the campaign, the Rams ensured their Premiership survival, which was fitting reward for superb defensive organisation, spirited all-round enterprise and one fabulous piece of finishing.

Though both sides were markedly under-strength, the game was lively enough, with Derby perhaps the more purposeful unit for most of the first half. With the clever Kinkladze and the classy Eranio impressing in midfield, they fashioned two early chances

1 DERBY COUNTY

34 CHRISTIE

1. Mart POOM
2. Horacio CARBONARI
23. Paul BOERTIEN
15. Danny HIGGINBOTHAM
5. Rory DELAP
21. Chris RIGGOTT
17. Youl MAWENE
20. Stefano ERANIO
12. Malcolm CHRISTIE
10. Giorgi KINKLADZE
11. Lee MORRIS

SUBSTITUTES

13. Thordur GUDJONSSON (10) 77
18. Richard JACKSON
22. Bjorn BRAGSTAD
31. Adam BOLDER (12) 89
32. Lee GRANT

for Christie, but both shots from the lively frontman were fielded comfortably by Barthez.

At the other end Chadwick buzzed encouragingly and twice he combined promisingly with Cole, almost opening the scoring after a sweet interchange with the England centre-forward.

But that honour fell to Christie, who was heavily marked and seemingly offering scant threat when he received a shrewd pass from Eranio inside United's box. He spun away from a posse of defenders and dispatched a brilliant left-footer into the far top corner of the Reds' net from 15 yards.

Old Trafford flinched collectively before sitting back for the inevitable riposte. However, Derby continued to play coherent football and after the break Christie should have doubled the Rams' lead but sidefooted wide of a gaping net from close range after being set up by Morris.

Now United surged forward in search of reprisal but, despite several frenetic pinball sequences in the County goalmouth, the breakthrough failed to materialise.

Poom made some fine saves, Mawene cleared off the line from Giggs, and Sheringham almost turned in a Beckham cross but, until the title party began at the final whistle, it was Derby's day.

Luke Chadwick twists away from Derby's Youl Mawene

SOUTHAMPTON 2

1. Paul JONES
25. Garry MONK
18. Wayne BRIDGE
4. Chris MARSDEN
5. Claus LUNDEKVAM
6. Dean RICHARDS
17. Marian PAHARS
8. Matthew OAKLEY
16. James BEATTIE
10. Kevin DAVIES
30. Hassan KACHLOUL

SUBSTITUTES

7. Matthew LE TISSIER
11. Uwe ROSLER
13. Neil MOSS
15. Francis BENALI (25) 85
21. Jo TESSEM (30) 76

BROWN (o.g.) 9
PAHARS 14

MATCH REPORT

The contrast with United's previous visit to The Dell, a little more than a year earlier, was marked, indeed. On that occasion, the Red Devils had been at full strength and they brushed aside Southampton to clinch the Championship.

This time, with the silverware already secure, the visitors adopted a low-key approach, fielding what was virtually a reserve team, and they were beaten on merit by their hosts, who recorded a first win for caretaker manager Stuart Gray.

Ryan Giggs leaps over a challenge from Southampton's Kevin Davies before shooting tamely at keeper Paul Jones

1 MANCHESTER UNITED

71 GIGGS

United started disastrously, falling two goals adrift in the first quarter of an hour. Brown dived towards a wicked cross from Pahars, but instead of heading clear he directed the ball unstoppably into his own net. Then Kachloul lobbed beyond United's static back line to Pahars, who paused, as if he believed he was offside, before sidefooting home from ten yards.

Southampton remained on top for the remainder of the first period, with Davies coming close to increasing the lead, only to be denied by Goram's athleticism. For United, there were efforts on goal from Stewart, Giggs and Fortune, but Jones saved them all with ease.

After the break, the Red Devils were more incisive and skipper-for-the-day Giggs strode through to reduce the arrears following a slick one-two passing interchange with Yorke. Giggs, Neville and Chadwick all went close, but the Saints repelled them and were worth the three points which lifted them into the top half of the Premiership table.

Thus, United recorded their fourth defeat in six visits to The Dell. When Southampton welcome the champions to the south coast in 2001-02 it will be at a spanking new stadium which should be the scene of a more meaningful contest.

| 14. Andy GORAM |
| 12. Phil NEVILLE |
| 3. Denis IRWIN |
| 28. Michael STEWART |
| 5. Ronny JOHNSEN |
| 24. Wesley BROWN |
| 36. Luke CHADWICK |
| 22. Ronnie WALLWORK |
| 25. Quinton FORTUNE |
| 19. Dwight YORKE |
| 11. Ryan GIGGS |

SUBSTITUTES

| 4. David MAY (22) 72 |
| 17. Raimond VAN DER GOUW (14) 58 |
| 23. Michael CLEGG |
| 26. Mark WILSON |
| 32. Bojan DJORDJIC |

Phil Neville breaks up another Saints' attack

TOTTENHAM HOTSPUR 3

13. Neil SULLIVAN

2. Stephen CARR

21. Luke YOUNG

25. Stephen CLEMENCE

12. Gary DOHERTY

30. Anthony GARDNER

15. Willem KORSTEN

29. Simon DAVIES

9. Les FERDINAND

17. Oyvind LEONHARDSEN

28. Matthew ETHERINGTON

SUBSTITUTES

1. Ian WALKER

4. Steffen FREUND

6. Chris PERRY (30) 16

31. Alton THELWELL

37. John PIERCY (28) 84

KORSTEN 17, 67
FERDINAND 75

MATCH REPORT

A third successive defeat for the Red Devils provided a wholly inappropriate finale to what was, by any standards, yet another glorious campaign. In the end, however, events on the field were eclipsed by Sir Alex Ferguson's earlier declaration that he would be severing all ties with United in a year's time.

The game itself was entertaining enough, with plenty of pretty football, but – with the Reds having tied up the title what seemed like an eternity ago, and with Spurs anchored safely in mid-table – the match lacked any real competitive edge.

From a United perspective, the contest meant most to two men at opposite ends of their careers, with veteran keeper Raimond van der Gouw claiming a Championship medal by making his tenth appearance of the season, and rookie midfielder Bojan Djordjic making his debut at senior level.

The action began with the visitors buzzing enterprisingly, but it was Tottenham who took the lead when a Davies corner was punched out by van der Gouw to Korsten, who netted with a beautiful dipping volley from 20 yards.

United retaliated rapidly when Neville's perfectly measured first-time cross was nodded down by Sheringham for Scholes to net with a smart half-volley from six yards.

Paul Scholes equalised after 22 minutes

1 MANCHESTER UNITED

22 SCHOLES

17. Raimond VAN DER GOUW
12. Phil NEVILLE
3. Denis IRWIN
4. David MAY
5. Ronny JOHNSEN
27. Mikael SILVESTRE
18. Paul SCHOLES
8. Nicky BUTT
9. Andy COLE
10. Teddy SHERINGHAM
11. Ryan GIGGS
SUBSTITUTES
14. Andy GORAM
22. Ronnie WALLWORK
25. Quinton FORTUNE
28. Michael STEWART
32. Bojan DJORDJIC (3) 76

Ryan Giggs was unlucky with a 25-yard shot saved by the flying Sullivan

Three minutes later Giggs danced across the home defence from right to left before unleashing a 25-yard drive which brought a flying save from Sullivan, then Cole spurned two opportunities to put the Reds ahead. First he miscued with a free header from a Giggs cross, then he skewed his shot wide from 12 yards after being sent in by Sheringham.

Instead, the decisive contribution came from the lively Davies, whose incisive running created second-half goals for Korsten and Ferdinand. United fans were left to contemplate a period of rare anti-climax and suffer twinges of apprehension about the future.

Andy Cole has the ball taken off his toes by Tottenham's Chris Perry

MAY IN REVIEW

PLAYER IN THE FRAME

Ronny Johnsen

He's never been one to hog the limelight, but Ronny Johnsen deserves enormous credit for the way he fought back from career-threatening knee injuries, which ruined his season, to claim a title medal at the death. On his return he appeared as pacy and decisive as ever, and it is to be hoped that the personable Norwegian will remain fit enough to be an integral part of Sir Alex Ferguson's central defensive options in the 2001-02 campaign.

FA CARLING PREMIERSHIP

FINAL TABLE

	P	W	D	L	F	A	Pts
MANCHESTER UNITED	38	24	8	6	79	31	80
Arsenal	38	20	10	8	63	38	70
Liverpool	38	20	9	9	71	39	69
Leeds United	38	20	8	10	64	43	68
Ipswich Town	38	20	6	12	57	42	66
Chelsea	38	17	10	11	68	45	61
Sunderland	38	15	12	11	46	41	57
Aston Villa	38	13	15	10	46	43	54
Charlton Athletic	38	14	10	14	50	57	52
Southampton	38	14	10	14	40	48	52
Newcastle United	38	14	9	15	44	50	51
Tottenham Hotspur	38	13	10	15	47	54	49
Leicester City	38	14	6	18	39	51	48
Middlesbrough	38	9	15	14	44	44	42
West Ham United	38	10	12	16	45	50	42
Everton	38	11	9	18	45	59	42
Derby County	38	10	12	16	37	59	42
Manchester City	38	8	10	20	41	65	34
Coventry City	38	8	10	20	36	63	34
Bradford City	38	5	11	22	30	70	26

2000-01 SEASON IN REVIEW

Defeat by Bayern Munich in the Champions League was monstrously disappointing. In the immediate aftermath, Roy Keane let emotion rule reason and made his famous 'end of the road' pronouncement. Whilst this was in keeping with many merchants of gloom, it is time for a more measured reflection on the 2000-01 campaign in which, lest we forget, the Reds claimed their seventh League title in nine seasons, and finished in the top two for the tenth consecutive term.

Sir Alex Ferguson became the first man to guide a club to three successive Championship crowns, overhauling even the stunning record of Liverpool's Bob Paisley. Despite the gleeful critics, on the continental front there were positive aspects. United are the only club in Europe to reach the quarter-finals in each of the last five years. Of course, improvement is desirable and there is certainly evidence that it will be forthcoming. The existing squad is young enough, and dripping quality, while the £19 million investment in Ruud van Nistelrooy offers evidence of real ambition.

Arguably, a prime cause of European under-achievement was the chronic lack of competition. So masterful were most of United's domestic displays as they scaled the Premiership that their main rivals were pretty well buried by January.

Maybe complacency crept in. Whatever, there have been many uplifting factors: the integration of Barthez, the meteoric development of Brown, the progress of Silvestre, the stirrings of Chadwick and Stewart, Sheringham's Indian summer and new long-term contracts agreed with the likes of Giggs, Scholes, Stam and Cole.

Much has been made of the renaissance of Leeds and Liverpool, and the continuing threat of Arsenal so, next season, surely United will not have it all their own way in the Premiership as they have had for the last two terms. Is it stretching credibility to imagine an eighth title in ten years, and an unheard-of four in a row, as Sir Alex's last hurrah?

With the 2002 Champions League Final in the great man's home town of Glasgow maybe no dream is impossible. Suffice it to say, it would not be the first time that the Red Devils had rewritten the laws of probability.

FIRST TEAM

APPEARANCES

substitute appearances shown in parenthesis

Legend:
- ▨ FA CARLING PREMIERSHIP
- ▨ UEFA CHAMPIONS LEAGUE
- ▨ WORTHINGTON CUP
- ▨ FA CUP
- ■ TOTAL

Player	FA CARLING PREMIERSHIP	UEFA CHAMPIONS LEAGUE	WORTHINGTON CUP	FA CUP	TOTAL
NEVILLE • Gary	32	14	0	2	48
BARTHEZ • Fabien	30	12	0	1	43
KEANE • Roy	28	13	0	2	43
BECKHAM • David	29 (2)	11 (1)	0	2	42 (3)
SILVESTRE • Mikael	25 (5)	13 (1)	0	2	40 (6)
SCHOLES • Paul	28 (4)	12	0	0	40 (4)
BROWN • Wesley	25 (3)	9 (2)	1	1	36 (5)
GIGGS • Ryan	24 (7)	9 (2)	0	2	35 (9)
BUTT • Nicky	24 (4)	8 (3)	0	2	34 (7)
SHERINGHAM • Teddy	23 (6)	8 (3)	0	1 (1)	32 (10)
NEVILLE • Phil	24 (5)	4 (2)	2	1	31 (7)
IRWIN • Denis	20 (1)	7	0	1	28 (1)
COLE • Andy	15 (4)	10	0	1	26 (4)
SOLSKJAER • Ole Gunnar	19 (12)	3 (8)	2	1 (1)	25 (21)
YORKE • Dwight	15 (7)	7 (4)	2	1 (1)	25 (12)
STAM • Jaap	15	6	0	1	22
JOHNSEN • Ronny	11	4	1	0	16
VAN DER GOUW • Raimond	5 (5)	2	2	1	10 (5)
CHADWICK • Luke	6 (10)	1 (2)	2	0 (1)	9 (13)
FORTUNE • Quinton	6 (1)	0 (1)	2	0	8 (2)
WALLWORK • Ronnie	4 (8)	0 (1)	2	0 (1)	6 (10)
GREENING • Jonathan	3 (4)	1 (1)	2	0	6 (5)
STEWART • Michael	3	0	0 (2)	0	3 (2)
CLEGG • Michael	0	0	2	0	2
GORAM • Andy*	2	0	0	0	2
O'SHEA • John	0	0	2	0	2
MAY • David	1 (1)	0	0	0	1 (1)
RACHUBKA • Paul	1	0	0 (1)	0	1 (1)
HEALY • David	0 (1)	0	0 (1)	0	0 (2)
BERG • Henning	0 (1)	0	0	0	0 (1)
DJORDJIC • Bojan	0 (1)	0	0	0	0 (1)
WEBBER • Danny	0	0	0 (1)	0	0 (1)

Loan from Motherwell, 22/3/2001-31/5/2001

GOALSCORERS

Player	FA CARLING PREMIERSHIP	UEFA CHAMPIONS LEAGUE	WORTHINGTON CUP	FA CUP	TOTAL
SHERINGHAM • Teddy	15	5	0	1	21
COLE • Andy	9	4	0	0	13
SOLSKJAER • Ole Gunnar	10	0	2	1	13
SCHOLES • Paul	6	6	0	0	12
YORKE • Dwight	9	1	2	0	12
BECKHAM • David	9	0	0	0	9
GIGGS • Ryan	5	2	0	0	7
BUTT • Nicky	3	1	0	0	4
KEANE • Roy	2	1	0	0	3
CHADWICK • Luke	2	0	0	0	2
FORTUNE • Quinton	2	0	0	0	2
IRWIN • Denis	0	2	0	0	2
JOHNSEN • Ronny	1	0	0	0	1
NEVILLE • Gary	1	0	0	0	1
NEVILLE • Phil	1	0	0	0	1
SILVESTRE • Mikael	1	0	0	0	1
JONES • Matthew (Leeds United)	1 o.g.	0	0	0	1 o.g.
PEARCE • Stuart (West Ham)	1 o.g.	0	0	0	1 o.g.
WATSON • Steve (Everton)	1 o.g.	0	0	0	1 o.g.
Total	**79**	**22**	**4**	**2**	**107**

Gary Neville

Teddy Sheringham

LEAGUE ATTENDANCES 2000-01

Home			Away		
67,637	v Coventry City		52,134	v Newcastle United	
67,603	v West Ham United		48,260	v Sunderland	
67,597	v Ipswich Town		44,806	v Liverpool	
67,583	v Tottenham Hotspur		40,889	v Aston Villa	
67,581	v Southampton		40,055	v Leeds United	
67,576	v Middlesbrough		38,541	v Everton	
67,568	v Chelsea		38,146	v Arsenal	
67,535	v Arsenal		36,072	v Tottenham Hotspur	
67,535	v Manchester City		34,960	v Chelsea	
67,533	v Aston Villa		34,429	v Manchester City	
67,533	v Liverpool		34,417	v Middlesbrough	
67,528	v Everton		32,910	v Derby County	
67,526	v Derby County		25,998	v West Ham United	
67,523	v Leeds United		22,132	v Leicester City	
67,516	v Leicester City		22,007	v Ipswich Town	
67,505	v Charlton Athletic		21,079	v Coventry City	
67,503	v Sunderland		20,551	v Bradford City	
67,477	v Newcastle United		20,043	v Charlton Athletic	
67,447	v Bradford City		15,246	v Southampton	

Home		Away	
Highest	v 67,637 (Coventry City)	Highest	v 52,134 (Newcastle United)
Lowest	v 67,447 (Bradford City)	Lowest	v 15,246 (Southampton)
Total	1,283,306	Total	622,675
Average	67,542	Average	32,772

OLD TRAFFORD ATTENDANCES

League & Cup

Total   1,810,900

Average 67,070

Includes: 19 FA Carling Premiership games

7 UEFA Champions League games

1 FA Cup

Sunday 13 August, 2000 • Wembley Stadium • 3.00pm • Attendance 65,148
Referee Mike Riley

 # MANCHESTER UNITED 0

 ## CHELSEA 2
22 HASSELBAINK
73 MELCHIOT

MATCH REPORT

Though Charity Shield defeat was hardly a cause for unbridled dismay in the United camp – after all, in each of the previous two campaigns the Red Devils had lost this low-key opener, then went on to lift the Premiership crown – the manner of their reverse was regrettable.

In this last club confrontation before Wembley's demolition, the famous old stadium deserved better than the scrappy, ill-tempered contest which materialised. The low point was the 62nd-minute dismissal of Roy Keane for a gruesome tackle from behind on Gus Poyet. It was the skipper's seventh dismissal in a United shirt and it would cost him a three-match suspension. In mitigation, earlier Keane had been the victim of a horrible challenge from Hasselbaink, which went unpunished despite being violent enough to draw a post-match apology from the Dutchman.

Football-wise, Chelsea thoroughly deserved their victory, their men looking sprightly where most of United's seemed a trifle lethargic. Three times the Londoners almost snatched an early lead, but the otherwise impressive Stanic shot and headed wide, then Hasselbaink went close. The breakthrough came when the Blues' new £15 million marksman executed a smart exchange of passes with Poyet, then beat Barthez with a low shot which took a deflection off Stam.

MANCHESTER UNITED 1 Fabien BARTHEZ, 2 Gary NEVILLE, 3 Denis IRWIN, 16 Roy KEANE, 5 Ronny JOHNSEN, 27 Mikael SILVESTRE, 7 David BECKHAM, 18 Paul SCHOLES, 20 Ole Gunnar SOLSKJAER, 10 Teddy SHERINGHAM, 11 Ryan GIGGS **Substitutes:** 6 Jaap STAM (27) 19, 8 Nicky BUTT, 9 Andy COLE (20) 70, 12 Phil NEVILLE, 17 Raimond VAN DER GOUW, 19 Dwight YORKE (10) 70, 25 Quinton FORTUNE (11) 78

CHELSEA 1 Ed DE GOEY, 15 Mario MELCHIOT, 3 Celestine BABAYARO, 16 Roberto DI MATTEO, 5 Frank LEBOEUF, 6 Marcel DESAILLY, 12 Mario STANIC, 8 Gustavo POYET, 9 Jimmy Floyd HASSELBAINK, 25 Gianfranco ZOLA, 11 Dennis WISE **Substitutes:** 14 Graham LE SAUX (8) 77, 18 Gabriele AMBROSETTI, 19 Tore Andre FLO, 20 Jody MORRIS (16) 70, 21 Bernard LAMBOURDE, 22 Eidur GUDJOHNSEN (25) 73, 23 Carlo CUDICINI

Paul Scholes controls the ball despite the close attentions of Zola and Melchiot

Scholes came close to equalising but narrowly missed the target after slipping behind the Chelsea rearguard shortly before the break, but De Goey was not called on to make a meaningful save until he dealt with Beckham's free-kick after 67 minutes.

Some five minutes later Melchiot settled matters when he cut inside. True, this was no more than preparation for more meaningful challenges that lay ahead, but few United fans would have been happy with their team's farewell to the scene of so many memorable triumphs.

Mikael Silvestre denies Chelsea's marauding Hasselbaink

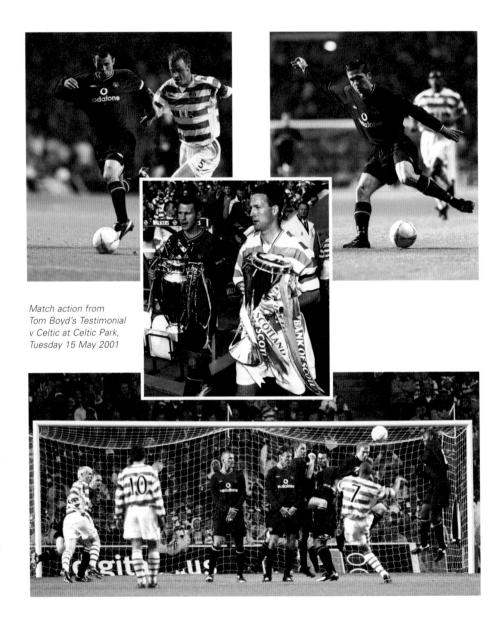

Match action from Tom Boyd's Testimonial v Celtic at Celtic Park, Tuesday 15 May 2001

names in bold indicate goalscorers

v YORK CITY (away) • Attendance: 9,003 • Won: 2-0   Saturday 29 July 2000

van der Gouw • Neville G. • Irwin • Wallwork • Silvestre • **Keane 2** • Beckham • Scholes • Notman • Yorke • Giggs
Substitutes: Hilton • Rachubka • Webber (for Notman) • Teather (for Neville G.) • Djordjic (for Giggs)

v SHREWSBURY TOWN (away) • Attendance: 8,000 • Won: 8-1   Sunday 30 July 2000

Bosnich • **Clegg M.** • Neville P. • Johnsen • Berg • **Fortune 2 (1 pen)** • **Healy** • **Butt** • **Solskjaer 2** • **Sheringham** • Blomqvist
*Substitutes: Brown (for Berg) • Wallwork (for Blomqvist) • Notman (for Solskjaer) • Teather (for Johnsen) •
Lynch (for Neville P.) • Webber (for Butt)*

BAYERN MUNICH CENTENARY TOURNAMENT

v REAL MADRID CF (Olympic Stadium, Munich) • Attendance: 39,000 • Won: 1-0   Friday 4 August 2000

van der Gouw • Neville G. • Irwin • Keane • Johnsen • Silvestre • Beckham • Scholes • **Solskjaer** • Sheringham • Giggs
Substitutes: Barthez • Berg • Stam • Butt • Cole • Neville P. • Fortune • Wallwork • Yorke (for Giggs)

v BAYERN MUNICH (Olympic Stadium, Munich) • Attendance: 43,000 • Lost: 1-3   Saturday 5 August 2000

Barthez • Neville G. • Neville P. • Berg • Silvestre • Keane • Beckham • Butt • Cole • Yorke • **Fortune**
*Substitutes: Irwin • Johnsen • Stam • Sheringham (for Cole) • Giggs (for Beckham) • van der Gouw •
Wallwork (for Silvestre) • Keane (for Scholes) • Solskjaer*

v BIRKIRKARA (Ta'Qali, Malta) • Attendance: 10,000 • Won: 5-1   Wednesday 9 August 2000

Barthez • Neville P. • Silvestre • Berg • Johnsen • Wallwork • **Beckham** • Keane • Cole • Sheringham • Blomqvist
*Substitutes: Stam (for Johnsen) • van der Gouw (for Barthez) • Neville G. (for Berg) • Giggs (for Blomqvist) •
Fortune (for Beckham) • Irwin (for Silvestre) • **Scholes** (for Keane) • **Yorke** (for Sheringham) • **Solskjaer 2** (for Cole)*

DENIS IRWIN TESTIMONIAL

v MANCHESTER CITY (home) • Attendance: 45,158 • Won: 2-0   Wednesday 16 August 2000

van der Gouw • Neville G. • Irwin • Neville P. • Johnsen • Scholes • Beckham • Butt • **Cole** • **Sheringham** • Fortune
*Substitutes: Wallwork (for Irwin) • Brown (for Johnsen) • Giggs • Rachubka • Greening (for Beckham) •
Stewart (for Scholes) • Clegg • Notman*

TOM BOYD TESTIMONIAL

v CELTIC (away) • Attendance: 57,268 • Won: 2-0   Tuesday 15 May 2001

van der Gouw • Neville P. • Irwin • Butt • May • Stam • Beckham • Scholes • **Silvestre** • Sheringham • Giggs
*Substitutes: Fortune (for Irwin) • Goram (for van der Gouw) • Stewart (for Beckham) •
Johnsen (for Stam) • **Djordjic** (for Giggs)*

FABIEN BARTHEZ

Position: goalkeeper
Born: Lavelanet, France, 28 June 1971
Height: 180 cms
Weight: 80 kgs
Transferred: from AS Monaco, 21 May 2000
Other clubs: Toulouse, Olympique Marseille, AS Monaco
Senior United debut: 13 August 2000 v Chelsea at Wembley
(FA Charity Shield)
United record: League: 30 games, 0 goals; FA Cup: 1 game, 0 goals; League Cup: 0 games, 0 goals; Europe: 12 games, 0 goals; Others: 1 game, 0 goals
Total: 44 games, 0 goals
Full International: France
In 2000-01: concerns about finding a long-term replacement for Peter Schmeichel were laid firmly to rest by the flamboyant Frenchman. Fabien is not tall for a keeper, but he is supremely athletic, he oozes charisma and his all-encompassing self-belief transmitted itself to team-mates and fans alike. In addition, he emerged as one of the most accomplished dribblers in the side!

DAVID BECKHAM

Position: midfielder
Born: Leytonstone, 2 May 1975
Height: 183 cms
Weight: 76 kgs
Signed trainee: 8 July 1991
Signed professional: 23 January 1993
Other club: Preston North End (loan)
Senior United debut: 23 September 1992 v Brighton & Hove Albion at the Goldstone Ground (League Cup, substitute for Andrei Kanchelskis)
United record: League: 187 (19) games, 45 goals; FA Cup: 18 (2) games, 5 goals; League Cup: 5 (2) games, 0 goals; Europe: 56 (2) games, 7 goals; Others: 7 (2) games, 1 goal
Total: 273 (27) games, 58 goals
Full international: England
In 2000-01: David appeared to be striding towards genuine greatness in the first half of the season. Later, however, despite receiving the massive boost of the England captaincy, his form dipped. He continued to work hard, though, and the blip is sure to be temporary.

WESLEY BROWN

Position: defender
Born: Manchester, 13 October 1979
Height: 185 cms
Weight: 87 kgs
Signed trainee: 8 July 1996
Signed professional: 4 November 1996
Senior United debut: 4 May 1998 v Leeds United at Old Trafford
(League, substitute for David May)

United record: League: 37 (7) games, 0 goals; FA Cup: 3 games, 0 goals; League Cup: 1 (1) games, 0 goals; Europe: 12 (3) games, 0 goals; Others: 0 games, 0 goals
Total: 53 (11) games, 0 goals
Full international: England
In 2000-01: after losing a season through injury, Wes re-established himself majestically. Quick and strong, composed and skilful, he replaced the sidelined Stam with maturity and authority, an achievement reflected by his selection for the PFA team of the season. Concentration and communication appear the only areas in need of marginal improvement.

NICKY BUTT

Position: midfielder
Born: Manchester, 21 January 1975
Height: 178 cms
Weight: 75 kgs
Signed trainee: 8 July 1991
Signed professional: 23 January 1993
Senior United debut: 21 November 1992 v Oldham Athletic at Old Trafford (League, substitute for Paul Ince)

United record: League: 164 (42) games, 19 goals; FA Cup: 18 (2) games, 1 goal; League Cup: 5 games, 0 goals; Europe: 38 (11) games, 2 goals; Others: 7 games, 2 goals
Total: 232 (55) games, 24 goals
Full international: England
In 2000-01: after admitting that his development had stood still last year, Nicky enjoyed what was arguably the most accomplished campaign of his career to date and his England recall was thoroughly deserved. A prodigious worker and abrasive competitor, he is much coveted by other clubs but his value to United, especially when Keane is out, remains inestimable.

PLAYER PROFILES

LUKE CHADWICK

Position: forward
Born: Cambridge, 18 November 1980
Height: 180 cms
Weight: 73 kgs
Signed trainee: 30 June 1997
Signed professional: 5 February 1999
Other club: Royal Antwerp (loan)
Senior United debut: 13 October 1999 v Aston Villa at Villa Park (League Cup)

United record: League: 6 (10) games, 2 goals; FA Cup: 0 (1) games, 0 goals; League Cup: 3 games, 0 goals; Europe: 1 (2) games, 0 goals; Others: 0 games, 0 goals
Total: 10 (13) game, 2 goals

In 2000-01: Luke made enormous strides during the season, proving that he is comfortable in the Premiership. Versatile enough to operate effectively on either flank, he troubled even the most clam-like of rearguards and offered an excitingly fresh attacking option. Luke's thrilling dance past three Bayern defenders was a telling illustration of his vast potential.

MICHAEL CLEGG

Position: defender
Born: Ashton-under-Lyne, 3 July 1977
Height: 173 cms
Weight: 74 kgs
Signed trainee: 5 July 1993
Signed professional: 1 July 1995
Other clubs: Ipswich Town (loan), Wigan Athletic (loan)
Senior United debut: 23 November 1996 v Middlesbrough at Riverside Stadium (League)

United record: League: 4 (5) games, 0 goals; FA Cup: 3 (1) games, 0 goals; League Cup: 7 games, 0 goals; Europe: 1 (2) games, 0 goals; Others: 0 games, 0 goals
Total: 15 (8) games, 0 goals

In 2000-01: Michael captained the Red Devils' reserves, invariably exuding calmness and efficiency in the process, but such was the wealth of talent at Sir Alex Ferguson's disposal that he appeared to be no closer to claiming a regular place in the senior set-up. For Michael, that must be mightily frustrating after performing competently on his rare first-team outings.

ANDY COLE

Position: forward
Born: Nottingham, 15 October 1971
Height: 180 cms
Weight: 77 kgs
Transferred: from Newcastle United, 12 January 1995
Other clubs: Arsenal, Fulham (loan), Bristol City, Newcastle United
Senior United debut: 22 January 1995 v Blackburn Rovers at Old Trafford (League)
United record: League: 154 (30) games, 89 goals; FA Cup: 19 (2) games, 9 goals; League Cup: 2 games, 0 goals; Europe: 42 (4) games, 18 goals; Others: 6 (1) games, 0 goals
Total: 223 (37) games, 116 goals
Full international: England
In 2000-01: after he began with six goals in his first five starts, outstripping Denis Law's European Cup scoring record in the process, Andy had achilles problems which affected his form. When fully fit, though, he looked sharp and more confident than ever, and his expected part in the club's future was emphasised by his signing of a new long-term contract.

NICK CULKIN

Position: goalkeeper
Born: York, 6 July 1978
Height: 188 cms
Weight: 87 kgs
Transferred: from York City, 25 September 1995
Other club: York City, Hull City (loan), Bristol Rovers (loan)
Senior United debut: 22 August 1999 v Arsenal at Highbury (League, substitute for Raimond van der Gouw)
United record: League: 0 (1) games, 0 goals; FA Cup: 0 games, 0 goals; League Cup: 0 games, 0 goals; Europe: 0 games, 0 goals; Others: 0 games, 0 goals
Total: 0 (1) games, 0 goals
In 2000-01: Nicky was absent from the Old Trafford scene for the whole season, which he spent on loan with Second Division Bristol Rovers. Having learned plenty during several years of observing Peter Schmeichel at close quarters, Nicky excelled for the Pirates, performing outstandingly in match after match as they struggled unsuccessfully to avoid relegation to the League's basement.

BOJAN DJORDJIC

Position: midfielder
Born: Belgrade, Yugoslavia, 6 February 1982
Height: 178 cms
Weight: 70 kgs
Transferred from: Brommapojkarna IF, 17 February 1999
Other club: Brommapojkarna IF
Senior United debut: 19 May 2001 v Tottenham Hotspur at
White Hart Lane (League, substitute for Denis Irwin)

United record: League: 0 (1) games, 0 goals; FA Cup: 0 games, 0 goals; League Cup:
0 games, 0 goals; Europe: 0 games, 0 goals; Others: 0 games, 0 goals
Total: 0 (1) games, 0 goals

In 2000-01: Bojan showed immense natural talent and application for the reserves, then took
the eye with an exquisitely chipped goal when the Red Devils met Celtic in Tom Boyd's
testimonial match. His reward was a call from the bench near the end of the final
Premiership game and plenty is expected of the youngster in the years ahead.

QUINTON FORTUNE

Position: forward or midfielder
Born: Cape Town, South Africa, 21 May 1977
Height: 175 cms
Weight: 74 kgs
Transferred: from Atletico Madrid, 21 August 1999
Other club: Atletico Madrid
Senior United debut: 30 August 1999 v Newcastle United at
Old Trafford (League, substitute for Paul Scholes)

United record: League: 10 (3) games, 4 goals; FA Cup: 0 games, 0 goals; League Cup:
2 games, 0 goals; Europe: 1 (4) games, 0 goals; Others: 1 (2) games, 2 goals
Total: 14 (9) games, 6 goals
Full international: South Africa

In 2000-01: Quinton experienced mixed luck. After impressing and scoring twice in the
Reds' September defeat of Bradford City, he netted in South Africa's victory over Brazil in the
Sydney Olympics and there seemed no clouds on the Fortune horizon. But then his
momentum was shattered by a knee injury which kept him out for 11 weeks, prior to his
springtime return.

RYAN GIGGS

Position: forward
Born: Cardiff, 29 November 1973
Height: 180 cms
Weight: 70 kgs
Signed trainee: 9 July 1990
Signed professional: 29 November 1990
Senior United debut: 2 March 1991 v Everton at Old Trafford
(League, substitute for Denis Irwin)
United record: League: 291 (30) games, 64 goals; FA Cup: 36 (3) games, 7 goals; League Cup: 17 (4) games, 6 goals; Europe: 51 (3) games, 13 goals; Others: 9 (1) games, 0 goals
Total: 404 (41) games, 90 goals
Full international: Wales
In 2000-01: Ryan won his seventh championship medal at the tender age of 27, an astonishing achievement even by the exalted standards of the world-class Welshman. As United were confronted serially with massed defences, so often it was his untrackable runs which broke through and a new five-year contract, signed in April, was uplifting news for Reds' fans.

JONATHAN GREENING

Position: forward or midfielder
Born: Scarborough, 2 January 1979
Height: 183 cms
Weight: 76 kgs
Transferred: from York City, 24 March 1998
Other club: York City
Senior United debut: 28 October 1998 v Bury at Old Trafford
(League Cup)
United record: League: 4 (10) games, 0 goals; FA Cup: 0 (1) games, 0 goals; League Cup: 6 games, 0 goals; Europe: 2 (2) games, 0 goals; Others: 1 (1) game, 0 goals
Total: 13 (14) games, 0 goals
In 2000-01: Jonathan spent another season on the fringe of the first team and, understandably for a talented and ambitious young man, he became frustrated with the situation. A pacy midfielder-cum-striker blessed with the ability to jink past defenders, the England Under-21 international was linked with several other clubs and was expected to move in the summer of 2001.

DENIS IRWIN

Position: defender
Born: Cork, 31 October 1965
Height: 173 cms
Weight: 68 kgs
Transferred: from Oldham Athletic, 8 June 1990
Other clubs: Leeds United, Oldham Athletic
Senior United debut: 25 August 1990 v Coventry City at Old Trafford (League)

United record: League: 346 (10) games, 22 goals; FA Cup: 42 (1) games, 7 goals; League Cup: 28 (3) games, 0 goals; Europe: 65 games, 4 goals; Others: 10 games, 0 goals

Total: 491 (14) games, 33 goals

Full international: Republic of Ireland

In 2000-01: though the evergreen Irishman continued to perform to his customary high standards, he began to play second fiddle to Mikael Silvestre as the Red Devil's left-back and hinted that he might look elsewhere to find a regular slot. Whatever happens, he will go down as one of the most accomplished and loyal servants the club has ever known.

RONNY JOHNSEN

Position: defender or midfielder
Born: Sandefjord, Norway, 10 June 1969
Height: 190 cms
Weight: 85 kgs
Transferred: from Besiktas, 10 July 1996
Other clubs: Stokke, EIK-Tonsberg, Lyn Oslo, Lillestrom, Besiktas
Senior United debut: 17 August 1996 v Wimbledon at Selhurst Park (League, substitute for Nicky Butt)

United record: League: 76 (13) games, 6 goals; FA Cup: 8 (2) games, 1 goal; League Cup: 3 games, 0 goals; Europe: 24 (2) games, 0 goals; Others: 3 games, 1 goal

Total: 114 (17) games, 8 goals

Full international: Norway

In 2000-01: Ronny made a goalscoring start at home to Newcastle in August, but soon his season degenerated into a battle against knee problems. He recovered from a career-threatening midwinter operation and by the spring was back in harness at the heart of United's defence. Hopes are high that there is still plenty of mileage in the versatile Norwegian.

ROY KEANE

Position: midfielder
Born: Cork, 10 August 1971
Height: 180 cms
Weight: 74 kgs
Transferred: from Nottingham Forest, 19 July 1993
Other clubs: Cobh Ramblers, Nottingham Forest
Senior United debut: 15 August 1993 v Norwich City at Carrow Road (League)

United record: League: 205 (8) games, 26 goals; FA Cup: 31 (1) games, 1 goal; League Cup: 9 (2) games, 0 goals; Europe: 53 games, 14 goals; Others: 9 games, 2 goals
Total: 307 (11) games, 43 goals
Full international: Republic of Ireland
In 2000-01: few disagree that the United skipper is the Premiership's finest all-round performer. Renowned for his strength and aggression, he is a ferocious motivator but is blessed also with remarkable skill and vision. However, his indiscretion against Manchester City means that he misses the start of the new term through suspension.

DAVID MAY

Position: defender
Born: Oldham, 24 June 1970
Height: 183 cms
Weight: 85 kgs
Transferred: from Blackburn Rovers, 1 July 1994
Other clubs: Blackburn Rovers, Huddersfield Town (loan)
Senior United debut: 20 August 1994 v Queen's Park Rangers at Old Trafford (League)

United record: League: 66 (16) games, 6 goals; FA Cup: 6 games, 0 goals; League Cup: 7 games, 1 goal; Europe: 12 (1) games, 1 goal; Others: 2 (1) games, 0 goals
Total: 93 (18) games, 8 goals
In 2000-01: with Jaap Stam and Ronny Johnsen suffering long spells on the sidelines, it might have been a campaign of renaissance for David but he was prevented from making a senior comeback by his own injury nightmare. As a centre-half proficient enough to oust Steve Bruce back in 1995-96, and only just into his thirties, he might yet have something to offer the United cause.

GARY NEVILLE

Position: defender
Born: Bury, 18 February 1975
Height: 180 cms
Weight: 78 kgs
Signed trainee: 8 July 1991
Signed professional: 23 January 1993
Senior United debut: 16 September 1992 v Torpedo Moscow at Old Trafford (UEFA Cup, substitute for Lee Martin)

United record: League: 199 (4) games, 3 goals; FA Cup: 23 (3) games, 0 goals; League Cup: 4 (1) games, 0 goals; Europe: 55 (3) games, 0 goals; Others: 6 (1) games, 0 goals
Total: 287 (12) games, 3 goals
Full international: England
In 2000-01: once again Gary was the hub of the Reds' rearguard. Not only was he almost metronomically consistent when employed in his regular right-back role, he was superb too when paired with Wes Brown in central defence during the long absence of Stam and Johnsen. A born organiser and astute reader of the game, Gary remains an enormous asset to the club.

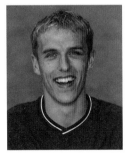

PHIL NEVILLE

Position: defender
Born: Bury, 21 January 1977
Height: 180 cms
Weight: 76 kgs
Signed trainee: 5 July 1993
Signed professional: 1 June 1994
Senior United debut: 28 January 1995 v Wrexham at Old Trafford (FA Cup)

United record: League: 129 (31) games, 2 goals; FA Cup: 15 (4) games, 0 goals; League Cup: 7 (1) games, 0 goals; Europe: 22 (11) games, 1 goal; Others: 6 (2) games, 0 goals
Total: 179 (49) games, 3 goals
Full international: England
In 2000-01: Phil rose above the hysterical but predictable abuse following his mistimed tackle for England against Romania to contribute another season of consistency. Able to perform in any full-back or midfield role, he tends to be a victim of his own versatility. Phil must be sick of being dubbed a great squad man, but that's about the size of it.

JOHN O'SHEA

Position: defender
Born: Waterford, Republic of Ireland, 30 April 1981
Height: 190 cms
Weight: 81 kgs
Signed professional: 3 August 1998
Other clubs: AFC Bournemouth (loan), Royal Antwerp (loan)
Senior United debut: 13 October 1999 v Aston Villa at Villa Park (League Cup)

United record: League: 0 games, 0 goals; FA Cup: 0 games, 0 goals; League Cup: 3 games, 0 goals; Europe: 0 games 0 goals; Others: 0 games, 0 goals

Total: 3 games, 0 goals

In 2000-01: after impressing in both of United's Worthington Cup outings, the lanky Irishman took the well-worn loan trail to Royal Antwerp in Belgium, where he continued to display immense promise. Having progressed steadily over his three seasons as a professional at Old Trafford, John will be raising his sights towards a regular berth in the senior squad during 2001-02.

PAUL RACHUBKA

Position: goalkeeper
Born: San Luis Obispo, California, 21 May 1981
Height: 185 cms
Weight: 83 kgs
Signed trainee: 30 June 1997
Signed professional: 1 July 1999
Senior United debut: 11 January 2000 v South Melbourne at the Maracana Stadium (Club World Championship, substitute for Raimond van der Gouw)

United record: League: 1 game, 0 goals; FA Cup: 0 games, 0 goals; League Cup: 0 (1) game, 0 goals, Europe: 0 games, 0 goals; Others: 0 (1) games, 0 goals

Total: 1 (2) games, 0 goals

In 2000-01: Paul's Premiership debut arrived unexpectedly when Fabien Barthez suffered a thigh strain before the home clash with Leicester City in March. The young Californian was not fazed, responding with a coolly competent performance which suggests he has the temperament to match his natural ability between the posts.

PAUL SCHOLES

Position: midfielder or forward
Born: Salford, 16 November 1974
Height: 170 cms
Weight: 70 kgs
Signed trainee: 8 July 1991
Signed professional: 23 January 1993
Senior United debut: 21 September 1994 v Port Vale at Vale Park
(League Cup)
United record: League: 145 (47) games, 47 goals; FA Cup: 8 (7)
games, 4 goals; League Cup: 6 (2) games, 5 goals; Europe: 40 (10) games, 16 goals; Others:
7 games, 0 goals
Total: 206 (66) games, 72 goals
Full international: England
In 2000-01: Paul continued to demonstrate vividly that he is one of Europe's premier talents.
At his best in central midfield, where his imaginative distibution makes him the creative
fulcrum of the team, he can help out on either flank, too. Wherever he plays, Paul is a potent
goal poacher and news of his new long-term contract was greeted ecstatically by United fans.

MIKAEL SILVESTRE

Position: defender
Born: Chambray-Les-Tours, France, 9 August 1977
Height: 183 cms
Weight: 83 kgs
Transferred: from Internazionale, 10 September 1999
Other clubs: Rennes, Internazionale
Senior United debut: 11 September 1999 v Liverpool at
Anfield (League)
United record: League: 55 (6) games, 1 goal; FA Cup: 2 games, 0 goals; League Cup:
0 games, 0 goals; Europe: 15 (3) games, 0 goals; Others: 4 games, 0 goals
Total: 76 (9) games, 1 goal
In 2000-01: as the season wore on, Mikael emerged as one of the most improved players at
the club, an achievement recognised by his elevation to full international status with
France. After working assiduously to eradicate occasional lapses of concentration from his
game, he laid persuasive claim to the left-back berth, his surging forward runs becoming
ever more impressive.

OLE GUNNAR SOLSKJAER

Position: forward
Born: Kristiansund, Norway, 26 February 1973
Height: 178 cms
Weight: 75 kgs
Transferred: from Molde, 29 July 1996
Other clubs: Clausenengen FK, Molde
Senior United debut: 25 August 1996 v Blackburn Rovers at Old Trafford (League, substitute for David May)

United record: League: 83 (50) games, 58 goals; FA Cup: 6 (9) games, 4 goals; League Cup: 6 games, 5 goals; Europe: 19 (25) games, 7 goals; Others: 5 (3) games, 0 goals
Total: 119 (87) games, 74 goals
Full international: Norway
In 2000-01: Sir Alex Ferguson dubbed Ole the best substitute in the world and, while obviously the Norwegian marksman would prefer to start every match, it is a tag which carries total conviction. A supremely dedicated professional and arguably the most clinical finisher at Old Trafford, he is at his predatory best as an out-and-out front man, but can also raid from the flanks.

JAAP STAM

Position: defender
Born: Kampen, Holland, 17 July 1972
Height: 190 cms
Weight: 95 kgs
Transferred: from PSV Eindhoven, 1 July 1998
Other clubs: Dos Kampen, FC Zwolle, Cambuur Leeuwarden, Willem II, PSV Eindhoven
Senior United debut: 12 August 1998 v LKS Lodz at Old Trafford (Champions League)

United record: League: 78 games, 1 goal; FA Cup: 7 (1) games, 0 goals; League Cup: 0 games, 0 goals; Europe: 32 games, 0 goals; Others: 6 (1) games, 0 goals
Total: 123 (2) games, 1 goal
Full international: Holland
In 2000-01: having been voted Europe's top defender for two successive years, Jaap started commandingly only to suffer an achilles problem which sidelined him for five months. On his return he gelled instantly with Wes Brown, exercising his customary defensive dominance.

MICHAEL STEWART

Position: midfielder
Born: Edinburgh, 26 February 1981
Height: 180 cms
Weight: 75 kgs
Signed trainee: 30 June 1997
Signed professional: 13 March 1998
Senior United debut: 31 October 2000 v Watford at Vicarage Road (League Cup, substitute for Ronnie Wallwork)

United record: League: 3 games, 0 goals; FA Cup: 0 games, 0 goals; League Cup: 0 (2) games, 0 goals; Europe: 0 games, 0 goals; Others: 0 games, 0 goals
Total: 3 (2) games, 0 goals
In 2000-01: made his senior entrance as a Worthington Cup substitute, then achieved a major impact when starting the Premiership encounter at Middlesbrough in April. Operating in central midfield in the absence of Roy Keane, the feisty Scottish redhead demonstrated aggression and technique in equal measure and he has a realistic chance of making the grade.

RAIMOND VAN DER GOUW

Position: goalkeeper
Born: Oldenzaal, Holland, 24 March 1963
Height: 190 cms
Weight: 87 kgs
Transferred: from Vitesse Arnhem, 1 July 1996
Other clubs: Go Ahead Eagles, Vitesse Arnhem
Senior United debut: 21 September 1996 v Aston Villa at Villa Park (League)

United record: League: 26 (10) games, 0 goals; FA Cup: 1 game, 0 goals; League Cup: 8 games, 0 goals; Europe: 11 games, 0 goals; Others: 2 games, 0 goals
Total: 48 (10) games, 0 goals
In 2000-01: Raimond's reputation for reliability was burnished further as he deputised capably for Fabien Barthez. When some second-string keepers step up then the fans feel a tremor of anxiety, but that has never been the case with the Dutchman, who completed his fifth season as a Red. His handling, agility and positional sense are impeccable; if only he were ten years younger.

RUUD VAN NISTELROOY

Position: forward
Born: Oss, Holland, 1 July 1976
Height: 190 cms
Weight: 80 kgs
Transferred: from PSV Eindhoven, 1 July 2001
Other clubs: Den Bosch, Heerenveen, PSV Eindhoven
United record: No record as yet
Full international: Holland

In 2000-01: Ruud completed his rehabilitation from the cruel knee injury which prevented his move from Eindhoven to Old Trafford a year earlier. His £19 million fee made him a British record signing, but the tall, pacy Dutchman is splendidly equipped to deliver value for money. Packing a fearsome shot with either foot, powerful in the air and blessed with the admirable all-round technique which tends to characterise his countrymen, he seems poised to add a new dimension to United's attack.

RONNIE WALLWORK

Position: defender or midfielder
Born: Manchester, 10 September 1977
Height: 178 cms
Weight: 83 kgs
Signed trainee: 11 July 1994
Signed professional: 17 March 1995
Other clubs: Carlisle United (loan), Stockport County (loan), Royal Antwerp (loan)
Senior United debut: 25 October 1997 v Barnsley at Old Trafford (League, substitute for Gary Pallister)
United record: League: 4 (14) games, 0 goals; FA Cup: 0 (1) games, 0 goals; League Cup: 3 (1) games, 0 goals; Europe: 0 (1) game, 0 goals; Others: 1 game, 0 goals
Total: 8 (17) games, 0 goals

In 2000-01: Ronnie made enough Premiership appearances to qualify for a title medal but his status remains that of a regular reserve. He has the attributes to thrive in the top flight as a central defender or midfielder, but would relish more opportunities to demonstrate them.

DANNY WEBBER

Position: forward
Born: Manchester, 28 December 1981
Height: 175 cms
Weight: 67 kgs
Signed trainee: 6 July 1998
Signed professional: 28 December 1998
Senior United debut: 28 November 2000 v Sunderland at the Stadium of Light (League Cup, substitute for Ronnie Wallwork)

United record: League: 0 games, 0 goals; FA Cup: 0 games, 0 goals; League Cup: 0 (1) games, 0 goals; Europe: 0 games, 0 goals; Others: 0 games, 0 goals
Total: 0 (1) games, 0 goals

In 2000-01: after catching the eye for United's reserve and Under-19 sides, Danny was rewarded with a senior entrance at Sunderland in the Worthington Cup, rising from the bench as an extra-time substitute. A quick-witted, mobile striker, he faces a stern challenge in breaking into the first-team set-up and only time will tell if he has the requisite mettle.

MARK WILSON

Position: midfielder
Born: Scunthorpe, 9 February 1979
Height: 183 cms
Weight: 79 kgs
Signed trainee: 10 July 1995
Signed professional: 9 February 1996
Other club: Wrexham (loan)
Senior United debut: 21 October 1998 v Brondby at the Parken Stadium (Champions League, substitute for Dwight Yorke)

United record: League: 1 (2) games, 0 goals; FA Cup: 0 games, 0 goals; League Cup: 2 games, 0 goals; Europe: 2 (2) games, 0 goals; Others: 1 game, 0 goals
Total: 6 (4) games, 0 goals

In 2000-01: Mark's campaign was blighted when he ruptured an achilles tendon during pre-season, but he showed enormous character by battling back to full fitness and reclaiming his England Under-21 place in the spring. He excelled for the reserves too, particularly in the 2-1 victory over Manchester City, and now he deserves a favourable nod from Lady Luck.

DWIGHT YORKE

Position: forward
Born: Canaan, Tobago, 3 November 1971
Height: 178 cms
Weight: 77 kgs
Transferred: from Aston Villa, 20 August 1998
Other club: Aston Villa
Senior United debut: 22 August 1998 v West Ham United at Upton Park (League)

United record: League: 76 (10) games, 47 goals; FA Cup: 6 (4) games, 3 goals; League Cup: 2 games, 2 goals; Europe: 27 (6) games, 11 goals; Others: 3 (2) games, 2 goals
Total: 114 (22) games, 65 goals
Full international: Trinidad and Tobago
In 2000-01: Dwight experienced mixed fortunes, losing his place to Teddy Sheringham early on and having his impetus disrupted by international calls. On the other hand, there were high points, most notably an exceptionally fine hat-trick against Arsenal, but Dwight will need to reach that standard more consistently if he is to hold his own amongst a plethora of quality marksmen in 2001-02.

'Others' include:
FA Charity Shield, UEFA Super Cup, Inter-Continental Cup, FIFA Club World Championship

YOUNG PROFESSIONALS

NICK BAXTER
Position: goalkeeper
Birthdate: 25 March 1983
Birthplace: Bridlington
Height: 190 cms
Weight: 87 kgs
Signed trainee: 18 October 1999
Signed professional: 12 July 2000

STEVEN CLEGG
Position: defender
Birthdate: 16 April 1982
Birthplace: Ashton-under-Lyne
Height: 175 cms
Weight: 80 kgs
Signed trainee: 5 July 1999
Signed professional: 12 July 2000

CRAIG COATES
Position: forward
Birthdate: 26 October 1982
Birthplace: Dryburn
Height: 173 cms
Weight: 78 kgs
Signed trainee: 5 July 1999
Signed professional: 26 October 1999

JOHN COGGER
Position: defender
Birthdate: 12 September 1983
Birthplace: Waltham Forest
Height: 178 cms
Weight: 85 kgs
Signed trainee: 3 July 2000
Signed professional: 1 July 2001

JIMMY DAVIS

Position: forward
Birthdate: 6 February 1982
Birthplace: Bromsgrove
Height: 173 cms
Weight: 83 kgs
Signed trainee: 6 July 1999
Signed professional: 31 August 1999

DARREN FLETCHER

Position: midfield
Birthdate: 1 February 1984
Birthplace: Edinburgh
Height: 183 cms
Weight: 83 kgs
Signed trainee: 3 July 2000
Signed professional: 1 February 2001

DAVID FOX

Position: midfield
Birthdate: 13 December 1983
Birthplace: Stoke-on-Trent
Height: 175 cms
Weight: 77 kgs
Signed trainee: 3 July 2000
Signed professional: 13 December 2000

COLIN HEATH

Position: forward
Birthdate: 31 December 1983
Birthplace: Chesterfield
Height: 183 cms
Weight: 83 kgs
Signed trainee: 3 July 2000
Signed professional: 31 December 2000

KIRK HILTON
Position: defender
Birthdate: 2 April 1981
Birthplace: Flixton
Height: 173 cms
Weight: 64 kgs
Signed trainee: 30 June 1997
Signed professional: 1 July 1999

CHRIS HUMPHREYS
Position: forward
Birthdate: 22 September 1983
Birthplace: Manchester
Height: 175 cms
Weight: 85 kgs
Signed trainee: 3 July 2000
Signed professional: 1 July 2001

JAMES JOWSEY
Position: goalkeeper
Birthdate: 24 November 1983
Birthplace: Scarborough
Height: 183 cms
Weight: 78 kgs
Signed trainee: 3 July 2000
Signed professional: 24 November 2000

MARK LYNCH
Position: defender
Birthdate: 2 September 1981
Birthplace: Manchester
Height: 183 cms
Weight: 83 kgs
Signed trainee: 6 July 1998
Signed professional: 31 August 1999

ALAN McDERMOTT
Position: defender
Birthdate: 22 January 1982
Birthplace: Dublin
Height: 188 cms
Weight: 87 kgs
Signed trainee: 6 July 1998
Signed professional: 22 January 1999

KALAM MOONIARUCK
Position: forward
Birthdate: 22 November 1983
Birthplace: Yeovil
Height: 173 cms
Weight: 74 kgs
Signed trainee: 3 July 2000
Signed professional: 22 November 2000

DAVID MORAN
Position: goalkeeper
Birthdate: 21 January 1983
Birthplace: Ballinasloe
Height: 183 cms
Weight: 91 kgs
Signed trainee: 5 July 1999
Signed professional: 12 July 2000

BEN MUIRHEAD
Position: forward
Birthdate: 5 January 1983
Birthplace: Doncaster
Height: 175 cms
Weight: 73 kgs
Signed trainee: 5 July 1999
Signed professional: 5 January 2000

PLAYER PROFILES

DANIEL NARDIELLO
Position: forward
Birthdate: 22 October 1982
Birthplace: Coventry
Height: 180 cms
Weight: 81 kgs
Signed trainee: 5 July 1999
Signed professional: 22 October 1999

DANNY PUGH
Position: midfield
Birthdate: 19 October 1982
Birthplace: Manchester
Height: 183 cms
Weight: 81 kgs
Signed trainee: 5 July 1999
Signed professional: 12 July 2000

JOHN RANKIN
Position: midfield
Birthdate: 27 June 1983
Birthplace: Bellshill
Height: 173 cms
Weight: 80 kgs
Signed trainee: 5 July 1999
Signed professional: 27 June 2000

LEE ROCHE
Position: defender
Birthdate: 28 October 1980
Birthplace: Bolton
Height: 178 cms
Weight: 68 kgs
Signed trainee: 30 June 1997
Signed professional: 5 February 1999

GARY SAMPSON
Position: midfield
Birthdate: 13 September 1982
Birthplace: Manchester
Height: 175 cms
Weight: 71 kgs
Signed trainee: 5 July 1999
Signed professional: 12 July 2000

ALAN TATE
Position: defender
Birthdate: 2 September 1982
Birthplace: Easington
Height: 185 cms
Weight: 85 kgs
Signed trainee: 5 July 1999
Signed professional: 12 July 2000

ANDREW TAYLOR
Position: midfield
Birthdate: 17 September 1982
Birthplace: Exeter
Height: 175 cms
Weight: 81 kgs
Signed trainee: 5 July 1999
Signed professional: 12 July 2000

KRIS TAYLOR
Position: midfield
Birthdate: 12 January 1984
Birthplace: Stafford
Height: 176 cms
Weight: 85 kgs
Signed trainee: 3 July 2000
Signed professional: 26 January 2001

PAUL TIERNEY
Position: midfield
Birthdate: 15 September 1982
Birthplace: Salford
Height: 178 cms
Weight: 81 kgs
Signed trainee: 5 July 1999
Signed professional: 12 July 2000

MARC WHITEMAN
Position: forward
Birthdate: 1 October 1982
Birthplace: St Hellier
Height: 178 cms
Weight: 88 kgs
Signed trainee: 5 July 1999
Signed professional: 12 July 2000

MATTHEW WILLIAMS
Position: forward
Birthdate: 5 November 1982
Birthplace: St Asaph
Height: 178 cms
Weight: 72 kgs
Signed trainee: 5 July 1999
Signed professional: 26 January 2000

NEIL WOOD
Position: forward
Birthdate: 4 January 1983
Birthplace: Manchester
Height: 178 cms
Weight: 92 kgs
Signed trainee: 5 July 1999
Signed professional: 4 January 2000

TRAINEE PROFESSIONALS 2001-02

FIRST YEAR

Name	Position	Birthdate	Birthplace	Date Signed
Philip BARDSLEY	defender	28 June 1985	Salford	2 July 2001
Danny BYRNE	midfield	30 November 1984	Frimley	2 July 2001*
Ben COLLETT	midfield	11 September 1984	Bury	2 July 2001
Eddie JOHNSON	forward	20 September 1984	Chester	2 July 2001
Jemal JOHNSON	midfield	3 May 1984	New Jersey, USA	2 July 2001*
David JONES	midfield	4 November 1984	Southport	2 July 2001
Lee LAWRENCE	defender	1 December 1984	Boston	2 July 2001
David POOLE	forward	12 November 1984	Manchester	2 July 2001*
Kieran RICHARDSON	midfield	21 October 1984	Greenwich	2 July 2001
Lee SIMS	defender	6 September 1984	Manchester	2 July 2001
Mads TIMM	forward	31 October 1984	Odense, Denmark	2 July 2001

* Registration was awaiting confirmation at time of going to press

UNDER-19 ACADEMY STUDENT

Ben WILLIAMS	goalkeeper	27 August 1982	Manchester	27 August 1999

DEPARTURES 2000-01

Name	Details	Date
Henning BERG	to Blackburn Rovers	15 December 2000
Jesper BLOMQVIST	free transfer	30 June 2001
Mark BOSNICH	contract cancelled by mutual consent	18 January 2001
George CLEGG	free transfer	30 June 2001
Stephen COSGROVE	free transfer	30 June 2001
Ashley DODD	free transfer	30 June 2001
Wayne EVANS	contract cancelled by mutual consent	31 January 2001
Kevin GROGAN	trainee registration cancelled	11 August 2000
David HEALY	to Preston North End	3 January 2001
Danny HIGGINBOTHAM	to Derby County	5 July 2000
Rhodri JONES	free transfer	30 June 2001
Alex NOTMAN	to Norwich City	28 November 2000
Michael ROSE	free transfer	30 June 2001
Teddy SHERINGHAM	free transfer	30 June 2001
Gareth STRANGE	free transfer	30 June 2001
Mark STUDLEY	free transfer	30 June 2001
Marek SZMID	free transfer	30 June 2001
Massimo TAIBI	to Reggina Calcio	28 August 2000
Paul TEATHER	retired through injury	14 March 2001
Joshua WALKER	free transfer	30 June 2001

FA PREMIER RESERVE LEAGUE – NORTH

Manchester United Reserves looked a good bet for honours early in the New Year when they strung together a run of four straight victories. It looked particularly good for Mike Phelan's team as two of those successes came against Sunderland, who were top of the table at the time, and second-placed Leeds United. But during March and April they ran into a sequence of mixed results, which saw them slip out of the running for the championship.

Reserve team coach must be one of the most difficult jobs in any football club because of the constant uncertainty regarding the availability of the players. One week it could be that several first-teamers are on their way back from injury and need to get in some match action, so there is an embarrassment of riches, whilst on other occasions there could be dearth of personnel. And that's where coaches like Mike Phelan really earn their corn dealing with a changing group of players of differing ages and ability almost every time they go out to play a match.

Overall the season provided several excellent matches and not all of them ended with United in front. The game against Everton at Gigg Lane in the last week of March was easily one of the best of the whole programme, but it was the Toffees who took the points following a 3-2 win. Then there was the seven-goal thriller against Middlesbrough at the Riverside which United lost 4-3. It was a terrific match that neither side deserved to lose.

Ultimately, success in the title race was not to be and there was no consolation in the Manchester Senior Cup either. United negotiated the group stage with a 100 per cent record, including a 5-1 win over Manchester City, before meeting City again in the final at Old Trafford. The Reds had won the competition in each of the previous two seasons, but they failed to claim the hat-trick with City taking the cup back to Maine Road after enjoying a 4-1 win over their closest rivals.

names in bold indicate goalscorers

v BRADFORD CITY (home, at Gigg Lane, Bury) • Won: 3-2 — Thursday 24 August 2000

Bosnich • Lynch • Studley • Clegg M. • Tate • Stewart • Davis • Greening • Healy • **Notman 2** • Djordjic
Substitutes: Evans • Rachubka • Cosgrove • Webber (for Greening) • Clegg G.

v SUNDERLAND (away) • Lost: 0-4 — Thursday 7 September 2000

Rachubka • Clegg M. • Studley • Brown • O'Shea • Stewart • Davis • Clegg G. • Healy • Notman • Djordjic
Substitutes: Webber (for Davis) • Williams B. • Lynch (for Brown) • Cosgrove (for Healy) • Szmid

v BLACKBURN ROVERS (home, at Gigg Lane, Bury) • Drawn: 0-0 — Thursday 14 September 2000

van der Gouw • Clegg M. • Studley • O'Shea • Wallwork • Stewart • Davis • Greening • Webber • Notman • Pugh
Substitutes: Evans • Rachubka • Cosgrove (for Stewart) • Lynch • Szmid

v ASTON VILLA (away) • Won: 1-0 — Thursday 21 September 2000

Rachubka • Lynch • Studley • Clegg M. • O'Shea • Stewart • Davis • Greening • **Healy** • Notman • Djordjic
Substitutes: Webber (for Davis) • Williams B. • Walker (for Healy) • Tate • Pugh

v LIVERPOOL (away) • Lost: 2-4 — Monday 2 October 2000

Rachubka • Clegg M. • Studley • O'Shea • Wallwork • Stewart • Fortune • **Solskjaer** • Yorke • Notman • **Djordjic**
Substitutes: Webber (for Yorke) • Lynch • Szmid • Cosgrove • Evans

v SHEFFIELD WEDNESDAY (home, at Gigg Lane, Bury) • Won: 1-0 — Thursday 19 October 2000

Bosnich • Clegg M. • Studley • May • O'Shea • Stewart • **Greening** • Wallwork • Healy • Notman • Djordjic
Substitutes: Webber • Rachubka • Davis (for Wallwork) • Szmid • Lynch (for May)

v MIDDLESBROUGH (away) • Lost: 3-4 — Wednesday 15 November 2000

Williams B. • Clegg M. • Studley • May • Wallwork • Stewart • Chadwick • Greening • **Healy** • **Notman 2 (1 pen)** • Djordjic
Substitutes: Webber (for Studley) • Jowsey • Lynch • Evans • Clegg G.

v NEWCASTLE UNITED (home, at Gigg Lane, Bury) • Won: 4-0 — Thursday 23 November 2000

van der Gouw • Clegg M. • Studley • May • O'Shea • **Stewart** • **Wallwork** • **Greening** • Healy • **Notman (pen)** • Djordjic
Substitutes: Webber • Rachubka • Lynch (for May) • Szmid • Clegg G.

RESERVES

Tuesday 5 December 2000 **v MANCHESTER CITY (away, at Ewen Fields, Hyde) • Lost: 1-2**

Rachubka • Clegg M. • Studley • May • Madou-Kah • Szmid • Chadwick • Wilson • Webber • Davis • **Djordjic**
Substitutes: Clegg G. • Cosgrove (for Studley) • Jones • Lynch (for May) • Wood (for Wilson)

Tuesday 16 January 2001 **v BRADFORD CITY (away) • Won: 3-2**

Bosnich • Clegg M. • Studley • May • Wallwork • Cosgrove • Chadwick • **Wilson 2 (1 pen)** • Clegg G. • **Stewart** • Djordjic
Substitutes: Evans • Williams B. • Lynch (for Studley) • Jones • Rose

---

Thursday 25 January 2001 **v SUNDERLAND (home, at Gigg Lane, Bury) • Won: 1-0**

Rachubka • Clegg M. • Pugh • May • Wallwork • Cosgrove • **Chadwick** • Wilson • Greening • Stewart • Djordjic
Substitutes: Wood (for Cosgrove) • Lynch • Evans • Clegg G. • Jones

---

Thursday 1 February 2001 **v LEEDS UNITED (home, at Gigg Lane, Bury) • Won: 3-0**

van der Gouw • Clegg M. • Pugh • May • Wallwork • Cosgrove • Greening • **Wilson** • **Clegg G. 2** • Stewart • Djordjic
Substitutes: Rose (for Stewart) • Rachubka • Lynch (for Greening) • Dodd • Jones (for Wallwork)

Thursday 15 February 2001 **v ASTON VILLA (home, at Gigg Lane, Bury) • Won: 4-2**

Rachubka • Clegg M. • Studley • May • Jones • Stewart • **Chadwick** • **Wilson** • Greening • **Yorke 2** • Djordjic
Substitutes: Lynch • Clegg G. • Webber (for Greening) • Rose • Walker

---

Thursday 22 February 2001 **v BLACKBURN ROVERS (away, at Christie Park, Morecambe) • Lost: 0-2**

Rachubka • Clegg M. • Neville P. • May • Wallwork • Stewart • Greening • Wilson • Webber • Yorke • Djordjic
Substitutes: Clegg G. (for Yorke) • Cosgrove (for Neville) • Dodd • Lynch

---

Thursday 8 March 2001 **v SHEFFIELD WEDNESDAY (away) • Won: 3-1**

Rachubka • Clegg M. • Pugh • May • Wallwork • Stewart • **Chadwick** • Wilson • **Fortune** • **Greening** • Djordjic
Substitutes: Webber (for Fortune) • Williams B. • Cosgrove • Tate (for May) • Lynch (for Chadwick)

Tuesday 20 March 2001 **v LEEDS UNITED (away, at Bootham Crescent, York) • Lost: 0-2**

Williams B. • Clegg M. • Studley • May • Lynch • Cosgrove • Muirhead • Wallwork • Webber • Fortune • Djordjic
Substitutes: Pugh (for Djordjic) • Moran • Tate • Williams M. • Sampson

---

names in bold indicate goalscorers

v EVERTON (home, at Gigg Lane, Bury) • Lost: 2-3 — Thursday 29 March 2001

Rachubka • Clegg M. • Tierney • **Tate** • Wallwork • Stewart • Muirhead • Wilson • Williams M. • **Fortune** • Djordjic
Substitutes: Lynch • Williams B. (for Rachubka) • Cosgrove • Nardiello (for Williams M.) • Pugh (for Wilson)

v NEWCASTLE UNITED (away, at Kingston Park, Kenton) • Lost: 1-2 — Monday 9 April 2001

van der Gouw • Clegg M. • Tierney • Lynch • Johnsen • Wallwork • Chadwick • Wilson • Webber • Fortune • Djordjic
(Caldwell o.g.)
Substitutes: Davis (for Chadwick) • Rachubka • Nardiello (for Johnsen) • Sampson • Cosgrove

v EVERTON (away, at Auto Quest Stadium, Widnes) • Won: 3-0 — Thursday 19 April 2001

Rachubka • Lynch • Tierney • May • Johnsen • Wallwork • **Davis** • Wilson • **Webber** • **Stewart** • Fortune
Substitutes: Djordjic (for Fortune) • Williams B. • Tate • Cosgrove

v MANCHESTER CITY (home, at Old Trafford) • Won: 2-1 — Thursday 26 April 2001

Goram • Clegg M. • Tierney • May • Tate • Wallwork • Muirhead • **Wilson** • **Webber** • Nardiello • Djordjic
Substitutes: Studley • Rachubka • Lynch (for Muirhead) • Williams M. • Rose (for Wallwork)

v MIDDLESBROUGH (home, at Old Trafford) • Lost: 0-3 — Monday 30 April 2001

Rachubka • Clegg M. • Tierney • May • Tate • Wallwork • Davis • Wilson • Webber • Nardiello • Djordjic
Substitutes: Lynch • Williams B. • Cosgrove • Williams M. (for Nardiello) • Muirhead (for Davis)

v LIVERPOOL (home, at Old Trafford) • Drawn: 2-2 — Monday 7 May 2001

Rachubka • Clegg M. • Tierney • May • Tate • Sampson • Muirhead • **Wilson (pen)** • Webber • **Davis** • Djordjic
Substitutes: Lynch (for Davis) • Williams B. • Nardiello (for Webber) • Cosgrove (for Sampson) • Studley

RESERVES

APPEARANCES

GOALSCORERS

Name	Appearances (as sub)	Name	Appearances (as sub)	Name	Goals (penalties)
CLEGG • Michael	21	BOSNICH • Mark	3	WILSON • Mark	6 (2)
DJORDJIC • Bojan	20 (1)	YORKE • Dwight	3	NOTMAN • Alex	5 (2)
STEWART • Michael	16	NARDIELLO • Daniel	2 (3)	CHADWICK • Luke	3
WALLWORK • Ronnie	16	WILLIAMS • Ben	2 (1)	DJORDJIC • Bojan	3
MAY • David	15	JOHNSEN • Ronny	2	GREENING • Jonathan	3
WILSON • Mark	13	JONES • Rhodri	1 (1)	STEWART • Michael	3
RACHUBKA • Paul	12	WILLIAMS • Matthew	1 (1)	FORTUNE • Quinton	2
STUDLEY • Mark	12	BROWN • Wesley	1	CLEGG • George	2
GREENING • Jonathan	11	GORAM • Andy	1	DAVIS • Jimmy	2
WEBBER • Danny	9 (7)	MADOU-KAH • Pa	1	HEALY • David	2
DAVIS • Jimmy	8 (2)	NEVILLE • Phil	1	WEBBER • Danny	2
NOTMAN • Alex	8	SAMPSON • Gary	1	YORKE • Dwight	2
CHADWICK • Luke	7	SOLSKJAER • Ole Gunnar	1	SOLSKJAER • Ole Gunnar	1
FORTUNE • Quinton	6	SZMID • Marek	1	TATE • Alan	1
HEALY • David	6	ROSE • Michael	0 (2)	WALLWORK • Ronnie	1
O'SHEA • John	6	WOOD • Neil	0 (2)		
TIERNEY • Paul	6	WALKER • Joshua	0 (1)	**Own Goals**	
LYNCH • Mark	5 (9)			CALDWELL • Gary	1
TATE • Alan	5 (1)			(Newcastle United)	
COSGROVE • Stephen	4 (5)				
PUGH • Danny	4 (2)				
MUIRHEAD • Ben	4 (1)				
VAN DER GOUW • Raimond	4				
CLEGG • George	3 (1)				

Michael Clegg

Mark Wilson

FA PREMIER RESERVE LEAGUE – NORTH

		P	W	D	L	F	A	Pts
FINAL TABLE 2000-01	Everton	22	14	2	6	35	22	44
	Sunderland	22	12	6	4	38	21	42
	Leeds United	22	11	4	7	40	24	37
	Blackburn Rovers	22	9	10	3	31	23	37
	MANCHESTER UNITED	22	11	2	9	39	36	35
	Manchester City	22	9	6	7	42	33	33
	Middlesbrough	22	9	6	7	39	38	33
	Liverpool	22	9	5	8	43	32	32
	Aston Villa	22	8	6	8	33	34	30
	Newcastle United	22	8	4	10	34	35	28
	Bradford City	22	3	2	17	30	63	11
	Sheffield Wednesday	22	1	3	18	25	68	6

The United line-up v Manchester City, Manchester Senior Cup Final, 11th May 2001: (back row, left to right) Bojan Djordjic, Mark Studley, Stephen Cosgrove, Gary Sampson, Paul Tierney, Alan Tate; (front row) Mark Lynch, Paul Rachubka, Ben Muirhead, Danny Webber, Jimmy Davis

Action from the Manchester Senior Cup Final v Manchester City at Old Trafford in May 2001

names in bold indicate goalscorers

MANCHESTER SENIOR CUP

v BURY (home, at Gigg Lane, Bury) • Won: 8-1   Thursday 28 September 2000

Rachubka • Clegg M. • Studley • **O'Shea** • **Wallwork** • **Stewart 2** • **Webber** • Fortune • **Healy** • **Notman** • Djordjic

*Substitutes: **Davis** (for Healy) • Lynch • Cosgrove • Evans (for Notman) • Szmid (for Fortune)*

v OLDHAM ATHLETIC (home, at Gigg Lane, Bury) • Drawn: 2-2*   Thursday 12 October 2000

Rachubka • Lynch • Studley • Tate • Jones • Szmid • Evans • Cosgrove • **Webber (pen)** • **Clegg G.** • Pugh

Substitutes: Walker • Williams B. • Dodd • Rose • Whiteman

*Won 4-2 on penalties *Penalty-scorers:* Webber • Evans • Cosgrove • Clegg G.

v MANCHESTER CITY (home, at Gigg Lane, Bury) • Won: 5-1   Thursday 26 October 2000

Rachubka • Clegg M. • Wallwork • May • O'Shea • Stewart • Greening • Fortune • **Healy 2** • **Notman 2** • Chadwick

*Substitutes: Lynch • Davis • Clegg G. • **Djordjic** (for Fortune) • Evans*

v BURY (away) • Won: 3-2   Wednesday 29 November 2000

Rachubka • Lynch • Studley • McDermott • Jones • Stewart • Evans • Cosgrove • **Healy 2** • **Davis** • Djordjic

Substitutes: Szmid (for Davis) • Clegg G. (for Healy) • Rose • Strange • Walker

v MANCHESTER CITY (away, at Ewen Fields, Hyde) • Drawn: 1-1*   Tuesday 27 March 2001

Rachubka • Clegg M. • Studley • May • Wallwork • Stewart • Muirhead • Djordjic • **Williams M.** • Fortune • Pugh

Substitutes: Nardiello (for Fortune) • Williams B. • Tate (for May) • Sampson (for Stewart) • Tierney

*Won 6-5 on penalties *Penalty-scorers:* Wallwork • Williams M. • Nardiello • Clegg M. • Muirhead • Pugh

v OLDHAM ATHLETIC (away) • Won: 2-0   Monday 23 April 2001

Rachubka • Lynch • Tierney • Tate • Jones • Cosgrove • Muirhead • Djordjic • **Webber** • **Nardiello** • Rose

Substitutes: Sampson • Williams B. • Strange • Heath

	P	W	L	F	A	Pts
MANCHESTER UNITED	6	6	0	21	7	18
Manchester City	6	4	2	16	9	12
Oldham Athletic	6	2	4	7	14	6
Bury	6	0	6	6	20	0

v MANCHESTER CITY Final (home, at Old Trafford) • Lost: 1-4   Friday 11 May 2001

Rachubka • Lynch • Studley • Tierney • Tate • Sampson • Muirhead • Cosgrove • **Webber** • Davis • Djordjic

Substitutes: Nardiello (for Muirhead) • Williams B. • Clegg G. • Strange • Szmid

FRIENDLIES

Thursday 20 July 2000   v RADCLIFFE BOROUGH (away) • Won: 6-3

Rachubka • Lynch • O'Shea • **Healy 2** • Studley • **Davis** • Stewart • Cosgrove • Djordjic • **Notman 2** • **Webber**
Substitutes: Clegg G. (for Webber) • Evans (for Davis) • Whiteman (for Healy)

Wednesday 26 July 2000   v LIVINGSTON (away) • Won: 2-1

van der Gouw • Clegg M. • Hilton • O'Shea • Johnsen • Wallwork • Fletcher • Greening • Healy • **Notman** • **Fortune**
Substitutes: Djordjic (for Fletcher) • Teather (for Wallwork) • Davis • Lynch • Cosgrove

Friday 28 July 2000   v SCARBOROUGH (away) • Lost: 2-3

Rachubka • Lynch • Hilton • Teather • Jones • Cosgrove • Evans • Greening • **Webber** • **Davis** • Djordjic
Substitutes: Studley (for Hilton) • Clegg G. (for Greening) • Pugh • Szmid

Tuesday 1 August 2000   v WREXHAM Gareth Owen Testimonial (away) • Won: 1-0

van der Gouw • Clegg M. • Hilton • Berg • Wallwork • Stewart • Healy • Greening • Notman • Yorke • **Giggs**
Substitutes: Teather (for Berg) • Rachubka • Lynch (for Hilton) • Studley (for Clegg M.) • Djordjic (for Giggs) •
Webber (for Yorke)

Saturday 5 August 2000   v CHELMSFORD CITY (away) • Won: 3-1

Bosnich • **Clegg M.** • Hilton • Teather • O'Shea • Stewart • Webber • Greening • Healy • **Notman 2 (1 pen)** • Djordjic
Substitutes: Evans (for Webber) • Rachubka • Clegg G. (for Healy) • Cosgrove (for Greening) • Studley • Lynch •
Strange (for Teather)

Sunday 6 August 2000   v PURFLEET (away) • Drawn: 0-0

Rachubka • Lynch • Studley • Clegg M. • O'Shea • Stewart • Cosgrove • Greening • Healy • Notman • Djordjic
Substitutes: Evans (for Cosgrove) • Clegg G. (for Healy) • Webber • Hilton (for Studley) • Strange (for Lynch)

Thursday 10 August 2000   v SHELBOURNE (away) • Drawn: 0-0

Bosnich • Lynch • Hilton • Clegg M. • O'Shea • Stewart • Cosgrove • Greening • Healy • Notman • Djordjic
Substitutes: Evans (for Lynch) • Rachubka (for Bosnich) • Davis (for Cosgrove) • Webber (for Notman) • Clegg G. • Studley

Wednesday 31 August 2000   v CAMEROON (Under 23) (home) • Lost: 0-4

Bosnich • Evans • Studley • Clegg M. • Wallwork • Clegg G. • Cosgrove • Butt • Fortune • Webber • Djordjic
Substitutes: Tate • Szmid • Dodd

names in bold indicate goalscorers

v BRISTOL CITY Buster Footman Testimonial (away) • Won: 4-0 — Monday 4 September 2000

Rachubka • Lynch • Studley • Brolin (trialist) • Jones R. • Cosgrove • Evans • Davis • **Webber 3** • Clegg G. • Pugh
*Substitutes: **Szmid** (for Davis) • Williams B. (for Rachubka) • Tierney (for Lynch) • Rose (for Pugh) • O'Shea (for Brolin)*

v DERRY CITY (away) • Won: 1-0 — Tuesday 14 November 2000

van der Gouw • Clegg M. • Silvestre • May • O'Shea • Wallwork • Webber • Stewart • Healy • **Notman** • Djordjic
Substitutes: Rachubka • Studley (for Silvestre) • Lynch (Clegg M.) • Evans (for Notman) Clegg G. (for Healy)

v HUDDERSFIELD TOWN Friendly/Training Match (home) • Lost: 0-1 — Thursday 21 December 2000

Rachubka • Clegg M. • Studley • O'Shea • Wallwork • Stewart • Lynch • Wilson • Webber • Davis • Clegg G.
Substitutes: Wood • Cosgrove (for Stewart) • Jones • Rose (for Lynch) • Szmid

v WREXHAM (away) • Drawn: 4-4 — Thursday 4 January 2001

Bosnich • **Clegg G. 2** • Wallwork • May • **Chadwick** • Stam • Greening • Wilson • Cole • **Sheringham** • Stewart
Substitutes: Studley (for Stam) • Rachubka • Djordjic (for Cole) • Cosgrove (for Chadwick) • Clegg G. (for Sheringham)

v NEWPORT COUNTY Friendly/Training Match (away) • Won: 3-1 — Saturday 6 January 2001

Moran D. • Clegg S. • **Pugh** • Sampson • Tate • Tierney • Muirhead • **Williams M.** • **Nardiello** • Fox • Rankin
Substitutes: Whiteman (for Nardiello) • Heaton (for Moran D.) • Cogger (for Tate) • Coates (for Williams M.) • Mooniaruck (for Muirhead) • Humphreys (for Sampson)

v CAERNARFON TOWN (away) • Won: 4-2 — Wednesday 31 January 2001

Moran D. • Clegg S. • Lynch • Sampson • Tate • Tierney • **Muirhead** • Dodd • **Williams M.** • **Coates 2** • Rose
Substitutes: Cogger (for Tate) • Heath (for Williams M.) • Mooniaruck (for Muirhead) • Fox (for Sampson) • Humphreys (for Coates)

v FK MOLDE (home) • Lost: 0-3 — Friday 23 March 2001

Rachubka • Lynch • Studley • Clegg • Tate • Cosgrove • Muirhead • Wallwork • Giggs • Fortune • Djordjic
Substitutes: Nardiello (for Giggs) • Williams B. • Pugh (for Cosgrove) • Walker • Sampson • Tierney (for Tate)

v NEWFOUNDLAND PROVINCIAL XI (home) • Won: 10-0 — Friday 11 May 2001

Moran D. • Clegg S. • **Rankin** • Strange • Taylor K. • **Fox 4** • Mooniaruck • **Williams M. 2** • Whiteman • **Coates** • Humphreys
*Substitutes: **Timm** (for Strange) • Jowsey (for Moran D.)*

FA PREMIER ACADEMY LEAGUE – UNDER 19s

Like the Reserves, there were times when David Williams' team looked capable of mounting a serious challenge for the group stage title. They were up there challenging with the leaders more than once, but again in keeping with the reserves, they slipped off the pace towards the close of the season and were eventually forced to concede the championship to Everton.

Three defeats in the opening seven matches saw them off to a less than ideal start, but results elsewhere meant that they were rarely very far off the pace. An excellent spell in October and November saw them collect maximum points from four out of five games and once again they were right back in amongst the front-runners. Impressive away wins in Staffordshire against Wolverhampton Wanderers and Stoke City were included in this sequence as was a 2-0 away victory over Manchester City.

They suffered a minor blip around Christmas losing to neighbours Bolton Wanderers and Blackburn Rovers in consecutive games but then entered another encouraging run of four games that produced three wins, including away successes at Liverpool and Crewe, a home win over Stoke and a draw at home to Bolton.

The last week of February saw them go down to eventual champions Everton 1-0 at Carrington. That was a match United really needed to win to preserve any real hopes of taking the title, but it wasn't to be.

A mixed-bag of results brought the campaign to a close with United finishing in fifth place, 17 points behind Everton.

The Youth Cup wasn't to provide any success either with the Reds being eliminated in the fifth round, losing 2-1 after extra time at Nottingham Forest. The earlier rounds saw United win at Reading and beat Scunthorpe United 8-0 at Old Trafford with the season's top scorer, Daniel Nardiello, netting four of the goals.

names in bold indicate goalscorers

v QUEENS PARK RANGERS (away) • Lost: 1-2   Saturday 26 August 2000

Williams B. • Taylor A. • Pugh • Szmid • Jones • Tierney • Muirhead • Dodd • **Webber** • Whiteman • Rankin
Substitutes: Walker • Moran • Coates (for Whiteman) • Sampson (for Dodd) • Clegg

v ASTON VILLA (home) • Drawn: 2-2   Saturday 2 September 2000

Williams B. • Clegg • Pugh • Szmid • Tate • Tierney • Sampson • Walker • Whiteman • **Coates** • Rose
(De Bolla o.g.)
Substitutes: Dodd • Moran • Rankin • Nardiello (for Whiteman) • Muirhead (for Coates)

v SUNDERLAND (away) • Won: 3-0   Saturday 9 September 2000

Williams B. • Clegg • **Rankin** • Lynch • Jones • Tierney • Muirhead • **Sampson** • Coates • Dodd • Rose
*Substitutes: Tate (for Rankin) • Moran • Wood (for Sampson) • **Nardiello** (for Coates) • Whiteman*

v HUDDERSFIELD TOWN (home) • Won: 4-0   Saturday 23 September 2000

Williams B. • Strange • Pugh • Taylor A. • Tate • Jones • **Dodd** • Szmid • **Nardiello 2** • **Whiteman** • Wood
Substitutes: Williams M. (for Nardiello) • Moran • Tierney (for Strange) • Muirhead • Sampson (for Dodd)

v DERBY COUNTY (away) • Lost: 1-3   Saturday 30 September 2000

Baxter • Clegg • Rankin • Walker • Tate • Tierney • Muirhead • Coates • Nardiello • Sampson • Rose
*Substitutes: **Pugh** (for Rankin) • Moran • Taylor A. • Wood (for Nardiello) • Williams M. (for Coates)*

v LEICESTER CITY (home) • Drawn: 1-1   Saturday 7 October 2000

Baxter • Taylor A. • Pugh • Lynch • **Jones** • Tate • Walker • Szmid • Whiteman • Muirhead • Dodd
Substitutes: Sampson • Moran • Wood (for Dodd) • Coates • Nardiello (for Muirhead)

v LEEDS UNITED (away) • Lost: 1-2   Tuesday 10 October 2000

Williams B. • Clegg • Taylor K. • Taylor A. • Tate • Jones • Sampson • Wood • **Nardiello** • Coates • Rose
Substitutes: Walker • Baxter • Muirhead (for Nardiello) • Whiteman • Williams M. (for Coates)

v BARNSLEY (home) • Won: 1-0   Saturday 21 October 2000

Baxter • Clegg • Pugh • Lynch • Tate • Szmid • Strange • Dodd • **Webber** • Whiteman • Wood
Substitutes: Coates • Moran • Sampson • Nardiello (for Webber) • Muirhead

JUNIORS

v MANCHESTER CITY (away) • Won: 2-0

Williams B. • Lynch • Tierney • Walker • Tate • Jones • Davis • **Rose (pen)** • Webber • Nardiello • **Djordjic**
Substitutes: Sampson • Moran • Pugh • Coates • Wood (for Nardiello)

v WREXHAM (home) • Lost: 1-2

Moran • Clegg • Pugh • Taylor A. • Strange • Dodd • Muirhead • Coates • Whiteman • Sampson • **Tierney**
Substitutes: Rate (for Clegg) • Baxter • Nardiello (for Coates) • Rose

v WOLVERHAMPTON WANDERERS (away) • Won: 3-1

Williams B. • Lynch • Tierney • Strange • Jones • Szmid • **Muirhead** • Davis • **Nardiello 2** • Rose • Rankin
Substitutes: Tate • Baxter • Sampson • Wood (for Rankin) • Coates

v STOKE CITY (away) • Won: 3-0

Moran • Taylor A. • Strange • **Tate** • Jones • Wood • Muirhead • Sampson • **Nardiello** • Coates • Rankin
*Substitutes: Clegg (for Wood) • Baxter • **Williams M.** (for Coates) • Szmid*

v LIVERPOOL (home) • Drawn: 1-1

Williams B. • Strange • Lynch • Szmid • McDermott • Jones • Davis • Walker • Webber • **Whiteman** • Rose
Substitutes: Taylor A. • Moran • Clegg • Sampson

v CREWE ALEXANDRA (home) • Won: 2-1

Moran • **Strange** • Tierney • Dodd • Clegg • Jones • Muirhead • Whiteman • **Webber** • Wood • Rose
Substitutes: McDermott (for Dodd) • Baxter • Williams M. • Szmid • Nardiello (for Whiteman)

v BOLTON WANDERERS (away, at Trafford Training Centre) • Lost: 0-3

Moran • Clegg • Strange • Sampson • Tate • Jones • Muirhead • Walker • Nardiello • Williams M. • Wood
Substitutes: Tierney (for Walker) • Williams B. (for Moran) • Coates (for Williams M.) • Whiteman

v BLACKBURN ROVERS (home) • Lost: 0-2

Williams B. • Lynch • Studley • Strange • Jones • Szmid • Dodd • Walker • Coates • Rose • Djordjic
Substitutes: Wood (for Studley) • Moran • Pugh (for Dodd) • Rankin (for Walker)

names in bold indicate goalscorers

v LIVERPOOL (away) • Won: 2-0   Friday 26 January 2001

Moran • Lynch • Tierney • Sampson • Tate • Jones • Muirhead • Coates • **Nardiello 2 (1 pen)** • Szmid • Rankin
Substitutes: Clegg (for Szmid) • Williams M. (for Coates) • Taylor K.

v STOKE CITY (home) • Won: 4-1   Saturday 3 February 2001

Moran • Clegg • Tierney • Strange • **Tate** • Dodd • **Muirhead** • Williams M. • **Nardiello 2** • Rose • Rankin
Substitutes: Coates (for Williams M.) • Taylor A. (for Clegg) • Sampson (for Rankin) • Pugh

v BOLTON WANDERERS (home) • Drawn: 1-1   Friday 9 February 2001

Moran • Clegg • Pugh • Sampson • Tate • Tierney • Muirhead • Coates • Williams M. • Wood • **Rankin**
Substitutes: Taylor A. (for Sampson) • Heath (for Coates) • Rose (for Wood)

v CREWE ALEXANDRA (away) • Won: 1-0   Saturday 17 February 2001

Moran • Strange • Tierney • Lynch • Tate • Taylor A. • Muirhead • Dodd • Williams M. • Coates • Pugh
*Substitutes: Clegg • Sampson • **Webber** (for Williams M.) • Rankin (for Muirhead)*

v EVERTON (home) • Lost: 0-1   Saturday 24 February 2001

Moran • Clegg • Pugh • Lynch • Tate • Taylor A. • Muirhead • Sampson • Williams M. • Coates • Rankin
Substitutes: Dodd (for Taylor A.) • Tierney (for Clegg) • Whiteman (for Coates)

v MANCHESTER CITY (home) • Won: 2-1   Saturday 10 March 2001

Moran • Clegg • Tierney • Lynch • Tate • Strange • Muirhead • Sampson • Whiteman • **Williams M. 2** • Rankin
Substitutes: Dodd • Williams B. • Coates • Nardiello (for Williams M.) • Pugh

v WREXHAM (away) • Lost: 1-2   Saturday 17 March 2001

Williams B. • Clegg • Pugh • Sampson • Tate • Tierney • Muirhead • Fox • **Nardiello (pen)** • Coates • Rankin
Substitutes: Whiteman (for Coates) • Moran • Humphreys • Taylor K. • Mooniaruck (for Muirhead)

v WOLVERHAMPTON WANDERERS (home) • Won: 1-0   Saturday 24 March 2001

Moran • Clegg • Pugh • Sampson • Tate • Tierney • Strange • Walker • Whiteman • Williams M. • Rankin
*Substitutes: **Nardiello** (for Whiteman) • Williams B. • Coates (for Williams M.) • Muirhead*

JUNIORS

Saturday 7 April 2001 **v NEWCASTLE UNITED (home) • Won: 3-2**

Moran • Clegg • Rankin • Szmid • Pugh • Studley • **Muirhead** • Sampson • **Nardiello** • **Coates** • Whiteman
Substitutes: Williams M. (for Coates) • Williams B. • Walker (for Szmid) • Tierney (for Whiteman)

Saturday 21 April 2001 **v MIDDLESBROUGH (away) • Lost: 2-3**

Moran • Clegg • Strange • **Sampson** • Jones • Tate • Muirhead • Walker • Whiteman • **Coates** • Rose
Substitutes: Rankin (for Walker) • Williams B. • Williams M. (for Whiteman)

Tuesday 24 April 2001 **v BLACKBURN ROVERS (away) • Lost: 0-1**

Williams B. • Clegg • Rankin • Strange • Cogger • Sampson • Mooniaruck • Humphreys • Whiteman • Williams M. • Heath
Substitutes: Coates (for Whiteman) • Moran • Timm (for Mooniaruck)

Saturday 28 April 2001 **v EVERTON (away) • Drawn: 0-0**

Moran • Clegg • Studley • Strange • Lynch • Williams M. • Muirhead • Sampson • Whiteman • Coates • Rankin
Substitutes: Tate (for Clegg) • Williams B. • Nardiello (for Coates) • Tierney (for Muirhead)

United's Under 19s squad pictured at Carrington: (back row, left to right) Alan McDermott, Danny Pugh, Alan Tate, Michael Rose, Rhodri Jones, Marek Szmid; (second row) Ben Williams, David Moran, Mark Studley, Gareth Strange, Paul Tierney; (third row) Joshua Walker, Andrew Taylor, Jimmy Davis, John Rankin, Daniel Nardiello, Craig Coates, Ben Muirhead, Neil Wood; (front row) Nick Baxter, Matthew Williams, Mark Lynch, Ashley Dodd, Gary Sampson, Danny Webber

UNDER 19s APPEARANCES

Name	Appearances (as sub)	Name	Appearances (as sub)
MUIRHEAD • Ben	19 (2)	WILLIAMS • Matthew	9 (7)
TATE • Alan	18 (3)	WALKER • Joshua	9 (1)
CLEGG • Steven	18 (2)	TAYLOR • Andrew	8 (2)
SAMPSON • Gary	17 (3)	WOOD • Neil	7 (6)
STRANGE • Gareth	16	WEBBER • Danny	5 (1)
COATES • Craig	15 (5)	BAXTER • Nick	3
TIERNEY • Paul	15 (5)	DAVIS • Jimmy	3
RANKIN • John	15 (3)	STUDLEY • Mark	3
WHITEMAN • Marc	14 (2)	DJORDJIC • Bojan	2
JONES • Rhodri	14	HEATH • Colin	1 (1)
MORAN • David	14	McDERMOTT • Alan	1 (1)
PUGH • Danny	12 (2)	MOONIARUCK • Kalam	1 (1)
LYNCH • Mark	12	COGGER • John	1
NARDIELLO • Daniel	11 (9)	FOX • David	1
ROSE • Michael	11 (1)	HUMPHREYS • Chris	1
WILLIAMS • Ben	11 (1)	TAYLOR • Kris	1
DODD • Ashley	10 (1)	TIMM • Mads	0 (1)
SZMID • Marek	10		

GOALSCORERS

Name	Goals (penalties)
NARDIELLO • Daniel	14 (2)
WEBBER • Danny	4
COATES • Craig	3
MUIRHEAD • Ben	3
WILLIAMS • Matthew	3
RANKIN • John	2
SAMPSON • Gary	2
TATE • Alan	2
WHITEMAN • Marc	2
DJORDJIC • Bojan	1
DODD • Ashley	1
JONES • Rhodri	1
PUGH • Danny	1
STRANGE • Gareth	1
TIERNEY • Paul	1
ROSE • Stephen	0 (1)

Own Goals

DE BOLLA • Mark (Aston Villa)	1

FA PREMIER ACADEMY LEAGUE UNDER 19s

GROUP B FINAL TABLE 2000-01	P	W	D	L	F	A	Pts
Everton	28	19	4	5	50	16	61
Manchester City	28	16	4	8	50	27	52
Blackburn Rovers	28	13	9	6	46	34	48
Crewe Alexandra	28	15	3	10	56	46	48
MANCHESTER UNITED	28	13	5	10	43	32	44
Liverpool	28	12	5	11	47	35	41
Wolverhampton Wanderers	28	11	4	13	38	39	37
Stoke City	28	6	7	15	37	59	25
Bolton Wanderers	28	5	3	20	31	61	18
Wrexham	28	2	4	22	24	77	10

JUNIORS

FA YOUTH CUP

v READING Third Round (away) • **Won: 1-0**

Jowsey • Clegg S. • Taylor K. • Sampson • Tate • Tierney • Muirhead • Williams M. • **Nardiello** • Wood • Rankin
Substitutes: Taylor A. (for Rankin) • Baxter (for Jowsey) • Whiteman (for Taylor A.) • Humphreys • Fox

v SCUNTHORPE UNITED Fourth Round (home) • **Won: 8-0**

Moran D. • Clegg S. • Pugh • Sampson • Tate • Tierney • Muirhead • **Williams M.** • **Nardiello 4** • **Wood** • **Rankin**
(Butler o.g.)
Substitutes: Coates (for Williams M.) • Heaton • Taylor K. • Fox (for Sampson) • Humphreys (for Nardiello)

v NOTTINGHAM FOREST Fifth Round (home, at City Ground, Nottingham)• **Lost: 1-2***

Moran D. • Clegg S. • Pugh • Sampson • Tate • Tierney • Muirhead • Coates • **Williams M.** • Wood • Rankin
Substitutes: Taylor A. • Heaton • Taylor K. • Fox • Heath (for Coates)
*After extra time, score after 90 minutes, 1-1

Action from the FA Youth Cup Fifth Round tie v Nottingham Forest, 14th February 2001

BAYERN MUNICH CENTENARY TOURNAMENT (UNDER 18s)

v FEYENOORD (Holland) Group A • Lost: 0-1   Saturday 5 August 2000

Williams • Clegg • Tierney • Szmid • Tate • Dodd • Taylor • Sampson • Nardiello • Davis • Pugh

Substitutes: Muirhead (for Nardiello)

v IFK GOTHENBURG (Sweden) Group A • Drawn: 2-2*   Saturday 5 August 2000

Baxter • Clegg • Tierney • **Szmid** • Tate • Dodd • **Muirhead** • Rose • Coates • Davis • Pugh

*Won on penalties: 5-4 *Penalty scorers: Rose, Muirhead, Davis, Coates, Szmid*

v FC BAYERN MUNICH (Germany) Group A • Lost: 2-3   Sunday 6 August 2000

Baxter • Clegg • Jones • Szmid • Tate • Dodd • Taylor • Sampson • **Nardiello** • **Davis** • Pugh

Substitutes: Rose (for Taylor) • Muirhead (for Sampson)

v SPARTAK MOSCOW (Russia) Third/Fourth Place Play-Off • Won: 3-0   Sunday 6 August 2000

Williams • Muirhead • Rose • Szmid • Tate • Dodd • Coates • **Sampson** • Nardiello • Whiteman • Pugh

*Substitutes: Clegg (for Dodd) • **Davis 2** (for Nardiello)*

TOURNAMENT SQUAD

Nick BAXTER	Michael ROSE
Steven CLEGG	Gary SAMPSON
Craig COATES	Marek SZMID
Jimmy DAVIS	Alan TATE
Ashley DODD	Andy TAYLOR
Rhodri JONES	Paul TIERNEY
Ben MUIRHEAD	Marc WHITEMAN
Daniel NARDIELLO	Ben WILLIAMS
Danny PUGH	

BV 04 DUSSELDORF JUNIOR FOOTBALL TOURNAMENT 2001

Saturday 14 April 2001   v FC BAYERN MUNICH (Germany) Group Stage • Won: 1-0

Williams • Clegg • Szmid • Fox • Tate • Tierney • Muirhead • Sampson • **Nardiello** • Heath • Djordjic

Saturday 14 April 2001   v HAMBURGER SV (Germany) Group Stage • Lost: 0-3

Williams • Clegg • Szmid • Humphreys • Tate • Tierney • Muirhead • Sampson • Davis • Coates • Djordjic
Substitutes: Cogger (for Tate) • Mooniaruck (for Davis) • Whiteman (for Humphreys)

Sunday 15 April 2001   v FORTUNA DUSSELDORF (Germany) Qualifying Round • Won: 3-1

Williams • Clegg • Szmid • Fox • Tate • Tierney • **Muirhead** • Sampson • **Davis** • Heath • **Djordjic**
Substitutes: Cogger (for Clegg)

Sunday 15 April 2001   v DEPORTIVO LA CORUNA (Spain) Quarter-Final • Won: 3-1

Williams • Cogger • Szmid • **Fox** • Tate • Tierney • Muirhead • Sampson • **Nardiello** • Davis • **Djordjic**
Substitutes: Humphreys (for Cogger) • Whiteman (for Djordjic) • Coates (for Nardiello)

Monday 16 April 2001   v VfB STUTTGART (Germany) Semi-Final • Drawn: 0-0*

Williams • Cogger • Szmid • Fox • Tate • Tierney • Muirhead • Sampson • Nardiello • Davis • Djordjic
Substitutes: Mooniaruck (for Cogger) • Heath (for Davis)
* Lost: on penalties

Monday 16 April 2001   v JAPAN NATIONAL XI Third/Fourth Place Play-Off • Lost: 1-3

Jowsey • Cogger • Szmid • Fox • Humphreys • Whiteman • Muirhead • Sampson • **Coates** • Heath • Mooniaruck
Substitutes: Tate (for Szmid) • Nardiello (for Cogger)

TOURNAMENT SQUAD

Steven CLEGG	Colin HEATH	Gary SAMPSON
Craig COATES	Chris HUMPHREYS	Marek SZMID
John COGGER	James JOWSEY	Alan TATE
Jimmy DAVIS	Kalam MOONIARUCK	Paul TIERNEY
Bojan DJORDJIC	Ben MUIRHEAD	Marc WHITEMAN
David FOX	Daniel NARDIELLO	Ben WILLIAMS

FRIENDLIES

v NEWPORT COUNTY (away) • Lost: 1-3 — Wednesday 19 July 2000

Baxter • Taylor A. • **Tierney** • Szmid • Tate • Jones R. • Muirhead • Fletcher • Nardiello • Coates • Rose
Substitutes: Strange (for Taylor A.) • Walker (for Fletcher) • Dodd (for Szmid) • Sampson (for Nardiello) • Williams M. (for Coates) • Pugh (for Rose)

v GLOUCESTER CITY (away) • Lost: 1-4 — Friday 21 July 2000

Baxter • Strange • Tierney • Walker • Tate • Jones R. • Muirhead • Dodd • **Williams M.** • Sampson • Pugh
Substitutes: Coates (for Muirhead) • Taylor A. (for Strange) • Rose (for Tate) • Fletcher (for Walker) • Szmid (for Dodd)

v PORTSMOUTH (home) • Won: 1-0 — Wednesday 26 July 2000

Baxter • Taylor A. • Studley • Strange • Szmid • Walker • Dodd • Nardiello • Webber • Rose • Pugh
Substitutes: Jones R. (for Taylor A.) • ***Coates (pen)*** *(for Rose) • Tierney (for Studley) • Tate (for Walker) • Clegg S. (for Strange) • Sampson (for Dodd) • Whiteman (for Webber) • Williams M. (for Nardiello)*

v UPTON ATHLETIC ASSOCIATION (away) • Drawn: 1-1 — Tuesday 1 August 2000

Williams B. • **Clegg S.** • Tierney • Strange • Tate • Szmid • Taylor A. • Sampson • Whiteman • Coates • Rose
Substitutes: Jones R. (for Tate) • Baxter • Dodd (for Szmid) • Nardiello (for Clegg S.) • Muirhead (for Coates) • Pugh (for Rose)

v QUEENS PARK RANGERS (home) • Drawn: 1-1 — Wednesday 9 August 2000

Baxter • Strange • Studley • Sampson • Tate • Tierney • Muirhead • Fletcher • Clegg G. • Coates • Rose
(Paquette o.g.)
Substitutes: Pugh • Williams M. • Clegg S. (for Fletcher) • Whiteman (for Strange)

v JERSEY (visit to Jersey) • Won: 3-0 — Tuesday 14 August 2000

Williams B. • Szmid • Studley • Dodd • Tate • Tierney • Muirhead • **Sampson** • **Webber** • Davis • Rose
Substitutes: Coates (for Webber) • ***Whiteman (pen)*** *(for Davis) • Rankin (for Dodd)*

v SPORTING LISBON (visit to Jersey) • Drawn: 2-2* — Saturday 19 August 2000

Baxter • Clegg S. • Studley • Dodd • Tate • Tierney • **Sampson** • Walker • Coates • **Davis** • Pugh
Substitutes: Rankin (for Clegg S.) • Rose (for Walker) • Muirhead (for Coates)
*Lost on penalties: 4-5 *Penalty scorers: Rose, Tate, Pugh, Davis*

v WREXHAM (home) • Won: 8-0 — Wednesday 8 November 2000

Baxter • Taylor A. • Tierney • Taylor K. • **Tate** • **Wood** • Muirhead • Sampson • **Nardiello (pen)** • **Coates 2** • **Pugh 2**
Substitutes: Heath (for Nardiello) • Rankin (for Taylor K.)

FA PREMIER ACADEMY LEAGUE – UNDER 17s

United's Under-17s entered their last group match of the campaign needing a win to be absolutely sure of collecting the laurels. And with a goal scored close to the end of the game by Kieran Richardson they succeeded in completing the mission.

Neil Bailey's lads were strong contenders for the title for most of the season losing just five of the 24-match league programme. Their best run of the entire season was sandwiched between two defeats inflicted by Manchester City. The first, 2-0, was at Carrington in mid-November, the second, 2-1, at City's Platt Lane five months later. In between times United completed ten matches, winning no fewer than nine of them.

Despite this marvellous run of consistency they were never alone in the chase for the title with Manchester City – not surprisingly – and Aston Villa proving the main challengers.

They had some outstanding victories during what was a highly satisfactory campaign. They trounced Queens Park Rangers 6-2 in London on the second Saturday of the season and three weeks later drew 4-4 with Sheffield Wednesday in Yorkshire. A 5-0 win over Crewe Alexandra in the build-up to Christmas was another success of note.

In the end-of-season Play-offs they were grouped together in a tough section with Sunderland, Liverpool and Blackburn Rovers. There was a goalless draw at Sunderland followed by a home win over Liverpool, which set up an intriguing final match with Rovers. United needed to win to go through to the knock-out stages, but they could only manage a draw and it was the lads from Ewood Park who stepped forward into the next phase.

names in bold indicate goalscorers

v ARSENAL (home) • Won: 1-0   Saturday 26 August 2000

Jowsey • Sims • Jones • Taylor • Cogger • Fox • Mooniaruck • Humpreys • **Heath** • Johnson J. • Johnson E.
Substitutes: Connor • Yeomans • Bardsley • Bruce (for Johnson J.) • Timm (for Johnson E.)

v QUEENS PARK RANGERS (away) • Won: 6-2   Saturday 2 September 2000

Jowsey • Sims • Lawrence • Taylor • Cogger • Fox • Mooniaruck • **Humphreys** • **Heath 2** • **Timm 3** • Richardson
Substitutes: Johnson J. (for Timm) • Heaton • Johnson E. (for Lawrence) • Connor • Jones (for Richardson)

v DERBY COUNTY (home) • Lost: 1-2   Saturday 16 September 2000

Jowsey • Sims • Lawrence • Taylor • Bardsley • Fox • Mooniaruck • Humphreys • Heath • Johnson E. • **Richardson**
Substitutes: Timm (for Richardson) • Heaton • Jones (for Lawrence) • Bruce • Poole (for Heath)

v SHEFFIELD WEDNESDAY (away) • Drawn: 4-4   Saturday 23 September 2000

Jowsey • Sims • Lawrence • **Moran** • Bardsley • Bruce • Mooniaruck • **Humphreys** • **Poole** • Johnson E. • **Richardson**
Substitutes: Jones (for Bruce) • Collett (for Lawrence) • Johnson J.

v LEEDS UNITED (home) • Drawn: 1-1   Saturday 30 September 2000

Jowsey • Sims • Lawrence • Taylor • Moran • **Fox** • Bardsley • Humphreys • Poole • Johnson E. • Richardson
Substitutes: Mooniaruck (for Bardsley) • Heaton • Johnson J. (for Johnson E.) • Bruce • Jones

v MIDDLESBROUGH (away) • Lost: 1-6   Saturday 7 October 2000

Jowsey • Sims • Lawrence • Taylor • Moran • Fox • Mooniaruck • Humphreys • **Heath** • Johnson J. • Richardson
Substitutes: Timm • Heaton • Poole • Johnson E. • Collett

v SUNDERLAND (home) • Drawn 0-0   Saturday 21 October 2000

Jowsey • Sims • Lawrence • Taylor • Bardsley • Fox • Mooniaruck • Humphreys • Heath • Timm • Fletcher
Substitutes: Jones • Heaton • Bruce (for Heath) • Poole • Johnson J. (for Timm)

v NOTTINGHAM FOREST (away) • Lost: 2-4   Tuesday 24 October 2000

Jowsey • Sims • Jones • Moran • Bardsley • Fox • Mooniaruck • Humphreys • **Heath 2** • Timm • Fletcher
Substitutes: Johnson J. (for Jones) • Heaton • Poole (for Collett) • Collett (for Fletcher) • Bruce

JUNIORS

Saturday 28 October 2000 **v WOLVERHAMPTON WANDERERS (home) • Drawn: 2-2**

Jowsey • Sims • Jones • Taylor • Hogg • Fox • Mooniaruck • Humphreys • Heath • Timm • **Richardson 2**
Substitutes: Bardsley • Heaton • Lawrence • Collett • Johnson E.

Saturday 4 November 2000 **v ASTON VILLA (away) • Drawn: 2-2**

Jowsey • Sims • Lawrence • Taylor • Hogg • **Fox** • Mooniaruck • Humphreys • **Heath** • Johnson E. • Richardson
Substitutes: Cogger (for Hogg) • Heaton • Poole • Collett • Jones

Saturday 11 November 2000 **v LIVERPOOL (home) • Won: 4-0**

Jowsey • Sims • Lawrence • **Taylor** • Cogger • Fox • Mooniaruck • Humphreys • Heath • **Johnson E.** • **Timm**
*Substitutes: Collett • Heaton • Bardsley • Bruce • **Poole** (for Johnson E.)*

Saturday 18 November 2000 **v MANCHESTER CITY (home) • Lost: 0-2**

Jowsey • Sims • Lawrence • Taylor • Hogg • Fox • Mooniaruck • Humphreys • Timm • Johnson E. • Richardson
Substitutes: Cogger • Heaton • Collett (for Richardson) • Jones • Bruce

Saturday 25 November 2000 **v EVERTON (home) • Won: 2-1**

Jowsey • Sims • Lawrence • Hogg • Cogger • Fox • **Mooniaruck** • Humphreys • **Poole** • Johnson E. • Richardson
Substitutes: Jones • Heaton • Collett • Moran • Bardsley

Saturday 2 December 2000 **v CREWE ALEXANDRA (home) • Won: 5-0**

Yeomans • Sims • Lawrence • Taylor • Cogger • **Fox 2** • Mooniaruck • Humphreys • Poole • **Johnson E.** • **Richardson**
*Substitutes: **Collett** (for Johnson E.) • Bardsley • Bruce • Moran*

Saturday 16 December 2000 **v BOLTON WANDERERS (away, at Trafford Training Centre) • Won: 3-2**

Yeomans • Sims • Lawrence • Taylor • Cogger • Fox • Mooniaruck • Humphreys • **Poole** • **Johnson E. 2** • Richardson
Substitutes: Collett (for Fox) • Jones • Bardsley • Timm • Johnson J.

Saturday 13 January 2001 **v EVERTON (away) • Won: 2-1**

Heaton • Sims • Lawrence • Stoor (trialist) • Cogger • **Fox** • Mooniaruck • Humphreys • Poole • **Johnson E.** • Richardson
Substitutes: Jones • Collett • Bardsley (for Stoor) • Bruce • Johnson J.

names in bold indicate goalscorers

v CREWE ALEXANDRA (away) • Won: 3-1   Saturday 27 January 2001

Heaton • Sims • Lawrence • Taylor • Cogger • Fox • Mooniaruck • Collett • **Heath 3** • Johnson E. • Richardson
Substitutes: Poole • Jones (for Lawrence) • Bardsley • Johnson J.

v BOLTON WANDERERS (home) • Won: 1-0   Saturday 3 February 2001

Heaton • Sims • Lawrence • Taylor • Cogger • Fox • Mooniaruck • Humphreys • **Heath** • Johnson E. • Richardson
Substitutes: Poole (for Humphreys) • Yeomans • Jones (for Richardson) • Bardsley • Johnson J.

v LIVERPOOL (away) • Drawn: 2-2   Saturday 10 February 2001

Heaton • Bardsley • Lawrence • Taylor • Cogger • Fox • Mooniaruck • **Humphreys** • Heath • **Johnson E.** • Richardson
Substitutes: Collett (for Lawrence) • Jones • Johnson J. (for Mooniaruck) • Byrne

v ASTON VILLA (home) • Won: 2-1   Saturday 17 February 2001

Heaton • Sims • Lawrence • Taylor • Cogger • **Fox** • Mooniaruck • **Humphreys** • Heath • Poole • Richardson
Substitutes: Collett (for Poole) • Johnson J. (for Heath) • Bardsley • Jones

v WOLVERHAMPTON WANDERERS (away) • Won: 2-0   Saturday 24 February 2001

Heaton • Sims • Lawrence • Taylor • Cogger • Fox • Mooniaruck • Humphreys • **Heath** • Johnson J. • Richardson
*Substitutes: Collett • Jones • Bardsley • **Timm** (for Johnson J.) • Byrne*

v BLACKBURN ROVERS (home) • Won: 1-0   Saturday 10 March 2001

Heaton • Sims • Lawrence • Taylor • Cogger • Fox • **Mooniaruck** • Humphreys • Heath • Johnson J. • Richardson
Substitutes: Johnson E. (for Johnson J.) • Collett • Jones • Bardsley

v MANCHESTER CITY (away) • Lost: 1-2   Saturday 24 March 2001

Heaton • Sims • Lawrence • Taylor • Cogger • Fox • **Mooniaruck** • Johnson E. • Heath • Johnson J. • Richardson
Substitutes: Poole (for Johnson J.) • Collett (for Richardson) • Jones • Bardsley • Byrne

v NEWCASTLE UNITED (away) • Won: 2-1   Saturday 31 March 2001

Heaton • Sims • Lawrence • Bardsley • Cogger • Fox • Mooniaruck • **Collett** • Heath • Poole • **Richardson**
Substitutes: Jones • Byrne • Picken (for Cogger) • Calliste • Eagles

Thursday 12 April 2001 v SUNDERLAND Play-Off, Group Two (away) • Drawn: 0-0

Heaton • Bardsley • Lawrence • Taylor • Cogger • Fox • Mooniaruck • Collett • Heath • Johnson E. • Richardson
Substitutes: Humphreys • Jowsey • Poole (for Mooniaruck) • Byrne • Picken

Saturday 21 April 2001 v LIVERPOOL Play-Off, Group Two (home) • Won: 2-1

Heaton • Sims • Lawrence • Bardsley • Cogger • Fox • Mooniaruck • Humphreys • **Heath** • **Poole** • Richardson
Substitutes: Collett (for Fox) • Jowsey • Jones • Byrne • Timm (for Heath)

Saturday 28 April 2001 v BLACKBURN ROVERS Play-Off, Group Two (home) • Drawn: 1-1

Heaton • Sims • Lawrence • Bardsley • Cogger • **Fox** • Mooniaruck • Humphreys • Poole • Timm • Richardson
Substitutes: Collett • Jowsey • Jones • Byrne • Picken (for Cogger)

United's Under 17s squad: (back row, from left to right) Lee Sims, Eddie Johnson, David Fox, Kalam Mooniaruck, Tom Heaton, John Cogger, Colin Heath, Chris Humphreys; (front row) Kris Taylor, Phil Bardsley, Lee Lawrence, Kieran Richardson, David Poole, Jemal Johnson, David Jones

UNDER 17s APPEARANCES

GOALSCORERS

Name	Appearances (as sub)	Name	Appearances (as sub)	Name	Goals (penalties)
MOONIARUCK • Kalam	26 (1)	BARDSLEY • Philip	10 (1)	HEATH • Colin	13
FOX • David	26	TIMM • Mads	7 (4)	FOX • David	7
SIMS • Lee	25	JOHNSON • Jemal	5 (6)	JOHNSON • Eddie	6
LAWRENCE • Lee	24	HOGG • Steven	4	RICHARDSON • Kieran	6
HUMPHREYS • Chris	23	MORAN • Martin	4	POOLE • David	5
RICHARDSON • Kieran	23	COLLETT • Ben	3 (9)	TIMM • Mads	5
TAYLOR • Kris	20	JONES • David	3 (5)	HUMPHREYS • Chris	4
HEATH • Colin	19	FLETCHER • Darren	2	MOONIARUCK • Kalam	3
COGGER • John	18 (1)	YEOMANS • Ryan	2	COLLETT • Ben	2
JOHNSON • Eddie	16 (2)	BRUCE • Alex	1 (2)	MORAN • Martin	1
JOWSEY • James	13	STOOR • Fredrik	1	TAYLOR • Kris	1
HEATON • Tommy	12	PICKEN • Philip	0 (2)		
POOLE • David	10 (6)				

FA PREMIER ACADEMY LEAGUE UNDER 17s

		P	W	D	L	F	A	Pts
GROUP B FINAL TABLE 2000-01	MANCHESTER UNITED	24	13	6	5	50	36	45
	Aston Villa	24	12	7	5	57	33	43
	Manchester City	24	13	3	8	48	34	42
	Wolverhampton Wanderers	24	10	4	10	36	44	34
	Liverpool	24	7	10	7	45	41	31
	Everton	24	7	6	11	42	42	27
	Bolton Wanderers	24	7	2	15	30	44	23
	Crewe Alexandra	24	6	4	14	23	49	22

FA PREMIER ACADEMY LEAGUE UNDER 17s PLAY-OFFS

		P	W	D	L	F	A	Pts
GROUP TWO FINAL TABLE 2000-01	Blackburn Rovers	3	2	1	0	8	4	7
	MANCHESTER UNITED	3	1	2	0	3	2	5
	Liverpool	3	1	0	2	5	6	3
	Sunderland	3	0	1	2	1	5	1

NIVEA UNDER 17s JUNIOR FOOTBALL TOURNAMENT – BLUDENZ, AUSTRIA

Saturday 14 April 2001   v USA SELECT XI Group A • Drawn: 0-0

Heaton • Sims • Lawrence • Taylor • Bardsley • Picken • Byrne • Collett • Poole • Johnson • Richardson
Substitutes: Eagles (for Byrne) • Calliste (for Poole)

Sunday 15 April 2001   v VORARLBERG COUNTRY SELECT XI (Austria)*

Due to heavy overnight snowfall and poor weather conditions the organisers decided that for each team one game would be replaced by a penalty shoot-out.
*Won: 9-7 on penalties Scorers: Heaton, Taylor, Bardsley, Byrne, Collett, Poole, Johnson, Richardson, Picken

Sunday 15 April 2001   v VfB STUTTGART (Germany) • Lost: 1-2

Heaton • Sims • Lawrence • Taylor • Bardsley • Picken • Byrne • Collett • Poole • **Johnson** • Richardson
Substitutes: Calliste (for Byrne) • Fox (for Collett)

Monday 16 April 2001   v AUSTRIA Semi-Final • Won: 1-0

Heaton • Sims • Eckersley • Taylor • Bardsley • Jones • Byrne • Collett • **Poole** • Johnson • Richardson
Substitutes: Lawrence (for Collett) • Eagles (for Byrne)

Monday 16 April 2001   v VfB STUTTGART (Germany) Final • Won: 3-0

Heaton • Sims • Lawrence • Taylor • Picken • Jones • Byrne • Collett • **Poole** • **Johnson 2** • Richardson
Substitute: Bardsley (for Poole)

TOURNAMENT SQUAD

Philip BARDSLEY	Eddie JOHNSON
Daniel BYRNE	David JONES
Ramon CALLISTE	Lee LAWRENCE
Ben COLLETT	Philip PICKEN
Christopher EAGLES	David POOLE
Adam ECKERSLEY	Kieran RICHARDSON
Mark FOX	Lee SIMS
Tommy HEATON	Kris TAYLOR

FRIENDLIES

v USA SUPERCLUBS NATIONAL TEAM (home) • Won: 2-0   Saturday 5 August 2000

Jowsey • Sims • Taylor K. • Moran M. • Cogger • Fox • Mooniaruck • Humphreys • **Johnson E.** • **Poole** • Jones D.
Substitutes: Johnson J. (for Sims) • Moran D. (for Jowsey) • Connor (for Moran M.) •
Bardsley (for Jones D.) • Bruce (for Humphreys)

v BELVEDERE (Republic of Ireland Tour) • Drawn: 0-0   Tuesday 8 August 2000

Jowsey • Sims • Lawrence • Taylor K. • Cogger • Fox • Mooniaruck • Humphreys • Heath • Poole • Bruce
Substitutes: Johnson E. (for Bruce) • Johnson J. (for Poole)

v DUBLIN SCHOOLBOYS' LEAGUE (Republic of Ireland Tour) • Won: 4-2   Thursday 10 August 2000

Jowsey • Sims • Eckersley • Taylor K. • Cogger • Fox • **Mooniaruck** • Humphreys • **Heath** • Johnson E. • **Bruce**
*Substitutes: Jones D. (for Eckersley) • Poole (for Humphreys) • **Johnson J.** (for Bruce)*

v BALLINASLOE (Republic of Ireland Tour) • Drawn: 0-0   Friday 11 August 2000

Moran D. • Picken • Eckersley • Taylor K. • Connor • Bardsley • Bruce • Johnson E. • Johnson J. • Poole • Jones D.
Substitutes: Mooniaruck (for Poole) • Heath (for Johnson J.) • Cogger (for Taylor K.) • Humphreys (for Eckersley)

v SAN DIEGO NOMADS (USA) (home) • Won: 1-0   Wednesday 16 August 2000

Jowsey • Sims • Richardson • Taylor K. • Cogger • Bardsley • Mooniaruck • Humphreys • **Heath** • Johnson J. • Johnson E.
Substitutes: Blandford (for Richardson) • Moran D. • Kouman (for Heath)

v WREXHAM (home) • Won: 10-0   Saturday 5 May 2001

Jowsey • Picken • Lawrence • Sims • Bardsley • **Jones D.** 2 • Timm • Byrne • **Gomez** 6 (trialist) • **Collett** • **Muntari** (trialist)
Substitutes: Fox (for Sims) • Moran D. • Humphreys (for Fox) • Mooniaruck (for Timm) •
Richardson (for Lawrence) • Fox (for Muntari)

MANCHESTER UNITED ACADEMY – UNDER 16s

Sunday 3 September 2000   v SUNDERLAND (home) • Won: 4-1

Heaton • Bardsley • Jones D. • Moran • Connor • Bruce • Kingsbury • **Kouman** • **Johnson J.** • Johnson E. • **Calliste**
Substitutes: Fox • Flanagan • Jones R. • Nevins

Sunday 1 October 2000   v ASTON VILLA (away) • Lost: 0-2

Heaton • Jones D. • Picken • Eckersley • Connor • Kouman • Bruce • Port • Johnson J. • Fox • Collett
Substitute: Flanagan

Sunday 8 October 2000   v BLACKBURN ROVERS (home) • Lost: 0-2

Heaton • Bardsley • Eckersley • Johnson E. • Connor • Jones D. • Byrne • Bruce • Poole • Timm • Collett
Substitute: Calliste

Wednesday 11 October 2000   v LIVERPOOL (home) • Drawn: 1-1

Heaton • Bardsley • Lawrence • Bruce • Connor • Moran • **Sims** • Collett • Johnson J. • Poole • Richardson
Substitutes: Byrne • Port • Eagles • Kingsbury

Sunday 29 October 2000   v BARNSLEY (home) • Won: 1-0

Heaton • Bardsley • Lawrence • **Bruce** • Connor • Moran • Byrne • Johnson E. • Johnson J. • Poole • Collett
Substitutes: Flanagan • Leather

Sunday 12 November 2000   v WREXHAM (home) • Drawn: 0-0

Heaton • Bardsley • Moran • Hogg • Connor • Jones D. • Bruce • Richardson • Johnson J. • Poole • Collett
Substitutes: Picken • Eckersley

Sunday 19 November 2000   v LEEDS UNITED (away) • Won: 5-0

Heaton • Bardsley • White • Leather • Connor • Jones D. • Picken • Bruce • **Flanagan 2** • **Kouman 2** • **Collett**

Sunday 26 November 2000   v LIVERPOOL (home) • Lost: 1-3

Heaton • Bardsley • Eckersley • Connor • Moran • **Jones D.** • Picken • Bruce • Flanagan • Kouman • Collett
Substitute: Nevins

names in bold indicate goalscorers

v BARNSLEY (home) • Won: 5-0 · Friday 8 December 2000

Yeomans • Bardsley • Lawrence • Hogg • Moran • **Jones D.** • **Byrne** • **Bruce** • Johnson J. • **Poole** • Collett
*Substitutes: Sims • Connor • **Johnson E.** • Calliste • Kouman*

v ASTON VILLA (at Moss Lane, Altrincham) • Won: 3-0 · Wednesday 20 December 2000

Heaton • Bardsley • **Lawrence** • Sims • Moran • **Jones D.** • Poole • Bruce • **Johnson J.** • Johnson E. • Collett
Substitute: Connor

v NEWCASTLE UNITED (away) • Lost: 0-2 · Sunday 28 January 2001

Yeomans • Nevins • White • Bardsley • Connor • Jones D. • Kingsbury • Bruce • Johnson J. • Poole • Eagles
Substitute: Flanagan

v LIVERPOOL (away) • Lost: 0-2 · Wednesday 7 February 2001

Heaton • Picken • Lawrence • Bardsley • Nevins • Jones D. • Byrne • Bruce • Johnson J. • Poole • Collett
Substitutes: Eagles • Calliste • Howard • Port

v LEICESTER CITY (away) • Won: 3-1 · Thursday 22 February 2001

Lee • Nevins • White • Bardsley • Howard • **Jones D.** • **Navaro** • Byrne • **Johnson J.** • Fox • Collett
Substitutes: Richardson • Flanagan • Nix • Greenwood

v NEWCASTLE UNITED (home) • Won: 1-0 · Sunday 25 February 2001

Heaton • Picken • Eckersley • Bardsley • Howard • **Jones D.** • Eagles • Byrne • Fox • Calliste • Collett
Substitutes: Kingsbury • Flanagan

v CREWE ALEXANDRA (home) • Won: 5-1 · Sunday 11 March 2001

Lee • Greenwood • Nix • Bardsley • Nevins • **Jones D.** • **Kingsbury** • **Byrne** • **Johnson E.** • Fox • **Collett**
Substitutes: Calliste • White

v MANCHESTER CITY (home) • Won: 3-1 · Sunday 18 March 2001

Lee • Picken • Eckersley • **Howard 2** • **Jones D.** • Poole • Byrne • Johnson J. • Johnson E. • Kouman • Collett
Substitutes: Kingsbury • Eagles

NORTHERN IRELAND MILK CUP
INTERNATIONAL YOUTH TOURNAMENT 2000 (UNDER 16s)

Monday 24 July 2000   v COUNTY ARMAGH (Northern Ireland) Group Six • Drawn: 1-1

Jowsey • Sims • Rankin • Taylor • Moran M. • Fox • Mooniaruck • Muirhead • **Heath** • Wood • Collett
Substitutes: Humphreys (for Wood) • Richardson (for Fox)

Tuesday 25 July 2000   v UNIVERSITAD CATOLICA (Chile) Group Six • Lost: 0-3

Jowsey • Sims • Rankin • Taylor • Cogger • Fox • Mooniaruck • Muirhead • Johnson • Richardson • Collett
Substitutes: Humphreys (for Collett) • Heath (for Johnson) • Poole (for Mooniaruck)

Wednesday 26 July 2000   v DUNDALK SCHOOLBOYS' LEAGUE (Republic of Ireland) Group Six • Won: 4-0

Moran D. • Sims • **Rankin (pen)** • Taylor • Cogger • Moran M. • **Mooniaruck** • Muirhead • Heath • **Poole** • Humphreys
Substitutes: Johnson (for Poole) • Richardson (for Humphreys) • Jones (for Muirhead)

Wednesday 26 July 2000   v WALES Quarter-Final • Won: 4-2

Moran D. • Sims • Rankin • **Taylor 2** • Cogger • Fox • Mooniaruck • Muirhead • Heath • **Johnson** • **Moran M.**
Substitutes: Collett (for Rankin) • Richardson (for Mooniaruck) • Jones (for Johnson)

Thursday 27 July 2000   v SUNDERLAND (England) Semi-Final • Lost: 0-2

Jowsey • Sims • Moran M. • Taylor • Cogger • Fox • Mooniaruck • Muirhead • Heath • Johnson • Collett
Substitutes: Richardson (for Collett) • Jones (for Moran M.)

Friday 28 July 2000   v WITS UNIVERSITY (South Africa) Third/Fourth Place Play-Off • Won: 3-0

Jowsey • Sims • **Jones** • Taylor • Cogger • Fox • **Mooniaruck** • Muirhead • **Heath** • Richardson • Collett

TOURNAMENT SQUAD

John COGGER	David JONES	David POOLE
Ben COLLETT	James JOWSEY	John RANKIN
David FOX	Kalam MOONIARUCK	Kieran RICHARDSON
Colin HEATH	David MORAN	Lee SIMS
Chris HUMPHREYS	Martin MORAN	Kris TAYLOR
Jemal JOHNSON	Ben MUIRHEAD	Neil WOOD

MANCHESTER UNITED ACADEMY – UNDER 15s

v USA SUPERCLUBS NATIONAL TEAM (home) • Drawn: 1-1   Wednesday 9 August 2000

Windram • Nevins • Nix • Lawlor • Howard • Jones (Reece) • Port • Eagles • Fox • Iniabere • White

*Substitutes: Hogg • Heaton • **Kitchen** • Laird • Thompson*

v SCUNTHORPE UNITED (away) • Won: 5-1   Monday 14 August 2000

Heaton • Nevins • **White** • Greenwood • **Howard** • Eagles • Kingsbury • **Kouman** • **Fox** • Kitchen • **Nix**

Substitutes: Hogg • Yeomans • Flanagan • Leather • Thompson

v BURY (home) • Won: 6-1   Sunday 20 August 2000

Heaton • **Thompson** • Nix • Lawlor • Howard • Greenwood • Kingsbury • **Jones (Reece)** • **Fox 2** • **Kitchen** • **Iniabere**

Substitutes: Bolton • Thompson

v PRESTON NORTH END (away) • Lost: 0-1   Sunday 27 August 2000

Heaton • Nevins • Eckersley • Greenwood • Howard • Guthrie • Thompson • Jones (Reece) • Fox • Flanagan • Iniabere

Substitute: Salmon A.

v EVERTON (home, Moss Lane, Altrincham) • Won: 5-1   Wednesday 20 September 2000

Heaton • Nevins • Eckersley • Picken • Howard • Greenwood • Kingsbury • Eagles • **Fox** • **Flanagan 2** • **Kouman**

*Substitutes: **Kitchen** • Coffey • Leather • Hogg*

v LIVERPOOL (away) • Drawn: 3-3   Wednesday 27 September 2000

Yeomans • Greenwood • Nix • Picken • Leather • Eckersley • Kingsbury • Eagles • Fox • **Calliste 2** • **Kouman**

Substitutes: Kitchen • Thompson • Howard • Coffey

v ASTON VILLA (away) • Lost: 0-4   Sunday 1 October 2000

Yeomans • Greenwood • Coffey • Thompson • Leather • Howard • Nevins • Eagles • Kitchen • Calliste • Nix

Substitute: Guthrie

v BARNSLEY (away) • Won: 3-2   Wednesday 4 October 2000

Yeomans • Picken • Nix • Greenwood • Leather • **Kouman** • Thompson • Eagles • **Flanagan 2** • Calliste • Coffey

Substitutes: Kitchen • Fox

ACADEMY

Sunday 8 October 2000 — **v BLACKBURN ROVERS (away) • Lost: 0-1**

Yeomans • Picken • Nix • Greenwood • Leather • Kouman • Thompson • Eagles • Fox • Flanagan • Port
Substitutes: Coffey • Kitchen

Sunday 22 October 2000 — **v HUDDERSFIELD TOWN (away) • Lost: 0-1**

Heaton • Greenwood • Eckersley • Picken • Howard • Nix • Thompson • Port • Flanagan • Fox • Coffey
Substitutes: Leather • Nevins • Hogg

Sunday 5 November 2000 — **v STOKE CITY (home) • Won: 3-1**

Yeomans • Picken • Eckersley • Leather • Howard • **Kouman** • Eagles • Kingsbury • **Flanagan** • Calliste • **Coffey**
Substitutes: Fox • Kitchen • Greenwood • Thompson

Sunday 26 November 2000 — **v LIVERPOOL (away) • Lost: 0-2**

Yeomans • Greenwood • Nix • Howard • Leather • Eagles • Jones (Richard) • Jones (Reece) • Calliste • Fox • Port

Sunday 3 December 2000 — **v BOLTON WANDERERS (home) • Won: 2-1**

Lee • Greenwood • White • Eckersley • Leather • **Jones (Reece)** • Kingsbury • Eagles • Calliste • **Kouman** • Port
Substitutes: Fox • Flanagan • Howard • Nevins

Wednesday 12 December 2000 — **v LEEDS UNITED (away) • Won: 4-1**

Yeomans • Greenwood • Eckersley • Howard • Leather • Kouman • Eagles • Jones (Reece) • Fox • **Calliste 4** • Kingsbury
Substitutes: Flanagan • Nevins • White • Port

Sunday 14 January 2001 — **v STOKE CITY (home) • Lost: 0-1**

Heaton • Nevins • White • Howard • Leather • Kouman • Hallit • Jones (Reece) • Flanagan • Fox • Woods
Substitutes: Greenwood • Port • Calliste

Sunday 28 January 2001 — **v SHEFFIELD WEDNESDAY (away) • Won: 3-0**

Lee • Greenwood • Talbot • Howard • Leather • Guthrie • Port • Jones (Reece) • Fox • **Calliste 2** • **Nix**

names in bold indicate goalscorers

v LIVERPOOL (home) • Drawn: 2-2   Sunday 4 February 2001

Yeomans • **Picken 2** • Eckersley • Howard • Nevins • Port • Kingsbury • Eagles • Flanagan • Fox • Nix

Substitutes: White • Talbot

v DERBY COUNTY (home) • Lost: 2-3   Sunday 11 February 2001

Yeomans • Picken • Talbot • Greenwood • Howard • **Nix** • Port • **Eagles** • Flanagan • Calliste • White

Substitutes: Fox • Jones (Reece) • Nevins

v EVERTON (away) • Won: 3-0   Sunday 18 February 2001

Yeomans • Greenwood • Eckersley • Nevins • **Howard** • Jones (Reece) • Eagles • Picken • **Marsh** • **Fox** • Nix

Substitute: White

v JAPAN XI (at Lancashire County FA, Leyland) • Won: 3-2   Thursday 15 March 2001

Lee • Pickin • Eckersley • Nevins • Howard • Jones (Reece) • Port • Eagles • **Fox** • Calliste • White

Substitutes: Kouman 2 • Kingsbury

v LEEDS UNITED (away) • Won: 2-0   Saturday 31 March 2001

Lee • Greenwood • Eckersley • Nevins • Howard • Jones (Reece) • Kingsbury • Kouman • **Flanagan 2** • Fox • Leather

v SHEFFIELD WEDNESDAY (home) • Won: 6-4   Sunday 8 April 2001

Newman • Picken • Eckersley • Nevins • Howard • Jones (Reece) • **Kingsbury** • Eagles • Fox • **Kouman 3** • **Nix**

*Substitutes: Leather • White • Greenwood • **Marsh** • Jones (Richard)*

v ASTON VILLA (home) • Won: 7-0   Sunday 22 April 2001

Heaton • Greenwood • Picken • Nevins • Howard • **Jones (Reece)** • Port • Eagles • **Calliste** • **Kouman 4** • White

*Substitutes: Fox • Flanagan • Leather • Marsh • **Jones (Richard)***

v BARNSLEY (home) • Won: 3-0   Thursday 26 April 2001

Heaton • Nevins • Picken • Howard • Leather • Kouman • Kingsbury • Eagles • **Flanagan** • **Fox 2** • Nix

Substitutes: Greenwood • Marsh • Jones (Richard)

Sunday 29 April 2001   v LEEDS UNITED (home) • Won: 5-1

Lee • Greenwood • White • Leather • Howard • **Jones (Reece)** • Kingsbury • Eagles • **Fox 2** • **Calliste** • Port
Substitutes: Kouman • Picken • Flanagan • Nix • Nevins • Marsh • ***Jones (Richard)***

Sunday 6 May 2001   v HUDDERSFIELD TOWN (home) • Won: 4-1

Heaton • Nevins • Greenwood • Leather • Howard • Jones (Reece) • Marsh • Eagles • **Flanagan** • **Kouman** • **Nix 2**
Substitutes: Picken • Byrne

MANCHESTER UNITED ACADEMY – UNDER 14s

Sunday 3 September 2000   v SUNDERLAND (away) • Lost: 0-2

Lee • Wilcox-Crookes • Adams N. • Simpson • Oxley • Guthrie • Salmon A. • McMahon • Marsh • Grimes • Bolton
Substitutes: White • Salmon K. • Holt • Hill • Usher

Sunday 1 October 2000   v ASTON VILLA (home) • Won: 6-2

Hartshorn • Wilcox-Crookes • Adams N. • Simpson • Oxley • McMahon • **Salmon A.** • Jones • **Marsh** • **Grimes 3** • Salmon K.
*Substitutes: **White** • Lee • Bolton*

Wednesday 4 October 2000   v LIVERPOOL (away) • Won: 5-1

Lee • Wilcox-Crookes • Adams N. • Simpson • **Oxley** • Guthrie • Salmon A. • Jones • **Marsh 3** • Grimes • McMahon
Substitutes: White • Salmon K. • Bolton • Holt

Sunday 8 October 2000   v BLACKBURN ROVERS (home) • Lost: 1-2

Hartshorn • Wilcox-Crookes • Adams N. • Simpson • Oxley • Guthrie • Salmon A. • Jones • Marsh • **Grimes** • McMahon
Substitutes: White • Lee • Salmon K. • Bolton • Holt

Thursday 12 October 2000   v BARNSLEY (away) • Won: 4-1

Hartshorn • Wilcox-Crookes • Adams N. • Simpson • Oxley • **Guthrie 3** • Salmon A. • Jones • Marsh • Grimes • McMahon
*Substitutes: **White** • Lee • Salmon K. • Bolton • Holt*

names in bold indicate goalscorers

v HUDDERSFIELD TOWN (home) • Won: 3-1   Sunday 22 October 2000

Hartshorn • Simpson • Adams N. • Holt • Oxley • **Guthrie 2** • Salmon K. • **Jones** • White • Grimes • McMahon

Substitutes: Salmon A. • Lee • Wilcox-Crookes

v LEEDS UNITED (home) • Drawn: 3-3   Sunday 19 November 2000

Lee • Simpson • Adams N. • Holt • Oxley • **Guthrie** • Salmon K. • Wilcox-Crookes • White • **Grimes 2** • McMahon

Substitute: Salmon A.

v LIVERPOOL (home) • Won: 4-3   Sunday 26 November 2000

Lee • Simpson • Adams N. • Holt • Oxley • **Guthrie** • Salmon K. • **Wilcox-Crookes** • **Marsh** • **Grimes** • McMahon

Substitute: White

v BOLTON WANDERERS (home) • Drawn: 0-0   Sunday 3 December 2000

Ratchford • Simpson • Adams N. • Holt • Oxley • Guthrie • Salmon K. • Wilcox-Crookes • Marsh • Grimes • McMahon

Substitute: White

v STOKE CITY (home) • Drawn: 2-2   Sunday 14 January 2001

Lee • Wilcox-Crookes • Adams N. • Holt • Oxley • Guthrie • Salmon K. • Jones • **Marsh** • **Grimes** • McMahon

Substitute: Salmon A.

v SHEFFIELD WEDNESDAY (home) • Drawn: 1-1   Sunday 28 January 2001

Ratchford • Wilcox-Crookes • Adams N. • Holt • Oxley • McMahon • Salmon A. • White • **Marsh** • Grimes • Burns

v LIVERPOOL (away) • Won: 6-2   Sunday 4 February 2001

Lee • Wilcox-Crookes • Adams N. • Holt • Oxley • **Guthrie** • Salmon A. • **Jones** • **Marsh 2** • **Grimes 2** • McMahon

Substitute: Salmon K.

v LEEDS UNITED (away) • Lost: 0-4   Tuesday 12 February 2001

Lee • Wilcox-Crookes • Adams N. • Holt • Oxley • Guthrie • Salmon A. • Jones • Marsh • Grimes • McMahon

Substitutes: Salmon K. • Simpson • White

Sunday 18 February 2001   **v EVERTON (home) • Won: 3-1**

Lee • Wilcox-Crookes • Adams N. • Holt • Oxley • **Guthrie** • Salmon A. • Jones • Salmon K. • **White 2** • McMahon
Substitute: Simpson

Tuesday 20 February 2001   **v DERBY COUNTY (home) • Lost: 0-2**

Lee • Wilcox-Crookes • Adams N. • Holt • Oxley • Guthrie • Salmon K. • Salmon A. • Marsh • White • McMahon

Sunday 11 March 2001   **v CREWE ALEXANDRA (away) • Drawn: 0-0**

Ratchford • Wilcox-Crookes • Adams N. • Holt • Oxley • Guthrie • McMahon • Jones • Marsh • Grimes • Fathali-Siah
Substitutes: White • Salmon K. • Salmon A. • Wharton

Sunday 18 March 2001   **v MANCHESTER CITY (away) • Lost: 1-7**

Daniels • Wilcox-Crookes • Adams N. • Jones • Oxley • Guthrie • Salmon K. • McMahon • **Marsh** • Grimes • Fathali-Siah
Substitute: Salmon A.

Wednesday 28 March 2001   **v EVERTON (home, at Moss Lane, Altrincham) • Lost: 1-3**

Lee • Wilcox-Crookes • Adams N. • Adams R. • Oxley • Guthrie • Salmon A. • McMahon • **Marsh** • Grimes • Fathali-Siah
Substitutes: Salmon K. • Burns

Saturday 31 March 2001   **v LEEDS UNITED (home) • Lost: 0-1**

Daniels • Wilcox-Crookes • Adams N. • Jones • Oxley • Guthrie • Salmon K. • Salmon A. • Marsh • Grimes • Fathali-Siah

MANCHESTER UNITED ACADEMY – UNDER 13s

v SUNDERLAND (away) • Drawn: 0-0   Sunday 3 September 2000

Daniels • Hunt • Lea • Priest • Shawcross • Baker • Evans • Baguley • Parillon • Campbell • Burns
Substitutes: Prince • Ratchford • Nix

v MANCHESTER CITY (home) • Lost: 0-1   Sunday 24 September 2000

Jones • Prince • Moore • Baker • Shawcross • Lea • Evans • Baguley • Parillon • Campbell • Burns
Substitute: Howard

v ASTON VILLA (home) • Lost: 0-3   Sunday 1 October 2000

Jones • Kendrick • Lea • Baker • Shawcross • Nix • Evans • Baguley • Burns • Brandy • Moore

v BLACKBURN ROVERS (away) • Drawn: 1-1   Sunday 8 October 2000

Daniels • Kendrick • Howard • Baker • Shawcross • Evans • Parillon • Baguley • Burns • Brandy • Moore
*Substitute: **Campbell***

v BARNSLEY (away) • Won: 6-1   Thursday 12 October 2000

Daniels • Kendrick • Howard • **Baker** • Shawcross • Evans • **Parillon** • Baguley • **Burns 3** • Campbell • Moore
*Substitutes: Drinkwater • **Mulholland** • Ellwood*

v HUDDERSFIELD TOWN (away) • Drawn: 1-1   Sunday 22 October 2000

Ratchford • Prince • Howard • Baker • Shawcross • Evans • **Parillon** • Baguley • Burns • Campbell • Moore
Substitutes: Ellwood • Mulholland

v EVERTON (away) • Drawn: 2-2   Tuesday 24 October 2000

Ratchford • Kendrick • Howard • Baker • Shawcross • Evans • **Parillon 2** • Baguley • Burns • Campbell • Moore
Substitute: Mulholland

v STOKE CITY (home) • Won: 4-1   Sunday 5 November 2000

Daniels • Baker • Lea • Moore • Shawcross • Evans • Mulholland • **Baguley** • **Burns 2** • Parillon • Howard
*Substitutes: Prince • Ratchford • **Campbell***

ACADEMY

Sunday 19 November 2000 **v LEEDS UNITED (home) • Lost: 1-5**

Ratchford • Kendrick • Howard • Baker • Shawcross • Evans • Parillon • Baguley • Burns • Campbell • Mulholland (1 o.g.)
Substitutes: Lea • Daniels • Moore

Sunday 26 November 2000 **v LIVERPOOL (away) • Lost: 1-2**

Daniels • Kendrick • Howard • Baker • Shawcross • Lea • **Baguley** • Lee • Burns • Parillon • Moore
Substitutes: Rowe • Ratchford

Sunday 3 December 2000 **v BOLTON WANDERERS (away) • Won: 3-2**

Daniels • Kendrick • Lea • Baker • Shawcross • **Campbell** • Parillon • Lee • **Burns** • **Evans** • Moore
Substitute: Howard

Sunday 14 January 2001 **v STOKE CITY (home) • Won: 4-0**

Ratchford • Kendrick • Howard • Baker • Shawcross • Lee • Campbell • Baguley • **Burns** • **Evans** • **Moore**
*Substitutes: **Parillon** • Daniels • Hewson*

Sunday 28 January 2001 **v SHEFFIELD WEDNESDAY (away) • Won: 3-2**

Daniels • Kendrick • Drinkwater • Baker • Shawcross • Lee • Campbell • **Baguley** • **Brandy** • Evans • **Moore**
Substitute: Hewson

Thursday 1 February 2001 **v LEEDS UNITED (away) • Lost: 0-6**

Ratchford • Kendrick • Moore • Baker • Shawcross • Lee • Hewson • Baguley • Burns • Evans • Campbell
Substitutes: Parillon • Daniels

Sunday 4 February 2001 **v LIVERPOOL (away) • Lost: 0-4**

Daniels • Kendrick • Drinkwater • Moore • Baker • Lee • Campbell • Baguley • Burns • Evans • Parillon
Substitutes: Howard • Ratchford

Sunday 11 February 2001 **v BOLTON WANDERERS (home) • Won: 4-2**

Ratchford • Kendrick • Drinkwater • Baker • Moore • Lee • **Campbell** • Baguley • **Burns 2** • Parillon • **Howard**
Substitute: Daniels

names in bold indicate goalscorers

v EVERTON (home) • Lost: 1-4 ⟨ Sunday 18 February 2001 ⟩

Daniels • Kendrick • Drinkwater • Moore • Baker • Lee • Campbell • Baguley • **Burns** • Parillon • Howard

Substitute: Evans

v HUDDERSFIELD TOWN (home) • Lost: 3-4 ⟨ Tuesday 20 February 2001 ⟩

Daniels • Hewson • Howard • Simpson • Baker • Lee • **Evans** • Baguley • **Burns** • Parillon • Moore

*Substitute: **Campbell***

v BLACKBURN ROVERS (home) • Lost: 1-2 ⟨ Sunday 25 February 2001 ⟩

Jones • Hewson • Drinkwater • Simpson • Baker • Lee • Evans • Baguley • Burns • **Parillon** • Moore

Substitutes: Howard • Daniels • Lea

v CREWE ALEXANDRA (home) • Drawn: 1-1 ⟨ Sunday 11 March 2001 ⟩

Daniels • Hewson • Drinkwater • Lea • Baker • Lee • **Parillon** • Baguley • Burns • Evans • Howard

Substitute: Moore

v MANCHESTER CITY (away) • Lost: 0-7 ⟨ Sunday 18 March 2001 ⟩

Ratchford • Hewson • Drinkwater • Baker • Lea • Lee • Parillon • Baguley • Burns • Evans • Howard

Substitute: Moore

v LIVERPOOL (away) • Won: 1-0 ⟨ Thursday 29 March 2001 ⟩

Daniels • Hewson • Howard • Drinkwater • Baker • Lee • Parillon • **Baguley** • Burns • Evans • Lee

Substitute: Moore

v LEEDS UNITED (home) • Lost: 2-3 ⟨ Sunday 1 April 2001 ⟩

Robinson • Kendrick • Howard • Drinkwater • Baker • Lee • Parillon • **Baguley 2** • Burns • Evans • Moore

Substitute: Hewson

v SHEFFIELD WEDNESDAY (home) • Won: 5-1 ⟨ Sunday 8 April 2001 ⟩

Ratchford • Hewson • Drinkwater • Lea • Baker • Lee • **Parillon** • Baguley • **Burns 3** • **Evans** • Howard

Substitute: Moore

Sunday 22 April 2001   **v ASTON VILLA (away) • Lost: 3-5**

Daniels • Hewson • Drinkwater • Lea • Baker • Lee • Parillon • Baguley • Burns • **Evans** • **Moore**
Substitutes: Howard • **Kuba-Kuba**

Thursday 26 April 2001   **v BARNSLEY (away) • Won: 4-2**

Daniels • Baker • Drinkwater • Lea • **Howard** • Lee • Parillon • **Baguley** • **Burns** • Brandy • Moore
Substitute: **Kuba-Kuba**

Sunday 6 May 2001   **v HUDDERSFIELD TOWN (home) • Lost: 0-1**

Daniels • Baker • Howard • Lea • Drinkwater • Lee • Thompson • Baguley • Burns • Parillon • Moore
Substitute: Brandy

UNDER 12s

SQUAD

Febian BRANDY
James CHESTER
Thomas CLEVERLEY
Theodore COLEMAN
Alexander DRINKWATER
Richard ECKERSLEY
Lee HANSON
Sam HEWSON
Adam INGRAM-HUGHES
Zacharaiah JONES
Matthew KENDRICK
Luke MORGAN

David OWENS
Daniel ROWE
Thomas ROWE
Joseph THOMPSON

UNDER 11s

SQUAD

Nicholas BLACKMAN
Antonio BRYAN
Jacob BUTTERFIELD
Jonathan CROMPTON
James DERBYSHIRE
Daniel DRINKWATER
Dominic INGRAM-HUGHES
Matthew MAINWARING
Daniel McDONALD
Michael McFALONE
Jay McGARVEY
Thomas MELLOR

Adriano MOKE
Matthew ROBERTS
Alex SKIDMORE
James WAGGETT
Gregory WILKINSON

UNDER 10s

SQUAD

Kristopher DICKINSON
Joseph DUDGEON
Shaun JOHNSON
Matthew JONES
Lee LATHAM
Jacob LAWLOR
Ben MARSHALL
Oliver NORWOOD
Daniel WELBECK

Jordan WHITE
David WILLIAMS
Jake WILLIAMS
Matthew WILLIAMS

UNDER 9s

SQUAD

Nicholas AJOSE
Ryan BARROW
Reece BROWN
Brad BYRNE
Mark DUNCAN
Thomas GARNETT
Peter GREGSON
Sam ILLINGWORTH
William MELLOR

Steven MURTY
Justin PICKERING
Oliver PLATT
Matthew REAM

HSBC SOUVENIR CUP, MAURITIUS (UNDER 15s)

v MAURITIUS YOUNG STARS • Won: 2-0 — Sunday 27 May 2001

Heaton • Picken • Howard • Nevins • Eckersley • Kingsbury • Eagles • Jones • Nix • Kouman • Flanagan
*Substitutes: Lee (for Heaton) • Leather (for Howard) • Port (for Kingsbury) • Greenwood (for Jones) •
White (for Nix) • Fox (for Kouman) •* **Calliste 2** *(for Flanagan) • Hogg*

v MAURITIUS YOUNG STARS • Won: 5-2 — Wednesday 30 May 2001

Heaton • Picken • Howard • Leather • Eckersley • Port • **Eagles 2** • **Kouman** • White • Fox • Flanagan
Substitutes: Kingsbury (for Port) • Jones (for Eagles) • Nevins (for Kouman) • Nix (for White) •
Calliste 2 *(for Flanagan) • Lee • Hogg • Greenwood*

v MAURITIUS YOUNG STARS • Won: 5-0 — Friday 1 June 2001

Lee • Picken • Nevins • Howard • Eckersley • Port • Eagles • Jones • Nix • **Flanagan** • **Calliste 2**
*Substitutes: Leather (for Nevins) • Hogg (for Eckersley) • Kingsbury (for Port) •
White (for Jones) •* **Kouman** *(for Nix) •* **Fox** *(for Flanagan) • Heaton • Greenwood*

TOURNAMENT SQUAD

Ramone CALLISTE	Chris KINGSBURY
Chris EAGLES	Amadou KOUMAN
Adam ECKERSLEY	Wayne LEATHER
Callum FLANAGAN	Tommy LEE
Mark FOX	Adrian NEVINS
Ross GREENWOOD	Kyle NIX
Tom HEATON	Phillip PICKEN
Steven HOGG	Graham PORT
Mark HOWARD	Chris WHITE
Reece JONES	

FIFTH INTERNATIONAL FRIENDLY CHAMPIONSHIP OF SEVEN-A-SIDE FOOTBALL (UNDER 13s) – TENERIFE, SPAIN

Wednesday 27 December 2000   v FC BARCELONA (Spain) Group One • Lost: 0-4

Daniels • Drinkwater • Kendrick • Parillon • Hewson • Evans • Brandy
Substitutes: Chester • Hanson • Rowe • Thompson

Wednesday 27 December 2000   v CANARY ISLANDS SELECT (Spain) Group One • Won: 2-1

Jones • Drinkwater • Kendrick • Parillon • Hewson • Evans • **Brandy**
*Substitute: **Thompson***

Wednesday 27 December 2000   v JUVENTUS (Italy) Group One • Won: 1-0

Jones • Drinkwater • Kendrick • Thompson • Hewson • Evans • **Brandy**
Substitute: Parillon

Thursday 28 December 2000   v CF REAL MADRID (Spain) Group One • Drawn: 0-0

Jones • Drinkwater • Kendrick • Parillon • Hewson • Evans • Brandy
Substitute: Thompson

TOURNAMENT SQUAD

Febian BRANDY
James CHESTER
Luke DANIELS
Alex DRINKWATER
Gareth EVANS
Lee HANSON

Sam HEWSON
Zak JONES
Matt KENDRICK
Ashley PARILLON
Danny ROWE
Joe THOMPSON

INTERNATIONAL INDOOR FIVE-A-SIDE FOOTBALL TOURNAMENT 'EUROKIDS' ROTTERDAM, HOLLAND (UNDER 13s)

Thursday 4 January 2001
v SPARTA ROTTERDAM (Holland) Pool One • Won: 4-3
Scorers: *Parillon 2, Hanson, Eckersley*

Thursday 4 January 2001
v CLUB BRUGGE (Belgium) Pool One • Won: 6-1
Scorers: *Brandy 2, Evans 2, Hanson 2*

Friday 5 January 2001
v SC FEYENOORD (Holland) Pool One • Lost: 2-3
Scorer: *Brandy 2*

Friday 5 January 2001
v PSV EINDHOVEN (Holland) Pool One • Lost: 1-4
Scorer: *Parillon*

Saturday 6 January 2001
v SC FEYENOORD (Holland) Third/Fourth Place Play-Off • Won: 2-1
Scorers: *Brandy, Hanson*

TOURNAMENT SQUAD

Febian BRANDY
Tom CLEVERLEY
Alex DRINKWATER
Richard ECKERSLEY
Gareth EVANS
Lee HANSON
Ashley PARILLON
Aaron RATCHFORD

TOURNOI SANS FRONTIERE
(UNDER 12s/13s) 2001, SENS, FRANCE

Friday 13 April 2001

v OLYMPIQUE LYONNAIS (France) First Phase • Drawn: 0-0

Daniels • Cleverley • Drinkwater • Kendrick • Chester • Lee • Thompson • Hewson • Brandy • Owens • Hanson
Substitute: Eckersley (for Drinkwater)

Saturday 14 April 2001

v PARIS ST GERMAIN (France) First Phase • Won: 3-0

Daniels • Ingram-Hughes • Eckersley • Kendrick • Chester • **Thompson** • **Rowe D. 2** • Brandy • Coleman • Lee • Rowe T.
Substitute: Hanson (for Coleman)

Saturday 14 April 2001

v FC METZ (France) First Phase • Lost: 0-3

Daniels • Cleverley • Ingram-Hughes • Drinkwater • Eckersley • Rowe D. • Hewson • Owens • Rowe T. • Hanson • Coleman

Saturday 14 April 2001

v RENNES (France) Second Phase • Lost: 0-1

Daniels • Cleverley • Drinkwater • Kendrick • Chester • Lee • Thompson • Hewson • Brandy • Rowe T. • Hanson
Substitutes: Rowe D. (for Thompson) • Owens (for Cleverley)

Saturday 14 April 2001

v RSC ANDERLECHT (Belgium) Second Phase • Drawn: 1-1

Daniels • Cleverley • Kendrick • Chester • Drinkwater • Hewson • Rowe D. • Lee • Owens • **Brandy** • Hanson
Substitute: Thompson (for Rowe D.)

Saturday 14 April 2001

v NANTES (France) Second Phase • Won: 3-1

Daniels • Cleverley • Kendrick • Chester • Drinkwater • **Rowe D.** • Hewson • **Lee** • **Hanson** • Brandy • Rowe T.

Sunday 15 April 2001

v OLYMPIQUE LYONNAIS (France) Fifth/Sixth Place Play-Off • Won: 2-1

Daniels • Eckersley • Ingram-Hughes • Chester • Drinkwater • Rowe D. • Lee • Thompson • Rowe T. • **Brandy** • Coleman
*Substitutes: Kendrick (for Ingram-Hughes) • Hewson (for Thompson) • Owens (for Rowe T.) • **Hanson** (for Coleman)*

TOURNAMENT SQUAD

Febian BRANDY	Richard ECKERSLEY	David OWENS
James CHESTER	Lee HANSON	Danny ROWE
Tom CLEVERLEY	Sam HEWSON	Tom ROWE
Theo COLEMAN	Adam INGRAM-HUGHES	Joe THOMPSON
Luke DANIELS	Matthew KENDRICK	
Alex DRINKWATER	Kieron LEE	

OTHER EVENTS AT OLD TRAFFORD

PUBLIC TRAINING SESSION | Friday 11 August 2000 |

(Sir Alex Ferguson, Steve McClaren and the Manchester United First Team Squad)

Attendance: 4,332

RUGBY SUPER LEAGUE GRAND FINAL | Saturday 14 October 2000 |

ST HELENS 29	WIGAN 16
Tries: Hoppe	Tries: Farrell
Joynt 2	Hodgson
Tuilagi	Smith T.
Jonkers	Goals: Farrell 2
Goals: Long 4	
Drop Goal: Sculthorpe	

Attendance: 58,132

RUGBY LEAGUE WORLD CUP FINAL | Saturday 25 November 2000 |

AUSTRALIA 40	NEW ZEALAND 12
Tries: Gidley	Tries: Vainkolo
Hindmarsh	Carroll
Lockyer	Goals: Paul H. 2
Sailor 2	
Fittler	
Barrett	
Goals: Rogers 6	

Attendance: 44,329

FA CUP (Sponsored by AXA) SEMI-FINAL | Sunday 8 April 2001 |

ARSENAL 2	TOTTENHAM HOTSPUR 1
Vieira, Pires	Doherty

Attendance: 63,541

BEAMED-BACK LIVE TO OLD TRAFFORD | Saturday 28 April 2001 |

MIDDLESBROUGH 0	MANCHESTER UNITED 2
	Neville P., Beckham

Attendance: 4,479

GENERAL INFORMATION

During the football season the Membership & Supporters' Club office hours are as follows:

Monday to Friday: 9.00am – 5.00pm
Home match days: 9.00am – kick-off
(and 20 minutes after the game)

The office will be open one hour prior to departure to our away venues.

MEMBERSHIP

Once we deem membership has reached its capacity, our books will close for the season and no further applications will be accepted. In the main, sales of match tickets for home games are restricted to members. It is therefore important to note that anyone wishing to attend a home game must become a member. Application forms are available upon request.

MEMBERS' PERSONAL ACCIDENT INSURANCE

Under our special personal accident insurance policy with Lloyds Underwriters, all members are insured whilst in attendance and travelling to and from the stadium (until safe return to current place of residence), for all competitive games played by the Manchester United first team, both home and away, anywhere in the world.

The following accidental death and bodily injury benefits apply:

1.   Death £10,000 (limited to £1,000 for persons under 16 years of age).
2.   Total and irrecoverable loss of sight of both eyes £10,000.
3.   Total and irrecoverable loss of sight in one eye £5,000.
4.   Loss of two limbs £10,000.
5.   Loss of one limb £5,000.
6.   Total and irrecoverable loss of sight in one eye and loss of one limb £10,000.
7.   Permanent Total Disablement (other than total loss of sight of one or both eyes or loss of limb) £10,000.

The above is subject to the policy conditions and exclusions. Further details are available from the Membership Secretary to whom any enquiries should be addressed.

BRANCHES OF THE SUPPORTERS' CLUB

A full list of all our official branches of the supporters club can be found on pages 218 to 224.

AWAY TRAVEL

Domestic Games:

All Club Members, which includes Private Box holders, Executive Suite & Club Class Members and Season Ticket holders, are automatically enrolled in our Away Travel Club and, as such, are entitled to book coach travel from Old Trafford to all Premiership venues. Full details can be found on the opposite page.

How to make a Booking:

You can book a place on a coach, subject to availability upon personal application at the Membership Office, in which case you must quote your MUFC customer number. Alternatively, you can make a postal application by submitting the relevant payment, a stamped addressed envelope and a covering letter quoting your MUFC customer number. Telephone reservations are also acceptable if making payment by credit/debit card. Cancellations must be made in advance of the day of the game.

Car Park attendants will be on duty should you wish to park your car on one of our car parks before travelling to an away game. This service is offered at no extra charge but we wish to point out that the Club will not be held responsible for any damage or theft from your vehicle.

Members are advised to check match ticket availability before booking a place on a coach. Details can be obtained by telephoning our Ticket and Match Information line on **0161-868-8020**.

MEMBERS' COACH TRAVEL FROM OLD TRAFFORD

Opponents	Executive Coach	Luxury Coach	*Departure Time	**Estimated Return Time to Old Trafford
Arsenal	£20.00	£15.00	8.30 am	9.30 pm
Aston Villa	£14.00	£10.00	11.30 am	7.30 pm
Blackburn Rovers	£11.00	£8.00	1.00 pm	6.15 pm
Bolton Wanderers	£11.00	£6.00	1.00 pm	6.15 pm
Charlton Athletic	£20.00	£15.00	8.00 am	10.00 pm
Chelsea	£20.00	£15.00	8.30 am	9.30 pm
Derby County	£12.00	£9.00	11.00 am	8.00 pm
Everton	£11.00	£8.00	1.00 pm	6.15 pm
Fulham	£20.00	£15.00	8.30 am	9.30 pm
Ipswich Town	£21.00	£16.00	8.30 am	10.30 pm
Leeds United	£11.00	£8.00	1.00 pm	6.15 pm
Leicester City	£12.00	£9.00	11.00 am	8.00 pm
Liverpool	£11.00	£8.00	1.00 pm	6.15 pm
Middlesbrough	£15.00	£11.00	11.00 am	8.00 pm
Newcastle United	£17.00	£13.00	10.30 am	8.30 pm
Southampton	£20.00	£15.00	8.30 am	10.00 pm
Sunderland	£17.00	£13.00	10.30 am	8.30 pm
Tottenham Hotspur	£20.00	£15.00	9.00 am	9.30 pm
West Ham United	£20.00	£15.00	8.30 am	9.30 pm
Millennium Stadium, Cardiff	£22.00	£18.00	7.00 am	11.00 pm

All times based on games with a 3.00pm kick-off
* Departure times are subject to change and it is vital to check the actual time when making your booking
** Return times shown are only estimated and are subject to traffic congestion

EUROPEAN TRAVEL

The Membership Office is also responsible for organising members' travel and the distribution of match tickets for our European away games. Full details will be made known when available, via all usual channels.

If you have any query or require further information regarding Membership, Away Travel, Personal Insurance or Branches of the Supporters Club, please write to this address: Membership Office, Manchester United Football Club, Old Trafford, Manchester M16 0RA.
Or, if you prefer, you can telephone the office on **0161-868-8450** or send a fax on **0161-868-8837**. Minicom Textphone **0161-868-8668**.

ABERDEEN Branch Secretary Michael Stewart, 15E Balnagask Road, Torry, Aberdeen AB11 8HU **Tel: 01224 890243 (home) Mobile 07740 980967.** *Departure points* 6.00am Guild Street, Aberdeen; 6.45am Forfar Bypass; 7.00am The Kingsway, Dundee; 8.15am Stirling Services (coach for home games only). New members welcome – contact Branch Secretary for further information.

ABERGELE AND COAST Branch Secretary Eddie Williams, 14 Maes-y-Dre, Abergele, Clwyd, North Wales, LL22 7HW **Tel 01745 823694.** *Departure points* Aber; Llanfairfechen; Penmaen Mawr; Conwy; Llandudno Junction; Colwyn Bay; Abergele; Rhyl; Rhuddlan; Dyserth; Prestatyn; Mostyn; Holywell; Flint; Deeside.

ABERYSTWYTH AND DISTRICT Branch Secretary Alan Evans, 6 Tregerddan, Bow Street, Dyfed, SY24 5AW **Tel 01970 828117** after 6pm. *Departure points* please contact Branch Secretary.

ASHBOURNE Branch Secretary Diane O'Connell, 1 Milldale Court, Ashbourne, Derbyshire, DE6 1SN **Tel: 01335 346105** (evenings). *Departure points* 11.30am The Maypole, Brook Street, Derby; 11.45am (4.45pm) Markeaton Roundabout, Derby; 12 noon (5.00pm) Hanover Hotel, Ashbourne; 12.05pm (5.05pm) Ashbourne Bus Station; Times in brackets denote 8.00pm evening fixtures. For 7.45pm fixtures depart 15 minutes earlier. Contact Branch Secretary for details of travel to away fixtures.

BARNSLEY Branch Secretary Mick Mitchell, 12 Saxon Crescent, Worsbrough, Barnsley, S70 5PY **Tel 01226 283 983.** *Departure points* 12.30pm (5.30pm) Locke Park Working Mens Club, Park Road, Barnsley via A628 or 2½ hours before any other kick-off times.

BARROW AND FURNESS Branch Secretary: Robert Bayliff, 31 Ashworth Street, Dalton-in-Furness, Cumbria, LA15 8SH **Mobile 07788 762936.** *Departure points* 9.30am (4.00pm) Barrow, Ramsden Square; 9.45am (4.15pm) Dalton; 10.00am (4.30pm) Ulverston and A590 route to M6 (times in brackets denote evening fixtures).

BEDFORDSHIRE Branch Secretary Nigel Denton, 4 Abbey Road, Bedford, MK41 9LG **Tel 01604 964329.** *Departure points* Bedford Bus Station, pick-up at Milton Keynes 'Coachways', Junction 14, M1.

BERWICK-UPON-TWEED Branch Secretary Margaret Walker, 17 Lords Mount, Berwick-upon-Tweed, Northumberland, TD15 1LY. *Departure points* Berwick, Belford, Alnwick, Stannington, Washington; 7.00am Shielfield Terrace, Berwick-upon-Tweed **Tel 01289 308671.** SAE for all enquiries please. *Departure points* Berwick, Belford, Alnwick, Stannington, Washington; Scotch Corner, Leeming Bar and anywhere on the main A1- by arrangement.

BIRMINGHAM Branch Secretary Paul Evans, 179 Longbridge Lane, Birmingham B31 4LA **Tel 0121 604 1385** (6.30-9.00pm). *Departure points* Longbridge; Birmingham (Rotunda; New Street); Tennis Courts Public House (A34); Junction 7, M6. Coach fares £10.00 (adults), £5.00 (juniors). Coaches operate for all home games. For times please telephone or send a stamped addressed envelope.

BLACK COUNTRY The branch attend all home/away games. Coach details are as follows *Departure points* St Lawrence Tavern, Darlaston 11.00am (4.00pm); Woden Public House, Wednesbury; 11.10am (4.10pm) Friendly Lodge Hotel, J10, M6 11.15am (4.15pm); Wheatsheaf Public House, off J11, M6 11.25am (4.25pm) (times in brackets denote evening fixtures). For further information contact Branch Secretary Ade Steventon **Tel 0121 531 0826** (6.30- 9.00pm) **Mobile 07931 714318** (6-9.30pm) or Ken Lawton **Tel 01902 636393** (6.30-9pm).

BLACKPOOL, PRESTON AND FYLDE For coach travel to all home matches please contact Mrs Jean Halliday on 01772 635887. For all other branch matters please contact Martin Day on 01253 891301. **E-mail m.r.day@amserve.net.**

BRADFORD AND LEEDS Branch Secretary Sally Hampshire, PO Box 87, Cleckheaton, West Yorkshire, BD19 6YN **Tel 07973 904554. E-mail ian.Hampshire@btinternet.com www.bradfordreds.co.uk.**

BRIDGNORTH AND DISTRICT Branch Secretary Ann Saxby, 30 Pitchford Road, Albrighton, Near Wolverhampton WV7 3LS **Tel 01902 373260.** *Departure points* Ludlow; Bridgnorth; Albrighton; Wolverhampton.

BRIDGWATER AND SOUTH WEST Branch Secretary Ray White, 4 Spencer Close, Bridgwater, Somerset, TA6 5SP **Tel 01278 452186.** *Departure points* Taunton; Bridgwater; Weston-Super-Mare; Clevedon, Aztec West (Bristol).

BRIGHTON Branch Secretary Colin Singers, 34 Meadowview Road, Sompting, Lancing, West Sussex **Tel 01903 761679.** *Departure points* 6.30am Worthing Central; 6.40am Shoreham (George Pub); 7.00am Brighton Railway Station; 7.45am Gatwick Airport.

BRISTOL, BATH & DISTRICT Branch Secretary Dennis Dunford, 26 Fontwell Drive, Downend, Bristol BS16 6RR **Tel 0117 9560636** (6.30pm – 9.00pm) **Mobile 07989 586613. E-mail denmusc@netscape.net** Travel Secretary Mrs Margaret Pettinger, 8 Rectory Close, Warminster, Wilts. BA12 8QP **Tel 01985 219616** (Mon-Fri 5.30pm – 8.30pm). *Departure points* Executive Coach 1: Keynsham Church; Bath Church; Nailsworth; Sainsbury's Stroud; M5 Junction 13; Executive Coach 2: Bristol Temple Meads; Bradley Stoke North; M5 Junction 14.

BURTON-ON-TRENT Branch Secretary Mrs Pat Wright, 45 Foston Avenue, Burton-on-Trent, Staffordshire, DE13 0PL **Tel 01283 532534.** *Departure points* Moira (garage); Swadlincote; Burton (B&Q Lichfield Street); Stoke area.

CARLISLE AND DISTRICT Branch Secretary Arnold Heard, 28 Kentmere Grove, Morton Park, Carlisle, Cumbria, CA2 6JD **Tel/Fax 01228 538262 Mobile 0860 782769.** *Departure points:* For departure times and details on the branch, please contact Branch Secretary.

CENTRAL POWYS Branch Secretary Bryn Thomas, 10 Well Lane, Bungalows, Llanidloes, Powys, SY18 6BA **Tel 01686 412391** (home) **01686 413 3200** (work). *Departure points* Crossgates 10.30am; Rhayader 10.45am; Llanidloes 11.05am; Newtown 11.25am.

CHEPSTOW AND DISTRICT Branch Secretary Anthony Parsons, 56 Treowen Road, Newbridge, Newport, Gwent, NP11 3DN **Tel 01495 246253.** *Departure points* Newbridge, Pontypool, Cwmbran Bus Station; Newport; Coldra Langstone; Magor; Caldicot; Chepstow. For departure times and further details contact Branch Secretary.

CHESTER AND NORTH WALES Branch Chairman Eddie Mansell, 45 Overlea Drive, Hawarden, Deeside, Flintshire, CH5 3HR **Tel 01244 520332** Branch Secretary Mrs Kate Reynolds, 139 Park Avenue, Bryn-Y-Baal, Mold, Flintshire CH7 6TR **Tel 01352 753962** Membership Secretary Mrs Irene Keidel, 3 Springfield Drive, Buckley, Flintshire CH7 2PH **Tel 01244 550943.** *Departure points* Oswestry; Ellesmere; Wrexham; Chester; Rhyl; Greenfield; Flint; Queensferry (ASDA Store); Whitby (Woodlands); Ellesmere Port (Bus Station); Frodsham.

CLEVELAND Branch Secretary John Higgins, 41 Ashford Avenue, Acklam, Middlesbrough TS5 4QL **Tel 01642 643112.** Treasurer Brian Tose, 5 Cowbar Cottages, Staithes, Cleveland TS13 5DA **Tel 01947 841628.** *Departure points* Please contact Branch Secretary for details.

COLWYN BAY AND DISTRICT Branch Secretary Clive Allen, 62 Church Road, Rhos-on-Sea, Colwyn Bay, North Wales, LL28 4YS **Tel 01492 546440.** Branch Chairman Bill Griffith, 'Whitefield', 60 Church Road, Rhos-on-Sea, Colwyn Bay, North Wales, LL28 4YS **Tel 01492 540240.** *Departure points* Bus Stop, Mostyn Broadway (opposite Asda stores) 11.00am (4.00pm); Bus Stop opposite Llandudno Junction Railway Station 11.15am (4.15pm); Guy's Newsagents, Conway Road, Colwyn Bay 11.30am (4.30pm); Bus Stop opposite Marine Hotel, Old Colwyn 11.35am (4.35pm); Top Shop, Abergele Road, Old Colwyn 11.40am (4.40pm); Bus Stop, Fair View Inn, Llandudno 11.45am (4.45pm); Slaters Showrooms Bus Stop, Abergele 11.50am (4.50pm); Talardy Hotel, St. Asaph 12.00noon (5.00pm); Plough Hotel, Aston Hill, Queensferry 12.45pm (5.45pm) (times in brackets denote evening fixtures).

CORBY Branch Chairman Andy Hobbs, 32 Lower Pastures, Great Oakley, Corby, Northants **Tel 01536 744 838 Mobile 07974 571353.** Branch Meetings 7.15pm 1st Sunday of the month, Lodge Park Sports Centre, Shetland Way, Corby. *Departure points* Co-op Extra Store, Alexandra Road, Corby 8.30am (1.30pm); Co-op Extra Superstore, Northfield Avenue, Kettering 8.40am (1.40pm) (times in brackets denote evening fixtures).

CRAWLEY Branch Secretary Jimmy Ahearne, 7 Greenwich Close, Broadfield, Crawley, West Sussex RH11 9LZ **Mobile 0797 0334660.**

CREWE AND NANTWICH Branch Secretary Andy Ridgway, 38 Murrayfield Drive, Willaston, Nantwich, Cheshire CW5 6QF **Tel 01270 568418.** *Departure points* Nantwich Barony 12.30pm (5.00pm); Earl of Crewe 12.40pm (5.10pm); Cross Keys 12.50pm (5.20pm). Away travel subject to demand (times in brackets denote evening fixtures).

DONCASTER AND DISTRICT Branch Secretary Albert Thompson, 89 Anchorage Lane, Sprotboro, Doncaster, South Yorkshire, DN5 8EB **Tel 01302 782964.** Branch Treasurer Sue Moyles, 217 Warningtongue Lane, Cantley **Tel 01302 530422 Fax 01482 591708.** Branch Chairman Paul Kelly, 58 Oak Grove, Conisbrough DN12 2HN **Tel 01709 324058** Membership Secretary Mrs L Sudbury, 8 Parkway, Armthorpe, Doncaster **Tel 01302 834323.** *Departure points* Broadway Hotel, Dunscroft 10.30am (4.30pm); Edenthorpe 10.40am (4.40pm); Waterdale (opposite main library) 10.45am (4.45pm); The Highwayman, Woodlands 11.00am (5.00pm) (times in brackets denote 8.00pm kick-off). Meetings held first Monday of every month (unless there is a home match) in the Co-op Social Club (At the back of B & Q) at 7.30pm.

DORSET Branch Secretary Mark Pattison,89 Parkstone Road, Poole, Dorset, BH15 2NZ **Tel 01202 744348.** *Departure points* Poole Train Station 6.15am (10.30am); Banksome (Courts) 6.20am (10.35am); Bournemouth, 6.30am (10.45am); Christchurch (Bargates) 6.45am (11.00am); Ringwood 7.00am (11.15am); Rownham Services 7.15am (11.30am); Chieveley Services 8.30am (12.30pm) (times in brackets denote evening fixtures).

DUKINFIELD AND HYDE Branch Secretary Marilyn Chadderton, 12 Brownville Grove, Dukinfield, Cheshire, SK16 5AS **Tel** 0161 338 4892. *Departure points* Details of meetings and travel available from the above or S Jones **Tel** 0161 343 5260.

EAST ANGLIA Branch Secretary Mark Donovan, 55 The Street, Holywell Row, Mildenhall, Bury St Edmonds, Suffolk, IP28 8LT **Tel** 01638 717075 (9.00am-6.00pm) (Details of your local representative can also be obtained by telephoning this number.) Executive travel available to all home fixtures via the following services: Service No.1 Clacton; Colchester; Braintree; Great Dunmow; Bishop Stortford Service No.2 Felixstowe; Nacton; Ipswich; Stowmarket; Bury St. Edmonds Service No.3 Thetford; Mildenhall; Newmarket; Cambridge; Huntingdon Service No.4 Lowestoft; Great Yarmouth; Norwich; East Dereham; Kings Lynn Coaches also operate to all away games for which departure details are dependent on demand and ticket availability.

EAST MANCHESTER Branch Secretary Tony McAllister, 10 Walmer Street, Abbey Hey, Gorton, Manchester M18 8QP **Tel** 0161 230 7098 **Mobile** 07867 797547. Branch meetings held on the last Thursday of each month (8.00pm) at Gorton Labour Club, Ashkirk Street, Gorton, Manchester.

EAST YORKSHIRE Branch Secretary Ian Baxter, 18 Soberhill Drive, Holme Moor, York YO43 4BH **Mobile** 07768 821844. Hull Administrator Fred Helas **Mobile** 07774 775 078. *Departure points* Hull Coach Hull Marina 10.30am(3.30pm); Howden Coach Bay Horse, Market Weighton; 10.30am (3.30pm); Redbrick Café, Howden; 11.00am (4.00pm) (times in brackets denote evening fixtures).

ECCLES Branch Secretary Gareth Morris, 11 Brentwood Drive, Monton, Eccles, Manchester, M30 9LP **Tel** 0161 281 9435. *Departure point* (Away games only) Rock House Hotel, Peel Green Road, Peel Green, Eccles. For departure times please contact Branch Secretary.

FEATHERSTONE & DISTRICT Branch Secretary Paul Kingsbury, 11 Hardwick Road, Featherstone, Nr Pontefract, W Yorks WF7 5JA **Tel** 01977 793910. **Mobile** 07971 778161 Treasurer Andrew Dyson, 46 Northfield Drive, Pontefract, W Yorks WF8 2DL **Tel** 01977 709561 **Mobile** 07979 326183. *Departure points* Pontefract Sorting Office 11.30am (4.30pm); Corner Pocket, Featherstone 11.40am(4.40pm); Green Lane, Featherstone 11.45am(4.45pm); Castleford Bus Station 11.55am(4.55pm); (times in brackets denote evening fixtures). Meetings held every fortnight (Mondays) at the Jubilee Hotel, Wakefield Road, Featherstone.

GLAMORGAN AND GWENT Branch Secretary Neil Chambers, 201 Malpas Road, Newport, South Wales NP20 5PP. Branch Chairman Cameron Erskine **Tel** 02920 623705 (10.00am - 1.00pm Monday - Friday. Answerphone at other times) **Mobile** 07885 615546. **E-mail** c.erskine@ntlworld.co.uk. *Departure points* Skewen; Port Talbot; Bridgend; Cardiff; Newport.

GLASGOW Branch Secretary David Sharkey, 45 Lavender Drive, Greenhills, East Kilbride G75 9JH **Tel** 01355 902592 (7-11pm). Coach run to all home games. *Departure points* 8.00am (1.00pm) Queen Street Station, Glasgow; 8.15am (1.15pm) The Angel, Uddingston; Any M74 Service Stations (times in brackets denote evening fixtures).

GLOUCESTER AND CHELTENHAM Branch Secretary Paul Brown, 59 Katherine Close, Churchdown, Gloucester, GL3 1PB **Tel** 01452 859553 **Mobile** 07801 802593 **E-mail** muscglos@aol.com. *Departure points* Bennetts Yard, Eastern Ave, Glos. 8.45am (1.45pm); Station Road, Gloucester 9.00am (2.00pm); Cheltenham Railway Station (outside Midland Hotel), 9.10am (2.10pm); Cheltenham Gas Works Corner 9.15am (2.15pm) (times in brackets denote evening fixtures).

GRIMSBY AND DISTRICT Branch Secretary Bob England, 5 George Butler Close, Laceby, Grimsby, DN37 7WA **Tel** 01472 752130. **E-mail** yipyapstam6@manutd.com. Travel Arrangements Craig Collins (Branch Chairman) **Tel** 01472 314273. Membership Secretary Sarah Bell **Tel** 01472 314273.

GUERNSEY Branch Secretary Eddie Martel, Ayia Napa, Rue des Barras, Les Maresqets, Vale, Guernsey, Channel Isles **Tel** 01481 46285.

GWYNEDD Branch Secretary Gwyn Hughes, Sibrwd y Don, Tan y Cefn, Llanwnda, Caernarfon, Gwynedd, LL54 7YB **Tel** 01286 830073 **Mobile** 07050 380804 **E-mail** Gwyn.Hughes@manutd.com *Departure points* Pwllheli; Llanwnda; Caernarfon; Bangor. For departure times, please contact branch secretary.

HAMPSHIRE Branch Secretary Pete Boyd, 22 Weavers Crofts, Melksham Wilts SN12 8BP **Tel** 01225 700354 **E-mail** pete@muschants.com. Website www.muschants.com Membership Secretary/Treasurer Roy Debenham, 11 Lindley Gardens, Alresford, Hampshire, SO24 9PU **Tel/Fax** 01962 734420. Chairman Paul Marsh, Oaktree Cottage, Commonhill Road, Braishfield, Hants. SO51 0QF **Tel** 01794 368951. *Departure points* (1) King George V Playing Field, Northern Road, Cosham 7.30am (12.00 noon); (2) Sainsburys, Hedge End 7.50am (12.20pm); (3) Bullington Cross Inn, Junction of A34 & A303 8.20am (12.50pm) (4) Chieveley Services, Newbury 8.50am (1.20pm).

HARROGATE AND DISTRICT Branch Secretary Michael Heaton, Railway Cottage, Grange Road, Dacre Banks, Harrogate, N Yorks HG3 4EF. **Tel/Fax** 01423 780679 **Mobile** 07790 798328. *Departure points include:* Nidderdale, Rippon, Northallerton, Leyburn, Harrogate, Skipton and Earby areas. Coaches also operate to all away games, inc. European. For further information contact Branch Secretary. Send s.a.e for membership details.

HASTINGS Branch Secretary Tim Martin, 30 Silvan Road, St Leonards-on-Sea, East Sussex TN38 9RD (NO PERSONAL CALLERS PLEASE)**Tel** 01424 853189 (6pm-8pm) **Mobile** 07973 656716 (Daytime). For match bookings phone Tim at the above. For Membership details and other enquiries, contact Chris Fry **Tel** 01424 437595 **Mobile** 07973 309382. Steve Whitelaw **Tel** 07881 610345. Rod Beckingham **Tel** 01424 443477 (6pm-8pm). *Departure points* Eastbourne, Tesco's Roundabout 5.40am; Bexhill, Viking Chip Shop 6.00am; Silverhill Traffic lights 6.15am; Hurst Green, George Pub 6.40am; Pembury, Camden Arms Pub 7.00am. All above times for 3 or 4pm kick-off. For details of travel to away games please contact Branch Secretary.

HEREFORD Branch Secretary Norman Elliss, 40 Chichester Close, Abbeyfields, Belmont, Hereford, HR2 7YU **Tel** 01432 359923 **Fax** 01432 342880. *Departure points* 8.30am (2.00pm) Leominster; 9.00am (2.30pm) Bulmers Car Park, Hereford; 9.30am (3.00pm) Ledbury; 9.45am (3.15pm) Malvern Link BP Garage; 10.00am (3.30pm) Oak Apple Pub, Worcester; (times in brackets denote mid-week fixtures).

HERTFORDSHIRE Organised travel to home & away games. Pick-up points at Hertford, Welwyn, Stevenage, Hitchin and Luton. Travel arrangements - contact Mick Prior **Tel** 01438 361900. Membership - contact Mick Slack **Tel** 01462 622451. Correspondence to Steve Bocking, 64 Westmill Road, Hitchin, Herts SG5 2SD **Tel** 01462 622076.

HEYWOOD Branch Secretary Denis Hall, 2 Hartford Avenue, Summit, Heywood, Lancs OL10 4XH **Tel** 01706 364475. Chairman Lee Swettenham, 30 Wilton Grove, Heywood, Lancs OL10 1AZ **Tel** 01706 368953. *Departure Point* Bay Horse, Torrington Street, Hopwood/Heywood 1.00pm (6.00pm midweek).

HIGHLANDS & ISLANDS Branch Secretary Kenneth MacAskill, 2 Claymore House, Croyard Road, Beauly, IV4 7DJ **Tel** 01463 783765 (6pm – 10pm only).

HIGH PEAK Branch Secretary Karen Matthews, 8 Market Street, New Mills, High Peak, SK22 4AE **Tel** 01663 742172 **E-mail** Karen.Matthews2@btinternet.com Website musg-highpeak.co.uk. Chairman Dave Rhodes, 21 Park Road, Whaley Bridge, High Peak SK23 7DJ **Tel** 01663 732484. Coaches to some games. Monthly meetings last Thursday in the month.

HYNDBURN & PENDLE Branch Secretary Alan Haslam, 97 Crabtree Avenue, Edgeside, Waterfoot, Rossendale, BB4 9TB. **Tel** 01706 831736 *Departure points* Barnoldswick 11.15am (4.45pm); Nelson 11.30am (5.00pm); Burnley 11.45am (5.15pm); Accrington 12.15pm (5.45pm); Haslingden 12.20pm (5.50pm); Rawtenstall 12.30pm (6.00pm) (times in brackets denote evening fixtures).

INVICTA REDS (KENT) Branch Secretary Vic Hatherly **Tel** 01634 865613 **Mobile** 0778 844 5627. Tickets and Travel Shaun Rogers or Louise Dodd **Tel** 01622 721344 (not after 9pm) **Mobile** 0797 382 6794 (not after 9pm). Correspondence to Invicta Reds, c/o 'Pop-In' Newsagents, 97 Boundary Road, Ramsgate, Kent CT11 7NP **E-mail** invictareds@manutd.com. *Departure points* Pop-In Newsagents, Ramsgate; Mill Lane, Herne Bay; Magistrates Court, Canterbury; M2 Medway Services; M2, Junction 3, Chatham; A2 by Cobham, Little Chef Services; Dartford Tunnel; M25, Junction 28; M25, Junction 26.

ISLE OF MAN Chairman Graham Barlow, 21 Thirlmere Drive, Onchan, Isle of Man **Tel** 01624 661270. Branch Secretary Gill Keown, 5 King Williams Way, Castletown, Isle of Man, IM9 1DH **Tel** 01624 823143 **E-mail** reddevil@manx.net.

JERSEY Branch Secretary Mark Jones, 5 Rosemount Cottages, James Road, St. Saviour, Jersey, Channel Islands **Tel** 01534 34786 (home) 01534 885885 (work). Should any members be in Jersey during the football season, the branch shows television games in private club. Free food provided, everybody welcome, including children. Contact Branch Secretary for details.

KEIGHLEY Branch Secretary Kevin Granger, 3 Spring Terrace, Long Lee, Keighley, West Yorkshire, BD21 4SZ **Tel** 01535 661862 **Mobile** 01709 555653 **Fax** 01535 600564 **E-mail** k.d.granger@talk21.com. *Departure points* Coach leaves from Keighley Technical College in Cavendish Street then travels to Colne, and joins M65 & M66 to Manchester. Contact Branch Secretary for more details.

KNUTSFORD Branch Secretary John Butler, 4 Hollingford Place, Knutsford WA16 9DP **Tel** 01565 651360 **Fax** 01560 634792 **E-mail** john.butler@cwcom.net. Fortnightly meetings, usually on Thursdays at the Angel Hotel, King Street, Knutsford.

LANCASTER AND DISTRICT Branch Secretary Ed Currie, 30 Dorrington Road, Lancaster LA1 4TG **Tel** 01524 36797 **Mobile** 07880 550247. *Departure points* 11.45am (4.45pm) Carnforth Ex Servicemens; 12.00pm (5.00pm) Morecambe Shrimp Roundabout; 12.20pm (5.20pm) Lancaster Dalton Square and A6 route to Broughton Roundabout for M6 (times in brackets denote evening fixtures).

LEAMINGTON SPA Branch Secretary Mrs Norma Worton, 23 Cornhill Grove, Kenilworth, Warwickshire, CV8 2QP **Tel 01926 859476**
E-mail Norma.Worton@manutd.com.
Departure points Newbold Terrace, Leamington Spa; Leyes Lane, Kenilworth; London Road, Coventry.

LINCOLN Branch Secretary Steve Stone, 154 Scorer Street, Lincoln, Lincolnshire, LN5 7SX **Tel 01522 885671.**
Departure points Unity Square at 10.00am on Saturday's (3.00pm kick-off). Midweek matches, depart at 3.00pm from Unity Square.

LONDON Branch Secretary Ralph Mortimer, 55 Boyne Avenue, Hendon, London, NW4 2JL **Tel 0181 203 1213** (after 6.30pm).
Departure points Home Games, Coaches depart from following points: Semley Place (alongside Victoria Coach Station 8.00pm (12.30pm); Staples Corner (opposite Courts) 8.30am (1.15pm); Junction 11, M1 (under motorway) 9.00am (1.45pm); (times in brackets denote evening fixtures). All coaches need to be reserved in advance by calling Ralph Mortimer **0208 203 1213** after 6.30pm.
Away games: A coach will run for all away games, subject to numbers/tickets. Please contact Ralph Mortimer for details.

LONDON ASSOCIATION Branch Secretary Najib Armanazi **Tel 07941 124591**
E-mail najcantona@hotmail.com. Membership Secretary Alison Watt
Tel 01322 558333 (7pm – 9pm only). E-mail alisonwatt@redlodge.freeserve.co.uk.

LONDON FAN CLUB Branch Secretary Paul Molloy, 65 Corbylands Road, Sidcup, Kent, DA15 8JQ Travel Secretary Mike Dobbin,
E-mail info@mulfc65.freeserve.co.uk.
Departure points Euston Station by service train - meeting point at top of escalator from Tube). Cheap group travel to most home and away games.

MACCLESFIELD Branch Secretary Ian Evans, 25 Pickwick Road, Poynton, Cheshire SK12 1LD. Chairman Mark Roberts **Tel 01625 434362.** Treasurer Rick Holland, 97 Pierce Street, Macclesfield SK11 6EX **Tel 01625 427762.** Membership Secretary Neil McCleland **Tel 01625 613183.**
Departure points Home games, meet Macclesfield Rail Station 11.45am (4.45pm midweek fixtures). For away games, please contact Branch Secretary.

MANSFIELD Branch Secretary Peggy Conheeney, 48 West Bank Avenue, Mansfield, Nottinghamshire, NG19 7BP **Tel/Fax 01623 625140**
Mobile 0776 1107104 E-mail peg.con.musc@faxvia.net.
Departure points Kirkby Garage 10.00am (4.00pm); Northern Bridge, Sutton 10.10am (4.10pm); Mansfield Shoe Co. 10.20am (4.20pm); Pegs Home 10.30am (4.30pm); Young Vanish, Glapwell 10.40am (4.40pm); Hipper Street School, Chesterfield 10.55am (4.55pm) (times in brackets denote evening fixtures). Away games are dependent on ticket availability - please contact branch secretary.

MID CHESHIRE Branch Secretary Leo Lastowecki, 5 Townfield Court, Barnton, Northwich, Cheshire, CW8 4U **Tel 01606 784790.**
Departure points: Please contact Branch Secretary.

MIDDLETON & DISTRICT Branch Secretary Kevin Booth, 8 Wicken Bank, Hopwood, OL10 2LW **Tel 01706 624196 Mobile 07762 741438.** Chairman Mike Conroy, 12 Lulworth Road, Middleton, Manchester 24 **Tel 0161 653 5696.**
Home Games: Coaches depart Crown Inn, Middleton 1 hour prior to kick-off. Away Games: Contact Secretary.

MILLOM AND DISTRICT Branch Secretary/Chairman Clive Carter, 47 Settle Street, Millom, Cumbria, LA18 5AR **Tel 01229 773565.** Treasurer Malcom French, 4 Willowside Park, Haverigg, Cumbria, LA18 4PT **Tel 01229 774850.**
Assistant Treasurer Paul Knott, 80 Market Street, Millom, Cumbria
Tel 01229 772826.

NEWTON-LE-WILLOWS Branch Chairman Mark Coleman, 14 Avocet Close, Newton-le-Willows **Tel 01925 222390.** Branch Secretary Mrs Joan Collins, Birley Street, Newton-le-Willows **Tel 01925 228959.** Ticket Secretary Anthony Hatch
Mobile 07909 580790. Travel Secretary Mark Cheshire **Tel 01925 276298.**
Meetings once a month in the Legh Arms Public House, Newton-le-Willows. Telephone any of the above for date of meeting – all telephone enquiries before 9.00pm. Coach travel for selected home games to be booked and paid in advance. Most games available at Legh Arms. Junior and family membership welcome.

NORTH DEVON Branch Secretary Dave Rogan, Leys Cottage, Hilltop, Fremington, Nr Barnstaple, EX31 3BL **Tel/Fax 01271 328280.**
Departure points: Please contact Branch Secretary.

NORTH EAST Branch Secretary John Burgess, 10 Streatlam Close, Stainton, Barnard Castle, Co Durham, DL12 8RQ **Tel 01833 69520.**
Departure points Central Station, Newcastle 8.30am (1.00pm); A19/A690 Roundabout 8.50am (1.20pm); 8.50am (1.20pm) Peterlee Roundabout 9.00am (1.30pm); Hartlepool Baths 9.15am (1.45pm); Owton Lodge, Hartlepool 9.20am (1.50pm); The Swan, Billingham 9.30am (2.00pm); Sappers Corner 9.40am (2.10pm); Darlington Bus Station 10.00am (2.30pm); Scotch Corner Roundabout 10.10am (2.40pm); Leeming Bar Services A1 10.20am (2.50pm).

NORTH MANCHESTER Branch meetings Leggatts Wine Bar, Oldham Road, Failsworth. Coaches to all home and away games. Secretary Graham May
Mobile 07931 505488. All home coach details: Garry Chapman **07748 970225.**
All away coach details: Dixie **07968 121872.** All other enquiries contact Graham **07931 505488.**

NORTH POWYS Branch Secretary Glyn T Davies, 7 Tan-y-Mur, Montgomery, Powys, SY15 6PR **Tel 01686 668841.** Area Officials Knighton – R Davies **01547 528318** Welshpool – C Harrington **01938 570571;** Montgomery (Branch Secretary); Newton – J Mitchell **01686 622391;** Llanfair – G Jones **01938 810902.** Vice-Chairman A L Jones, Newton **07780 805313.** For all information on coach travel & tickets contact Branch Secretary. Tickets must be ordered six weeks in advance. *Departure times* – Midweek: 4.00pm Newtown; 4.10pm Abermule; 4.30pm Welshpool; 5.00pm Mile End; Saturdays 3pm k.o.: 10.30am Newton Bus Station; 10.40am Abermule; 11.00am Weshpool; 11.20 Mile End; Saturdays early k.o.: 8.30am Newton Bus Station; 8.45am Abermule; 9.00am Weshpool; 9.20 Mile End; Branch meetings take place every 8 weeks in areas of branch in rotation.

NORTH STAFFORDSHIRE Branch Secretary Peter Hall, Cheddleton Heath House, Cheddleton Heath Road, Leek ST13 7DX **Tel 01538 360364.** *Departure points* 12.30pm (5.15pm) Leek Bus Station (times in brackets denote evening fixtures).

NORTH YORKSHIRE Branch Secretary Miss Jacky Potter, c/o MUSC N. Yorkshire, PO Box 480, York YO24 3ZW **Tel/Fax 01904 787291** (6.00-8.00pm)
Mobile 07980 854042 E-mail musc@jaks.freeserve.co.uk.
Departure points Executive coaches to all home games from Whitby, Scarborough, Malton and York, booking in advance is required. Please phone secretary for further details.

NOTTINGHAM Branch Secretary Wayne Roe, Vine Cottages, 15 Platt Street, Pinxton, Notts NG16 6NX **Tel 07870 604269** (home travel) **E-mail wainy@aol.com** Martyn Meek **Tel 01773 768424** (away travel). *Departure points* 10.00am (3.00pm) Nottingham; 10.30am (3.30pm) Ilkeston; 10.45am (3.45pm) Eastwood; 11.00am (4.00pm) Junction 28, M1 (times in brackets denote evening fixtures).

OLDHAM Branch Secretary Dave Cone, 67 Nelson Way, Washbrook, Chadderton, Lancashire, OL9 8NL **Tel 0161 626 9734 Mobile 07973 939255.** Chairman Martyn Lucas, 1 Greenhills Holt, Norden, Rochdale OL12 7PQ **Tel 01706 355728.** Meeting every Tuesday night 7.30-9.00pm at Horton Arms, 1 Ward Street, off Middleton Road, Chadderton, Oldham. Match Travel Coach to all home matches; Mid-week - leaves at 6.00pm; Weekend 3.00pm k.o. - leaves at 1.00pm; Weekend 4.00pm k.o. - leaves at 1.30pm; Away Travel - subject to receiving match tickets.

OXFORD, BANBURY AND DISTRICT Branch Secretary Mick Thorne, "The Paddock", 111 Eynsham Road, Botley, Oxford OX2 9BY **Tel 01865 864924** (6.00-8.00pm Monday-Friday only) **Fax 01865 864924** (Anytime).
Departure points McLeans Coach Yard, Witney 8.00am (2.00pm); Botley Road Park-n-Ride, Oxford 8.30am (2.30pm); Plough Inn, Bicester 8.45am (2.45pm); Bus Station, Banbury 9.00am(3.00pm) (times in brackets denote evening fixtures). Mid-week European matches, coaches depart 30 minutes earlier. Coach fare for home games adults £11.00, Junior & OAP's £8.00. All coach seats must be booked in advance. Away travel, including European, subject to match tickets. New members welcome. Large sae for copy of branch review.

PETERBOROUGH AND DISTRICT Branch Secretary Andrew Dobney, 3 Northgate, West Pinchbeck, Spalding, Lincs, PE11 3TB **Tel 01775 640743**
E-mail andrew@dobney.fsnet.co.uk.
Departure points Spalding Bus Station 8.30am (1.15pm); Peterborough, Key Theatre 9.15am (2.00pm); Grantham, Foston Services 10.00am (2.45pm) (times in brackets denote evening fixtures).

PLYMOUTH Branch Secretary Dave Price, 34 Princess Avenue, Plymstock, Plymouth PL9 9EP **Tel 01752 482049** or Branch Information Line **01579 348497.**
Departure Points Tamar Bridge 6.30am (10.30am); Bretonside 6.45am (10.45am); Plympton 7.00am (11.00am); Ivybridge 7.10am (11.10am); Buckfastleigh 7.25am (11.25am); Exeter Services 7.50am (11.50am) (times in brackets denote evening fixtures).

PONTYPRIDD Branch Secretary Lawrence Badman, 11 Laura Street, Treforest, Pontypridd, Mid Glamorgan, South Wales, CF37 1NW **Tel 01443 400894.** *Departure points:* for coach departure and pick-up points please contact Branch Secretary.

REDDITCH Branch Secretary Mark Richardson, 90 Alcester Road, Hollywood, Worcs. B47 5NS **Tel/Fax 07890 584676.**
Departure points Redditch & Drumsgrove.

ROCHDALE Branch Chairman Paul Mulligan, 54 Norden Road, Bamford, Rochdale, Lancs OL11 5PN **Tel 01706 368909.** Regular coach service to home games.

ROSSENDALE Branch Secretary Ian Boswell, 44 Cutler Lane, Stacksteads, Bacup, Lancs OL13 0HW **Tel 01706 874764 Mobile 07802 502356** (all enquiries).
Meetings: The Royal Hotel, Waterfoot – see local press or
E-mail ROYALREDS@theroyal-hotel.co.uk . Coach travel arrangements – Contact Paul Stannard **Tel 01706 214493 Fax 01706 215371** or **Paul@theroyal-hotel.co.uk.**

RUGBY AND NUNEATON Branch Secretary Greg Pugh, 67 Fisher Avenue, Rugby, Warwickshire CV22 5HW **Tel 01788 567900.** Chairman Mick Moore, 143 Marston Lane, Attleborough, Nuneaton, Warwickshire **Tel 01203 343 868.** *Departure points* St Thomas Cross Pub, Rugby; McDonalds Junction 2, M6, Coventry; Council House, Coton Road, Nuneaton. Departure times vary according to kick-off.

RUNCORN AND WIDNES Branch Secretary Elizabeth Scott, 39 Park Road, Runcorn, Cheshire, WA7 4SS.

SCUNTHORPE Branch Secretary Pat Davies **Tel 01724 851359.** Chairman Guy Davies **Tel 01724 851359.** Transport Manager Tony Fish **Tel 01724 341029.**

SHEFFIELD & ROTHERHAM Branch Secretary Roger Everitt, 27 South Street, Kimberworth, Rotherham, South Yorkshire, S61 1ER **Tel 01709 563613.** Coach Travel available to all home games. *Departure points* Saturdays: Rotherham (Nellie Denes) 11.00am; Sheffield (Midland Railway Station) 11.20am; Stockbridge 11.50am; Midweek games: Rotherham (Nellie Denes) 4.30pm; Meadowhall Coach Park 4.45pm. Kick-off times vary Sat/Sun, please contact Branch Secretary.

SHOEBURYNESS, SOUTH END AND DISTRICT Branch Secretary Bob Lambert, 23 Royal Oak Drive, Wickford, Essex, SS11 8NT **Tel 01268 560168** Chairman Gary Black **Tel 01702 219072.** *Departure points* Cambridge Hotel, Shoeburyness; 7.15am Bell Public House, A127; 7.20am Rayleigh Weir; 7.30am McDonalds Burger Bar, A127; 7.40am Fortune of War Public House, A127; 8.00am Brentwood High Street; 8.05am Little Chef, Brentwood By-pass. Additional pick-ups by arrangement with Branch Secretary. All coach seats should be booked in advance. Ring for details of midweek fixtures.

SHREWSBURY Branch Secretary Martyn Hunt, 50 Whitehart, Reabrook, Shrewsbury, SY3 7TE **Tel 01743 350397.** Chirk Secretary Mike Davies **Tel 01691 778678.** *Departure points* Reabrook Island; Abbey Church; Monkmoor Inn; Heathgates Island; Harlescott Inn; Hand Hotel, Chirk 3.00 & 4.00pm kick-off: Depart Reabrook 10.30am; 7.30 & 8.00pm kick-off:Depart Reabrook 3.00pm;

SOUTH ELMSALL & DISTRICT Branch Secretary Bill Fieldsend, 72 Cambridge St, Moorthorpe, South Elmsall, Pontefract, West Yorkshire WF9 2AR **Tel 01977 648358 Mobile 07818 245954.** Treasurer Mark Bossons **Tel 01977 650316.** Meetings held every Tuesday at the South Kirkby Royal British Legion Club. *Departure points* Cudworth Library 11.30am (4.30pm); Hemsworth Market 11.45am (4.45pm); Mill Lane 11.50am (4.50pm); Pretoria WMC 12 noon(5.00pm) (times in brackets denote evening fixtures).

SOUTHPORT Branch Secretary Robert Stephenson, 143 Heysham Road, Southport, Merseyside, PR9 7ED **Tel 01704 220685.** Weekly meetings held Tuesday evening at The Mount Pleasant Hotel, Manchester Road. *Departure point* The Mount Pleasant Hotel, Manchester Road, Southport, picking-up en route.

STALYBRIDGE Branch Secretary Walt Petrenko **Mobile 07788 491977.** Chairman S Hepburn, **Tel 0161 344 2328.** Treasurer R A Wild **Tel 0161 338 7277.** Membership Secretary A Baxter **Tel 01457 838 764.** Away Travel Nigel Barrett **Mobile 0802 799482.** Home Travel B Wiliamson **Tel 0161 338 6832.** *Departure points* Branch is based at The Pineapple, 18 Kenworthy Street, Stalybridge Landlord Addy Dearnaley **Tel 0161 338 2542.** Home coach leaves from The Pineapple 1½ hours before kick-off. Away coaches are arranged when applicable per game, coaches run most games.

STOKE-ON-TRENT Branch Secretary Geoff Boughey, 63 Shrewsbury Drive, Newcastle, Staffordshire, ST5 7RQ **Tel/Fax 01782 561680** (home) **Mobile 0468 561680 E-mail geoffboughey@cwcom.net.** *Departure points* 12.00noon (5.00pm) Hanley Bus Station; 12.10pm (5.10pm) School Street, Newcastle; 12.15pm (5.15pm) Little Chef A34; 12.30pm (5.30pm) The Millstone Pub, Butt Lane (times in brackets denote evening fixtures). Branch meetings every Monday night. Contact Branch Secretary for details.

STOURBRIDGE & KIDDERMINSTER Branch Secretary, Robert Banks, 7 Croftwood Road, Wollescote, Stourbridge, West Midlands DY9 7EU **Tel 01384 826636.** *Departure Points* Contact Branch Secretary for departure points and times.

SURREY Branch Membership Secretary Mrs Maureen Acker, 80 Cheam Road, Ewell, Surrey, KT17 1QF **Tel 0208 393 4763.** Home League Games Co-ordinator John Ramsden, 22 Pound Lane, Godalming, Surrey **Tel 01483 420909;** Cup Games Co-ordinator John Fuggle, Flat 9, The Shrubbery, 22 Hook Road, Surbiton, Surrey **Mobile 07703 650869.**

SWANSEA Branch Secretary Dave Squibb, 156 Cecil Street, Manslebon, Swansea, SA5 8QJ **Tel 01792 641981 E-mail david.squibb@manutd.com.** *Departure points* Swansea (via Heads of Valleys Road); Neath; Hirwaun; Merthyr; Tredegar; Ebbw Vale; Brynmawr; Abergavenny; Monmouth.

SWINDON Branch Secretary Martin Rendle, 19 Cornfield Road, Devizes, Wiltshire, SN10 3BA **Tel 01380 728358** (between 8.00pm-10.00pm Monday to Friday). *Departure points* Kingsdown Inn; Stratton St Margaret; Swindon.

TELFORD Branch Secretary Sal Laher, 4 Hollyoak Grove, Lakeside, Priorslee, Telford, TF2 9GE **Tel 01952 299224.** *Departure points* Saturday (3pm kick-off) 10.30am Cuckoo Oak, Madeley; 10.40am Heath Hill, Dawley; 10.50am Bucks Head, Wellington; 11.00am Oakengates; 11.10am Bridge, Donnington; 11.20am Newport. Midweek (8.00pm kick-off) departure starts 4.30pm with ten minutes later for each of the above locations. Contact Branch Secretary for membership and further details.

TORBAY Branch Secretary Vernon Savage, 5 Courtland Road, Shiphay, Torquay, Devon TQ2 6JU **Tel 01803 616139 Fax 01803 616139 Mobile 07765 394238.** *Departure points* 7.00am Upper Cockington Lane, Torquay; 7.20am Newton Abbot Railway Station; 7.30am Kingsteignton Fountain; 7.45am Countess Wear Roundabout, Exeter; Taunton 8.15am; Other departure times by arrangement with the Branch Secretary. Midweek coach departure times, add 5 hours to above times.

UTTOXETER & DISTRICT Branch Secretary Mr T Bloor, 63 Carter Street, Uttoxeter, Staffs ST14 8EY. Branch Chairman Ray Phillips **Tel 01889 567323.**

WALSALL Branch Secretary Ian Robottom, 157 Somerfield Road, Bloxwich, Walsall WS3 2EN **Tel 01922 861746.** *Departure points* 10.50am (4.15pm) Junction 9 (M6); 11.15am (4.50pm) Bell Pub, Bloxwich; 11.30am (5.15pm) Roman Way Hotel, A5 Cannock; 11.50am (5.35pm) Dovecote Pub, Stone Road, Stafford.

WARRINGTON Branch Secretary Su Buckley, 4 Vaudrey Drive, Woolston, Warrington, Cheshire, WA1 4HG **Tel 01925 816966.** *Departure points* Blackburn Arms 1.00pm (6.00pm); Churchills 1.10pm (6.10pm); Chevvies 1.15pm (6.15pm); Highway Man/Kingsway 1.20pm (6.20pm); Rope 'n' Anchor 1.25pm (6.25pm); (times in brackets denote evening fixtures).

WELLINGBOROUGH Branch Secretary Paul Walpole, 7 Cowgill Close, Cherry Lodge, Northampton NN3 8PB **Tel/Fax 01604 787612.** *Departure points* Shoe Factory, Irchester Road, Rushden 8.30am (1.30pm); Doc Martins Shoe Factory, Irchester 8.35am (1.35pm); The Cuckoo Public House, Woolaston 8.45am (1.45pm); Police Station, Wellingborough 8.55am (1.55pm); Duke of York Public House, Wellingborough 9.00am (2.00pm); Trumpet Public House, Northampton 9.10am (2.10pm); Abington Park Bus Stop, Northampton 9.15 am (2.15pm); Campbell Square, Northampton 9.20am (2.20pm); Mill Lane Layby (opposite Cock Hotel Public House), Kingsthorpe 9.25am (2.25pm); Top of Bants Lane (opposite Timken), Dugton 9.30am (2.30pm).

WEST CUMBRIA Branch Secretary Robert Wilson, 23 Calder Drive, Moorclose, Workington, Cumbria CA14 3NZ **Tel 01900 872804 Mobile 07799 666610 E-mail robertwilson3@btinternet.com.** *Departure points* Coach 1 departs: Egremont 9.45am (3.15pm); Cleator Moor 10am (3.30pm); Whitehaven 10.15am (3.45pm); Distington 10.20am (3.50pm); Cockermouth 10.35am (4.05pm) Coach 2 departs: Salterbeck 9.45am (1.45pm); Harrington Road 9.50am (1.50pm); Workington 10am (2.00pm); Station Inn 10.10am (2.10pm); Netherhall Cr 10.12am (2.12pm); Netherton 10.15am (2.15pm); Dearham 10.20am (2.20pm) Times in brackets denotes 8pm kick-off – contact Branch Secretary for other kick-off times.

WEST DEVON Branch Secretary Mrs R M Bolt, 16 Moorview, North Tawton, Devon, EX20 2HW **Tel 01837 82682** (all enquiries). *Departure points* North Tawton; Crediton; Exeter.

WESTMORLAND Branch Secretary Dennis Alderson, 71 Calder Drive, Kendal, Cumbria, LA9 6LR **Tel 01539 728248 Mobile 0973 965373.** *Departure points* Ambleside; Windermere; Staveley, Kendal and Forton Services. For departure times and further details, please contact Branch Secretary.

WORKSOP Branch Secretary Mick Askew, 20 Park Street, Worksop, Nottinghamshire **Tel 01909 486194.**

YEOVIL Branch Secretary Richard Chapman-Cox, 34 Crofton Avenue, Yeovil, Somerset, BA21 4DL **Tel 01935 478285 Mobile 07930 505349 E-mail richard.chapmancox@btinternet.com.** *Departure points* Yeovil and Taunton. Transport available to non-branch members. Please contact Branch Secretary for departure times.

MANCHESTER UNITED DISABLED SUPPORTERS' ASSOCIATION - (MUDSA) Branch Secretary Phil Downs, M.U.D.S.A., PO Box 141, South D.O., M20 5BA **Tel 0161 434 1989 Fax 0161 445 5221 E-mail phil.downs@cwcom.net.**

IRISH BRANCHES

ANTRIM TOWN Branch Secretary Alex Mould, 20 Repulse Court, Townparks, Antrim, Northern Ireland, BT41 4HU **Mobile 07899 818623.** Chairman William Cameron, 92 Doragone Drive, Parkhall, Antrim, N Ireland **Tel 02894 461634.** Club meetings held every other Thursday in the Top of the Town Bar, Antrim. All members must be registered with Manchester United's official membership scheme.

ARKLOW Branch Secretary James Cullen, 52 South Green, Arklow, Co Wicklow, Eire **Tel** 087 2327859 or 0402 39816. All trips arranged via local committee members. Pick-ups Waterford to Dublin. Anyone interested in joining, please contact the Secretary.

BALLYCASTLE Branch Secretary Cathy McLaughlin, 7 Strand Cottages, Ballycastle, Co Antrim, Northern Ireland, BT54 6HR **Mobile** 07720 826586. Branch Chairman Derek McKendry. Branch Meetings: First Sunday in every month.

BALLYMONEY Branch Secretary Malachy McAleese, 8 Riverview Park, Ballymoney, Co Antrim, Northern Ireland, BT53 7QS **Tel** 028 276 67623. Chairman Gerry McAleese, 11 Greenville Avenue, Ballymoney, Co Antrim, Northern Irelan **Tel** 028 276 65446. *Departure Points* Ballymoney United Social Club, Grove Road, Ballymena; Belfast Harbour or Belfast International Airport; Meetings: Last Thursday of every month, Ballymoney United Social Club, 35 Castle Street, Ballymoney **Tel** 028 276 66054 – New Members always welcome. **Website** www.musc-ballymoney.co.uk **E-mail** info@musc-ballymoney.co.uk.

BANBRIDGE Branch Secretary James Loney, 83 McGreavy Park, Derrymacash, Lurgan, Northern Ireland BT66 6LR **Tel** 028 38 345058 **Mobile** 07901 833076. Chairman Kevin Nelson, 10 Ballynamoney Park, Derrymacash, Lurgan, N Ireland **Tel** 028 38 344232 **Mobile** 07879 436358. *Departure Points* Corner House, Derrymacash; Lurgan Town Centre; Newry Road, Banbridge.

BANGOR Branch Secretary Gary Wilsdon, 4 Bexley Road, Bangor, Co Down, BT19 7TS **Tel** 028 91 458485 **E-mail** gary.wilsdon@virgin.net. Branch Meetings: Every other Monday 8.00pm at the Imperial Bar, Central Avenue, Bangor.

BELFAST REDS Branch Secretary John Bond, 53 Hillhead Crescent, Belfast, Northern Ireland, BT11 9FS **Tel** 028 90 627861.

BUNDORAN Branch Secretary Danny Tighe, "United Cottage", The Rock, Bundoran, Co Donegal, Eire **Tel/Fax** 072 42080 **Mobile** 086 859 7718. *Departure point* The Holyrood Hotel and additional pick-up points en route to Dublin Port. All bookings to be made through Branch Secretary only. Bookings should be made well in advance as travel arrangements have to be made. New members are welcome.

CARLINGFORD LOUTH Branch Secretary Harry Harold, Mountain Park, Carlingford, Co Louth, Ireland **Tel** 00 353 42 9373379.

CARLOW Branch Secretary Michael Lawlor, Trafford House, 20 New Oak Estate, Carlow, Ireland **Tel** 0503 43759 **Mobile** 086 8950030 (Mon-Friday 7.00-9.00pm only). Treasurer William Carroll **Mobile** 086 8593062 (Mon-Fri 9.00am-5.00pm only).

CARRICKFERGUS Branch Secretary Gary Callaghan, 3 Red Fort Park, Carrickfergus, Co Antrim, Northern Ireland, BT38 9EW **Tel** 028 93 355362 **Fax** 028 93 369995 **E-mail** aca@globalnet.co.uk. The branch holds their meetings fortnightly on a Monday evening at 8.00pm in the Quality Hotel, Carrickfergus. New members are welcome, especially Family and Juniors. The branch presently has a membership of 165 and organises trips to Old Trafford for all home games. They also travel to away matches including European whenever possible.

CARRYDUFF Branch Secretary John White, 'Stretford End', 4 Baronscourt Glen, Carryduff, Co Down, Northern Ireland, BT8 8RF **Tel** 028 90 812377 **E-mail** whitedevil@nireland.com. Chairman John Dempsey. Vice-Chairman Wilson Steele **Tel** 028 94 464987. *Departure points*: The branch organise coach trips to Old Trafford for every home game from The Royal Ascot, Carryduff and The Grand Opera House, Belfast. Branch meetings are held every week. No alcohol and no other club colours are permitted on the coach. Junior members particularly welcome as we are a family orientated branch. Branch Membership exceeds 400 and ALL members must be registered with Manchester United's Official Membership Scheme. The branch owns a number of Season Tickets, used on trips.

CASTLEDAWSON Branch Secretary Niall Wright, 22 Park View, Castledawson, Co Londonderry, Northern Ireland **Tel** 028 79 468779.

CASTLEPOLLARD Branch Secretary Anne Foley, Coole, Mullingar, Co Westmeath, Ireland **Tel/Fax** 00 353 44 61613 **E-mail** muscpollard@hotmail.com. *Departure points* The Square, Castlepollard. Additional pick-up points by arrangement with Branch Secretary. Branch meetings on 3rd Monday of every month. Notification of additional meetings by 'newsletter'.

CASTLEWELLAN Branch Secretary Seamus Owens, 18 Mourne Gardens, Dublin Road, Castlewellan, Co Down, Northern Ireland, BT31 9BY **Tel** 028 437 78137 **Fax** 028 437 70762 **Mobile** 07714 756 455. Chairman Tony Corr **Tel** 028 437 22885. Treasurer Michael Burns **Tel** 028 437 78665.

CITY OF DERRY Branch Secretary Mark Thompson, 210 Hillcrest, Kilfennan, Londonderry, Northern Ireland, BT47 6GF **Tel** 028 7134 6537 **E-mail** mthompson@freeuk.com. Meetings: First Tuesday of every month at the Upstairs Downstairs Bar, Dungiven Road, Londonderry at 8.30pm.

CLARA Branch Secretary Michael Kenny, River Street, Clara, Co Offaly, Ireland.

COLERAINE Branch Secretary Noel Adair, 106 Lisnablaugh Road, Harper's Hill, Coleraine, Co Derry, Northern Ireland **Tel** 01265 57744.

COMBER Branch Secretary Derek Hume, 14 Carnesure Hts., Comber, Co Down **Tel** (028) 91 872608 **E-mail** Derekhume@onetel.net.uk. Chairman Stephen Irvine **Tel** (028) 91 811517 **E-mail** Stevieirvine@Hotmail.com. Branch **E-mail** Comberbranch@onetel.net.uk. Branch meetings are held on Tuesday evenings at the social rooms of Comber Rec FC. Family run branch. New adult & Junior members welcomed. Ask for Michael or Brian. Dates of meetings printed in local 'Chronicle' newspaper and also on our **Website** www.aasq35.manufree.net.

COOKSTOWN Branch Secretary Geoffrey Wilson, 10 Cookstown Road, Moneymore, Co Londonderry, Northern Ireland, BT45 7QF **Tel** 028 86748625 **Mobile** 07833 945847. Meeting: First Monday of every month at Royal Hotel, Cookstown - 9.00pm. All members must be registered with Manchester United's official membership scheme.

CORK AREA Branch Secretary Paul Kearney, Beech Road, Passage West, Co Cork, Republic of Ireland **Tel** 021 841190.

COUNTY CAVAN Chairman Owen Farrelly **Tel** 046 42184. Secretary: Jimmy Murray **Tel** 046 42501. Assistant Secretary Gerry Heery **Tel** 042 9665226 **Email** co.cavanbranch@eircom.net **Website** www.cocavanbranch.homestead.com. Meetings third Monday of each month in Jimmy's Bar, Main St, Mullagh, Co. Cavan.

COUNTY LONGFORD Branch Secretary Seamus Gill, 17 Springlawn, Longford, Republic of Ireland **Tel** 043 47848 **Fax** 043 41655. Chairman Harry Ryan, 58 Teffia Park, Longford, Co. Longford. Treasurer Noel Daly, 18 Shannonvale, Longford, Co Longford.

COUNTY MONAGHAN Branch Secretary Seamus Gallagher **Tel** 047 57232. Chairman Gerard Treanor **Tel** 087 57232. Meetings fortnightly Bellevue Tavern, Dublin Street, Monaghan **Tel** 047 84311 **Fax** 047 83265.

COUNTY ROSCOMMON Branch Secretary Noel Scally, Cashel, Boyle, Co Roscommon, Ireland **Tel** 079 64995. Chairman Seamus Sweeney, Croghan, Boyle, Co. Roscommon **Tel** 079 68061. Treasurer Padraig McCrann, Garrow, Boyle, Co Roscommon. President George Tiernan, 8 Termon Road, Boyle, Co Roscommon. Meetings are held once a month, usually on the third Thursday of each month at the Royal Hotel, Boyle.

COUNTY TIPPERARY Branch Secretary Mrs Kathleen Hogan, 45 Canon Hayes Park, Tipperary, Republic of Ireland **Tel** 062 51042.

COUNTY WATERFORD Branch Secretary Mr K. Moore, 92 Childers Estate, Dungarvan, Co Waterford, Ireland **Tel** 058 48925. Chairman Oliver Drummy, 8 Cloneety Terrace., Dungarvan, Co. Waterford **Tel** 058 42365. Vice-Chairman Pat Grant, "Old Trafford", Ballinamuck, Dungarvan, Co Waterford, Ireland **Tel/Fax** 058 44219. Treasurer Judy Connors, 26 Hillview Drive, Dungarvan, Co Waterford. Membership Secretary Ann Houlihan, Feddans Cross, Rathgormac.

CRAIGAVON Branch Secretary Eamon Atkinson, 8 Rowan Park, Tullygally Road, Craigavon, Co Armagh, Northern Ireland, BT65 5AY **Tel** 028 38 343870. Chairperson James Nolan **Tel** 028 38 341434. Treasurer Susan Atkinson. *Departure Points* Lurgan Town Centre; Tullygally Road, Craigavon; Mayfair Centre, Portadown; Tandragee & Banbridge.

DONEGAL Branch Secretary Liam Friel **Tel** 00 353 87 6736967. Chairman Paul Dolan Treasurer Paddy Delap. Travel Organiser Tony Murray Public Relations Officer W Diver.

DOWNPATRICK Branch Secretary Terry Holland, 20 Racecourse Road, Downpatrick, Co Down, Northern Ireland **Tel/Fax** 028 44 616467 **Mobile** 07712 622242.

DUNDALK Chairman Michael McCourt, Secretary Joan Kirk, Assistant Secretary Arthur Carron, Treasurer Mary Laverty, Ticket & Travel Dickie O'Hanrahan, Committee Members Ollie Kelly, Gerry Dullaghan.

DUNGANNON Branch Secretary Ian Hall, 'Silveridge', 229 Killyman Road, Dungannon, Co Tyrone, Northern Ireland, BT71 6RS **Tel** 028 87 723085 (home) **Tel**: 028 87 752255 (work) **Mobile** 00787 124765. Meetings every 2 weeks (all year) at 30 Church Street, Dungannon. For details on membership, meetings, and trips contact Branch Secretary or Keith Houston on 028 87 722735 or Lawrence McKinley 07867 941163.

ENNIS Branch Secretary Seamus Hughes, 'Old Trafford', Quin, Ennis, Co Clare, Republic of Ireland **Tel** 065 68 20282 **Mobile** 086 239 3975. Branch Chairman Eamon Murphy, Knockboy, Ballynacally, Co Clare, Ireland **Tel** 065 68 28105. Meetings held at Roslevan Arms, Tulla Road, Ennis.

FERMANAGH Branch Secretary Gabriel Maguire, 80 Glenwood Gardens, Enniskillen, BT74 5LT **Tel** 028 66 325 950 **Mobile** 07788 421739. Chairman Eric Brown, 166 Main Street, Lisnaskea. Treasurer Raymond McBrien, Ardlougher Road, Irvinestown. Meetings held in Charlie's Lounge, Enniskillen.

FIRST BALLYCLARE Branch Secretary Alan Munce, 7 Merion Park, Ballyclare, Co Antrim, Northern Ireland, BT39 9XD **Tel** 028 93 324126.

FIRST NORTH DOWN (BANGOR) Branch Secretary Robert Quee, "Stretford End", 67 Springhill Road, Bangor West, Co Down, Northern Ireland, BT20 3PD. 1st North Down meet at the Bangor Sports Complex on the Old Belfast Road, Bangor (near cemetery) on alternative Tuesdays at 8pm. For details please ring 028 91 453094.

FIRST PORTAFERRY Branch Secretary David Peacock, 5 Loughshore Road, Portaferry, Northern Ireland, BT22 1PD **Tel** 028 427 28420/28646 **Fax** 028 427 29834. Chair Tony Cleary. Treasurer Hugh Conlon. Branch meetings held first Tuesday every month @ 9.00pm at McNamara's, High Street, Portaferry.

FOYLE Branch Secretary Martin Harkin, 2 Harvest Meadows, Dunlade Road, Greysteel, Co Derry, Northern Ireland, BT47 3BG. Meeting point Ulsterbus Club, Bishop Street, Derry City. Travel Arrangements: Meet Ulsterbus at midnight, boat at 0250 on matchday. Hotel Comfort Friendly, Hyde Road. Return boat 1430, arrive Ulsterbus Club 2030.

GALWAY Branch Secretary Patsy Devlin, 37 Gortgreine, Rahoon, Galway, Ireland **Tel** 00 353 091 582634 **Fax** 00 353 91 582634. (1) Meetings held monthly in Currans Hotel, Eyre Square. (2) All live TV games at Brennans Bar, New Docks. (3) Membership open all year round.

GLENOWEN Branch Secretary Jim Turner, 4 Dermot Hill Drive, Belfast, Northern Ireland BT12 7GG **Tel** 02890 242682 **Mobile** 07990 848 961 (day). **E-mail** Jimmy.Turner@tesco.net

IVEAGH YOUTH Branch Secretary Russell Allen, 2 Iveagh Crescent, Belfast, Northern Ireland, BT12 6AW **Tel** 028 90 542651 (office) 028 90 329621 (home). Assistant Branch Secretary Brendan McBride, 3 Gransha Park, Belfast BT11 8AT **Tel** 028 90 522400 (work) 028 90 203171 (home).

IRELAND (DUBLIN) Branch Secretary Eddie Gibbons, 19 Cherry Orchard Crescent, Ballyfermont, Dublin 10 **Tel** 01 626 9759 **Fax** 01 6236388. Membership Secretary Michael O'Toole, 49 Briarwood Lawn, Mulmuddart, Dublin 15 **Tel** 01 821 5702.

KILKENNY Branch Secretary John Joe Ryan **Tel** 056 6565827 (day) 056 65136 (after 6.00pm) **Fax** 056 64043. Branch Chairman Pat Murray **Tel** 056 71772.

KILLALOE Branch Secretary Michael Flynn, 611 Cross Road, Killaloe, Co Clare, Ireland **Tel** 061 376031.

KILLARNEY Branch Secretary Frank Roberts, St Margaret's Road, Killarney, Co Kerry, Republic of Ireland. Chairman Bill Keefe Treasurer Denis Spillane. Meetings held on the first Wednesday of each month at which future trips are organised.

LAGAN Branch Secretary Errol Hall, 11 Arthur Park, Newtownabby, N Ireland BT36 7EL **Tel** 028 90 861949.

LAOIS Branch Secretary Denis Moran, Newpark, Portlaoise, Co Laois, Ireland **Tel** 0502 22681.

LARNE Branch Secretary Brian Haveron, 69 Croft Manor, Ballygally, Larne, Co Antrim BT40 2RU **Tel** 028 28 261197 (day) 028 28 583027 (night) **Mobile** 07785 388959. Branch Chairman John Hylands, 43 Olderfleet Road, Larne, Co Antrim BT40 1AS **Tel** 028 28 277888. Meetings: Every Monday night 8.00pm at St. John's Social Club, Mill Brae, Larne. The branch has an allocation for every home fixture and is a family orientated branch. New members always welcome.

LIMERICK Branch Secretary Dennis O'Sullivan, 14 Rossa Avenue, Mulgrave Street, Limerick, Republic of Ireland **Tel** 061 311502 **Mobile** 600 743.

LISBURN Branch Secretary Colin Scott, 7 Barban Hill, Dromore, Co Down, Northern Ireland, BT25 1PR **Tel** 028 92 699608 **Mobile** 07808 532951. **E-mail** lisburnmusc@gcs-internet.com
The Branch meets each Tuesday night at 8.30pm at the Club Rooms on Sackville Street. To join the branch you must be an official member of Manchester United. The branch travel to all games, league and European, and some away. Anyone interested in joining, families and kids welcome, please contact the Branch Secretary.

LISTOWEL Branch Secretary Aiden O'Connor, 55 Pytha Fold Road, Withington, Manchester M20 4UR **Tel** 0161 434 4713. Assistant Secretary David O'Brien, Bedford, Listowel, Co Kerry Ireland **Tel** 068 22250.

LURGAN Branch Secretary John Furphy, 123 Drumbeg North, Craigavon, Co Armagh, N Ireland BT65 5AE **Tel** 028 38 341842.

MAYO Branch Secretary Seamus Moran, Belclare, Westport, Co Mayo, Ireland **Tel** 00 353 982 7533 (h) 00 353 985 5202 **Mobile** 00 353 872 417966 **Fax** 00 353 982 8874. Chairperson Liam Connell, 70 Knockaphunta, Castlebar, Co Mayo, Ireland. Treasurer T J Gannon, 4 The Paddock, Castlebar Road, Westport, Co Mayo, Ireland. PRO Kieran Mongey, Blackfort, Castlebar, Co Mayo, Ireland.

MEATH Branch Secretary Colm McManus, 46 Beechlawn, Kells, Co Meath, Republic of Ireland **Tel** 046 49831. Pick-up points for travel to Old Trafford: Jack's Railway Bar, Kells; Fairgreen, Naven.

NEWRY Branch Secretary Brendan McConville, 14 Willow Grove, Newry, Co Down, Northern Ireland, BT34 1JH **Tel** 028 3026 6996.
E-mail brendan.mcconville@manutd.com Chairman Jeffrey Clements **Tel** 028 3026 7158. Meetings: first Tuesday of each month at the Cue Club, Newry **Tel** 028 3026 6066.

NEWTOWNARDS Branch Secretary Leo Cafolla, 11 Strangford Gate Drive, Newtownards, Co Down, Northern Ireland, BT23 8ZW **Tel** 07710 820300 **Fax** 028 91 811822.
Meeting every other Monday 7.30pm at Nixx Sport's Bar, Newtownards. Junior Branch also.

NORTH BELFAST Branch Secretary Robert Savage, 59 Hollybrook Manor, Glenganely, Belfast, Northern Ireland, BT36 7XR **Tel** 028 90 713164. Our meetings are held every second Sunday of the month in the Shamrock Social Club.

OMAGH Branch Secretary Brendan McLaughlin, 4 Pinefield Court, Killyclougher, Omagh, Co Tyrone, Northern Ireland, BT79 7YT **Tel** 028 82 250025 **Mobile** 077 10 366 486.

PORTADOWN Branch Secretary Harold Beck, 23 Kernan Grove, Portadown, Co Armagh, BT63 5RX **Tel** 028 3 833 6877 **Mobile** 07703 360423.

PORTAVOGIE Branch Secretary Robert McMaster, 6 New Road, Portavogie, Co Down BT22 1EN.

PORTRUSH Branch Secretary James Friel, 15-17 Causway Street, Portrush, Northern Ireland.

PORTSTEWART Branch Secretary Ryan McLaughlin, 45 Drumavalley, Bellarena, Limavady, Co. Derry, Northern Ireland BT49 0LT **Tel** 028 777 50281 after 6.00pm. Club Meetings held every second Wednesday of the month at 7.30pm, Anchor Bar, Portstewart.

ROSTREVOR Branch Chairman John Parr, 16 Drumreagh Park, Rostrevor BT34 3DU **Tel** 028 417 39797. Branch Secretary Roger Morgan, 23 Ardfield Crescent, Warrenpoint, Co Down **Tel** 028 417 54783. Treasurer John Franklin, 14 Rosswood Park, Rostrevor, Co Down BT34 3DZ **Tel** 028 417 38906. Asst. Secretary M. Rea, 8 The Square, Rostrevor, Co. Down **Tel** 028 417 39808. Club President Paul Braham.

SION MILLS Branch Secretary Jim Hunter, 122 Melmount, Sion Mills, Co Tyrone, Northern Ireland, BT82 9EU **Tel** 028816 58226 (home) 02882 252491 (work).

SLIGO Branch Chairman Eddie Gray, 27 Cartron Heights, Sligo, Republic of Ireland **Tel** 00 353 71 44387 **Mobile** 086 6075 855. Branch Secretary Martin Feeney, 40 Cartron Bay, Sligo, Republic of Ireland **Mobile** 087 2971842.

SOUTH BELFAST Branch Secretary James Copeland, 17 Oakhurst Avenue, Blacks Road, Belfast BT10 0PD **Tel** 028 90 615184 or 028 90 871231 **Mobile** 07767 271648. Chairman Danny Nolan; Vice-Chairman Michael Murphy; Treasurer James McLaughlin; Fundraising Officer Simon Murray.
Departure Point Balmoral Hotel, Blacks Road.

STEWARTSTOWN Branch Secretary Robert O'Neill, 6 Castle Farm Road, Stewartstown, Co Tyrone, Northern Ireland.

STRABANE Branch Secretary Gerry Donnelly, 27 Dublin Road, Strabane, Co Tyrone, Northern Ireland, BT82 9EA **Tel** 028 417 83337.

TALLAGHT Branch Secretary Jimmy Pluck, 32 Kilcarrig Cresent, Fettercairn, Tallaght, Co Dublin 24, Republic of Ireland **Tel** 086 333 5303.

TIPPERARY TOWN Branch Secretary John Ryan, 14 Marian Terrace, Tipperary Town, Co Tipperary, Republic of Ireland **Tel** 086 8831456 (24 hours) **Fax** 086 8934635 (24 hours).

TOWER ARDS Branch Secretary Stephen Rowley **Tel** 028 91 810457 (home) 028 90 432014 (work). Meetings held every second Sunday at the Tower Inn, Mill Street, Newtownards.

TRALEE Branch Secretary Johnny Switzer, Dromtacker, Tralee, Co Kerry, Republic of Ireland **Tel** 066 7124787

WARRENPOINT Branch Secretary Pat Treanor, 31 Oakland Grove, Warrenpoint **Tel** 028 417 73921 **Mobile** 0775 968595. Chairman John Bird, 23 Greendale Crescent, Rostrevor, Co Down Tel: 028 417 3837. Treasurer Leo Tohill, 46 Carmen Park, Warrenpoint, Co Down **Tel** 028 417 72453. Club **Website** address is http://www.muwp/manutd.htm Club based at Cearnogs Bar, The Square, Warrenpoint, Co Down, N Ireland **Tel** 028 417 53429. Branch meets last Friday of every month at 8.00pm.

WEST BELFAST Branch Secretary John McAllister, 25 Broadway, Belfast BT12 6AS **Tel** 028 90 329423 **Fax** 0870 0637348 **E-mail** hoyt@lineone.net Branch Chairman George McCabe, 21 Beechmount Street, Belfast, BT12 7NG. Treasurer Mr G Burns Committee Mr Liam Curran, Mr Mark Mallon, Mr Michael Curran. Meetings held fortnightly on Tuesday evening in "The Red Devil Bar", Falls Road, Belfast For information contact Branch Secretary.

OVERSEAS BRANCHES

BELGIUM Chairman Peter Bauwens, Merellaan 52, 9060 Zelzate, Belgium **Tel/Fax 00 32 934 40578** Branch Secretary Bjørn Tack **Tel/Fax 00 32 934 45860.**

CANADA Manchester United Supporters Club, 12 St Clair Avenue East, PO Box 69057, Toronto, Ontario, M4T 3AI, Canada **E-mail chairman@muscc.com Fax 00 1 416 480 0501** FAO Maureen Website **www.muscc.com**

CYPRUS Branch President Ronis Soteriades, P.O.Box 51365, 3504 Limassol, Cyprus **Tel 05 337690 Fax 05 388652.**

GERMAN FRIENDS Branch President Marco Hornfeck, Silberstein 36, 95179 Geroldsgrün, Germany **Tel 09267 8111.**

GERMAN KREFELD REDS Branch Secretary Andy Marsh, Innsbrucker Str, 47807 Krefeld, Germany **Tel/Fax 00 49 (0) 2151 392908 Mobile 00 49 (0) 173 250 3390.** Assistant Branch Secretary. Stuart Dykes, Grete Schmitz Str. 8, 47829 Krefeld, Germany **Tel 00 49 (0) 2151 435 167 Fax 00 49 2151 435 168 Mobile 00 49 (0) 172 398 5152 E-mail stuart.dykes@t-online.de.**

GERMAN REDS Branch Secretary Thomas Rochel, Lessingstr 23, D-39108 Magdeburg, Germany **Tel 00 49 391 733 8275 Fax 00 49 391 7313127. E-mail th.rochel@t-online.de**

GIBRALTAR Manchester United Supporters Gibraltar Branch, PO Box 22, Gibraltar Branch Chairman Clive A Moberley; Branch Secretary Robert Beiso; Treasurer Brian Cardona; Committee Members Manolo Ferro, Wilfred Gavito, Billy Lima, Denis Peralta.

HOLLAND Branch Chairman Ron Snellen, PO Box 33742, 2503 BA Den Haag, Holland **Tel 00 31 70 329 8602 Fax 00 31 70 367 2247. Internet www.dutch-mancunians.nl E-mail dennisvandervin@hetnet.nl**

HONG KONG 12B Shun Ho Tower, 24-30 Ice House Street, Central, Hong Kong **Tel 00 852 2869 1993 Fax 00 852 2869 4312.** Branch Secretary/Treasurer Rick Adkinson Chairman Mark Saunders.

ICELAND Branch Secretary Bubbi Avesson, Studningsmannaklubbur, Manchester United á Íslandi, PO Box 12170, 132 Reykjavik, Iceland.

LUXEMBOURG Branch Secretary Steve Kaiser **Tel 00 352 4301 33073** (work) 00 352 340265 (home).

MALTA Quarries Square, Msida MSD 03, Malta (since 1959) **Tel 00 356 223531 Fax 00 356 231902 E-mail musc@maltanet.net.mt** Website **www.maltazone.com/hosted/mufc** Branch President John Buttigieg.

MAURITIUS Branch Secretary Yacoob Atchia, Flamingo Pool House, Remeno Street, Rose Hill, Mauritius, Indian Ocean **Tel 464 7382/454 7761/454 3570/464 7750 Fax 454 7839. E-mail abyss.manutd@intnet.mu** Chairman Swallay Banhoo **Tel 464 4450** (home). Treasurer Naniel Baichoo **Tel 454 3570** (work) **465 0387** (home).

NEW SOUTH WALES Chairperson Steve Griffiths Vice-Chairperson Tony Redman. Treasurer Jeanette Frost. Secretary John Panaretto. Founders Fred & Ann Pollitt. Branch Address P.O.Box 693, Sutherland, New South Wales 1499, Australia **Tel/Fax 00 61 2 982 29781. Website http://manutd-nsw.one.net.au/index.htm**

NEW ZEALAND Branch Chairman Brian Wood, 55 Pine Street, Mount Eden, Auckland, New Zealand. Secretary Gillian Goodinson, 20 Sandown Road, Rothesay Bay, Auckland, New Zealand **E-mail woody.utd@xtra.co.nz**

SCANDINAVIA Branch Secretary Per H Larsen, PO Box 4003 Dreggen, N-5835 Bergan, Norway **Tel +47 5530 2770** (Mon - Fri 08.00-16.00) **Fax +47 5596 2033. E-mail muscsb@unitel.no**

SOUTH AFRICA PO Box 2540, Capetown 8000, S Africa **Tel 00 27 82 231 64364** (Customer care) **Fax 00 27 21 438 8295. E-mail m.united@mweb.co.za**

SOUTH EAST ASIA Manager Jeremy Goon, 6-B Orange Grove Road, Singapore 258332 **Tel 00 65 737 0677 Fax 00 65 733 5073. E-mail members@manutd-sea.com.sg**

SOUTH AUSTRALIA PO Box 276, Ingle Farm, South Australia 5098 **Fax 08 82816731.** Branch Secretary Mick Griffiths **Tel 08 82644499.** Branch Chairman Chris Golder **Tel 08 82630602.** Vice-Chairma John Harrison **Tel 08 82603413.** Treasurer Charlie Kelly **Tel 08 82628245.** Meetings are held at the Para Hills Soccer Club, Bridge Road, Para Hills, SA. The Manchester United Supporters Amateur League Soccer team train and play at Para Hills Soccer Club.

SWISS DEVILS Branch Secretary Marc Tanner, Dorfstrasse 30d, 5430 Wettingen, Switzerland **Tel (00 41 56) 426 94 80. Website www.swissdevils.ch E-mail vonisan@yahoo.co.uk**

TOKYO Branch Secretary Hiroki Miyaji, 2-24-10 Minami-Ayoma, Minato-ku, Tokyo, Japan **Tel +81 3 3470 3441.** English Information Stephen Ryan **Tel +81 3 3380 8441 E-mail best-oz@kk.iij4u.or.jp**

U.S.A. Branch Secretary Peter Holland, MUSC USA Branch HQ, 139 West Neck Road, Huntingdon, N.Y. 11743, U.S.A. **Tel 00 1 516 547 5500** (day) **Fax 00 1 516 547 6800** (day) **Tel/Fax 00 1 516 261 7314** (evening). **E-mail muscusa@datacapture.com** (day) **muscusa@muscusa.com** (evening) Website **www.muscusa.com** Webmaster **jpkell@ix.netcom.com**

VICTORIAN AUSTRALIA President Kieran Dunleavy, PO Box 1199, Camberwell, 3124 Victoria **Tel/Fax 9 804 0244.** Web Page **http://www.strug.com.au~sidcol E-mail muscovic@vicnet.net.au**

WESTERN AUSTRALIA Branch Chairman Graham Wyche, 19 Frobisher Avenue, Sorrento 6020, Perth, Western Australia **Tel/Fax (08) 9 447 1144 Mobile 0417 903 101 E-mail freobook@omen.com.au**